NEIGHBORHOODS UNDER SIEGE

The Memoirs of a Brooklyn Don

———————

Calvin "Klein" Bacote

PREE PUBLISHING

NEIGHBORHOODS UNDER SIEGE

Ordering information: Quantity sales. Special discounts are available on quantity purchases by corporations, associations, and others. For details, contact the publisher at the email address above.
ISBN (978-0-9916308-1-3)
Printed in the United States
First Printing, 2014

www.CalvinKleinBacote.com

Design and Illustration: HGXmarketing
Publisher: Pree Publishing
Editor: Charnise Sutton-Bacote

DEDICATION

I dedicate this book to my late grandmother Sarah Bacote. *"Grandma, I know you've always expected better of me. Although I've fallen short at times, I know it is never too late for me to bring out the best in myself and deliver the true talents that God has given me. I strive to rewrite my legacy and become more meaningful in the life I'm blessed to live today. I know you are now looking down on me with pride, proud to tell the other angels that I'm your Grandbaby, as I am proud to say You're my Grandma. May you rest in peace and know that I not only miss you, but I love you."*

TABLE OF CONTENT

ACKNOWLEDGEMENTS

I want to first and foremost thank God for blessing me and giving me the gifts that I humbly take advantage of using today. I want to thank the greatest parents in the world, Jo-Ann and Kenneth for being the ones God has chosen to give birth to me. You did everything right in raising me. It was I who set out on the wrong path and did wrong. I want to thank my siblings, Sonya and Tyrone for all of the wonderful memories we shared growing up. I want to thank my beautiful wife and Chief editor Charnise, for your sacrifice, love and patience in me. You've done what no one could by giving me inspiration daily to stay focused and to be the best that I can be for myself, our children and our loved ones. I want to thank my children, Angelique, Kodi, Jalyn and Persais. You are the better half of who I am and the reason why I do what I do today. I want to thank Mekeze Okoro and the HGXmarketing team, for all the hours put in to making this project as big as it has become. I want to thank, Pree Publishing, for taking this project to the next level. I want to thank, Damon Ruiz and Wendy Day. You stood by me during trying times and pushed me to greatness. I don't want to leave anyone out so I'll just say this, thank you Brooklyn, thank you

Red-Hook, thank you New York and most of all, thank you to all the readers.

PROLOGUE

"All rise; As the Honorable Judge Elaine Spielberg enters the courtroom!" Those in attendance, stood up as the judge entered the room and took her seat. The court officer instructed everyone to be seated. Soon after, the judge informed the court officer that she was ready to proceed. The court officer directed the US Marshals to bring out the first case on the docket.

As my brother and I entered the courtroom, the court officer yelled out for all to hear, *"Court is now in session! On November 8, 1991 The UNITED STATES vs. CALVIN BACOTE and KENNETH BACOTE on charges in violation of title 21 U.S.C. Sections 846 and 841 (b)(1)(b)(iii), a class C felony. Today is set for the sentencing of said defendants."*

This day felt like a funeral. The room's temperature was frigid, making my body feel like a lifeless corpse. My brother and I walked to the table where our lawyers stood. We had our eyes fixated on our mother, our girlfriends and a close friend of the family who came to lend a hand of support. The pain in everyone's eyes expressed what words couldn't. My brother and I decided against having a courtroom full of family and friends. We didn't want to increase the attention that this case was already receiving, due to it being a high profile case.

As we stood at our lawyers' side, we periodically looked over our shoulders to whisper words of endearment to our mother and girlfriends. My brother and I were facing charges for conspiracy to distribute crack-cocaine base and for possession with the intent to distribute crack-cocaine base to an undercover agent.

Since it felt like we were attending our own funerals, we felt it was only fitting to dress for the occasion. My brother dressed casually, wearing a cream Coogi sweater, beige slacks and brown gator shoes. Against his advice, I took more of the dapper approach. I wore an Armani suit and gator shoes, along with a pair of Cartier glasses. If only it were for a different occasion, our mother would have been proud of her boys for the way we looked and represented.

My brother and I stood in front of the judge, with an empty feeling of agony and defeat. This was a rough day for our family to say the least. The D.E.A, FBI and several local task force agencies apprehended my brother and myself ten months prior on February 12, 1991, in an eleven people sting operation. An investigation ensued for approximately six months in one of the most noted neighborhoods in Brooklyn, New York; The Red Hook Projects.

Brooklyn itself was a very notorious borough. Other parts of the city had their notoriety, but Brooklyn had an established reputation that was renowned. It was recognized not only by those in New York, but by those worldwide as well. Brooklyn wore its status as a badge of honor. From the day Brooklyn was discovered, every hood in the borough played its part in building the Brooklyn brand to what it is today.

Red-Hook was a well-known area, considered forbidden due to its heinous reputation. A cloud of danger often lurked in the air. Even during the day, it wasn't safe to go outside. Every man, woman and child had to move with great precaution; fearing danger would erupt at any given moment.

With the unruliness of the hood at an all-time high, the government agencies enforced a diversion plan, luring me from the hood and finally arresting me in Bay Ridge, Brooklyn. With all forces in place, they simultaneously moved on all targets in separate locations. The hood was taken down by the element of surprise.

As if that wasn't enough, The Government went

on a rampage seizing and confiscating anything that belonged to my brother or myself. The District Attorney claimed that my brother and I played major roles in the corruption of drugs and mayhem that were destroying the neighborhoods.

COURT PROCEEDINGS:

THE COURT: *"All right, we have certain steps that must be gone through before sentence can be imposed under the guidelines. Let me ask you, counsel, have you fully reviewed the probation report and had a chance to talk it over with your clients?"*

MR.SIEGEL: *"Yes, I have with my client Calvin Bacote, Your Honor."*

MR.HOROWITZ:*" I have as well with my client Kenneth Bacote, Your Honor."*

THE COURT: *"Are there any facts contained in the report to which you wish to take exception other than those that have already been addressed by the court?"*

MR.SIEGEL: *"No, Your Honor."*

MR. HOROWITZ: *"No, Your Honor."*

THE COURT: *"I don't believe there are any outstanding legal issues now that we've resolved the question of withdrawal of the guilty plea, is that correct?"*

MR. SIEGEL: *"That's correct Your Honor."*

MR. HOROWITZ: *"Correct, Your Honor."*

THE COURT: *"Is there any dispute as to the probation department's guideline calculation, other than those you've already noted?"*

MR SIEGEL: *"No, Your Honor."*

MR. HOROWITZ: *"No, Your Honor."*

THE COURT: *"All right. For the reasons I've stated in this case, I find that the defendant Calvin Bacote's total offense level is 34 with a criminal history category of 6. The guidelines provide for 262 to 327 month term of incarceration, a 4 to 5 year term of supervised release, a $17,500 to $2,000,000 fine and a $50 order of special assessment. Other than those objections noted, any further objections Mr. Siegel?"*

MR. SIEGEL: *"No, Your Honor"*

MR. SHEFFIELD: *"Your Honor, for the record, The Government is taking the position in requesting that both defendants receive the top of what their guidelines require."*

THE COURT: *"All right, noted. Mr. Siegel, if you're prepared to go forward, I'll be happy to hear you as to anything you'd like to say on Calvin Bacote's behalf."*

MR. SIEGEL: *"Yes, my client's a twenty-five year old that has obviously made some very bad choices in his life. He is very much aware of what is at stake here today Your Honor. He can either face the minimum, serving every year that he has lived thus far, or the maximum, serving his natural life in prison. We ask that the courts take that into account.*

THE COURT: *"All right, Mr. Bacote. While I cannot speak to the issue in large terms, I do think that the net result of everything in this case results in a very harsh sentence for you, someone who has plead guilty to this crime. Although I feel I may be giving you too much time, 262 months is the least that I will be able to impose to you under the guidelines. As I said, I already think that's too severe."*

MRS. BACOTE: *"Excuse me, Your Honor, I'm Calvin and Kenneth's mother. Did you receive my letters?"*

THE COURT: *"I know who you are Mrs. Bacote, and yes I did receive your letters. As a mother, I do understand what you must be going through. I am simply telling you that 262 months is the lowest amount that the law allows me to impose on Calvin. I see no reason to impose anything more on him. It's already a very, very harsh penalty, but I did get your letters. You do have to understand that your children have committed some very serious crimes, Calvin more so."*

MRS. BACOTE: *"But that's my baby!"*

Hearing the pain in my mother's voice made time rewind. In that very moment I regressed back to my beginnings. The prosecution made me out to be this evil villain, but every villain started out as someone's baby.

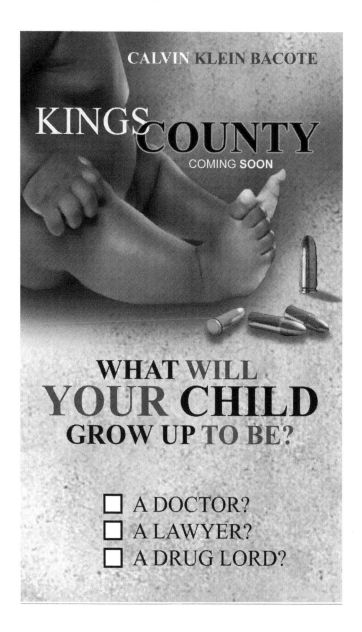

I was born in Brooklyn, New York at Brooklyn Jewish Hospital on May 30, 1966 to John and Jo-Ann Bacote. I was the youngest of three raised in the Red-Hook Housing Projects. My father was born and raised in Darlington, South Carolina while my mother was born in Hackensack, New Jersey. Tragedy struck my mom at seven months old when her mother took to a sudden death. My mom was sent with family to be raised in Darlington where she met my father, eventually becoming his childhood sweetheart.

With nearly a ninth grade education my father received the news from my mother that she was pregnant with their first child, my sister Sonya. To make good on trying to provide a better living for what was to come in his future, my father packed up with three of his best friends and headed to the Big Apple. It was the early 60's and my father was an aspiring singer with great potential. Soon to make a mark with his style of music, he and his friends settled in Harlem and my dad went full throttle into the music industry. He became close friends with Archie Bell from the group "*Archie Bell and the Drells*".

He did the majority of his networking at the Famous Apollo Theater and the Cotton Club. While making decent strides of progress with his music, my father and his boys sent for their girlfriends and children. They all shared an apartment in Harlem until everyone was able to move out on their own. My parents were soon married and were ready to branch out. My father moved his wife and daughter to Bed-Stuy, Brooklyn on Halsey St. and Broadway Ave. Two years later my brother Kenneth was born.

My father worked Downtown Brooklyn on Atlantic Ave. parking cars. He was doing his best to balance out taking care of his family and pursuing his music career. Two years after my brother was born my father received the unexpected news from my mother that she was once again pregnant. The apartment they lived in was too small to suit their expanding family, so they decided to move to The Red-Hook housing projects for a much-needed larger living space.

The Red-Hook housing projects is the largest low-income housing development in Brooklyn. It consist of over thirty residential buildings some as high as fourteen stories, 1,753 apartments and approximately 4,000 residents, a city within a city. My family laid their roots at 135 Richard St. on the thirteenth floor, where they welcomed my arrival. As they settled in, our home became the place where all family members and friends would congregate.

My parents owned a huge collection of music that they stored in milk crates. It included every artist and genre from James Brown to Alvin and the Chipmunks. Our home was filled with the sound of music all the time. Gospel was played all day on Sundays, before and after church.

My parents bought a pool table for entertainment, holding many games and tournaments. They made extra money serving drinks and selling plates of my mom's home cooked meals. During these times my sister, brother and I would sleep over at our friend's homes or stay the weekend with my aunt Liz and cousin Willie in East New York. These were the best times growing up. We were a very close-knit family.

It felt like a family reunion every summer. We would hold get-togethers in New York, South Carolina or New Jersey. All my relatives were adamant about our bond remaining strong. They instilled in all of us at a very young age the importance of knowing our roots and heritage.

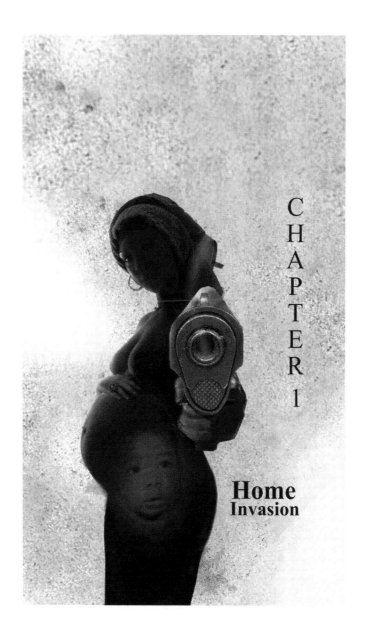

CHAPTER 1

Home
Invasion

One day around the tender age of two, while in the living room playing with my sister, brother and oldest cousin Pat, there was a knock at the door. It was a man who lived in the building on the eleventh floor with his wife and children. My mother looked through the peephole. Recognizing him, she parted the door slightly to see what he wanted. He began to make irrelevant conversation, knowing that my father had already left for work. My mother attempted to close the door and he quickly stopped it with his foot. He began to make a pass at her. He said he knew that she was married but wanted to be there for her in any way possible, while holding an envelope of money in his hand.

Once she declined his offer, he violently forced himself into our apartment. His sudden actions startled my mother. Her first instinct was to protect us. Noticing that we had stopped playing and directed our attention towards the man who was now pulling her arm, my mother asked if she could take us in the back room. He agreed with harsh demands for her to hurry up and return.

My mother knew she had to think and act fast, knowing that this man's intentions were to violate her womanhood. She gathered us together, directing us towards the back of the apartment and into the bathroom. She told us not to come out until we hear her say otherwise. The man was yelling for her to come back into the living room. My mother responded; saying she was coming.

It seemed as if all in one motion my mom was able to place us in the bathroom, quickly go into her bedroom and travel down the hallway back into the living room. Once the man saw my mother enter the living room, he moved forward with his arms open gesturing for her to come to him. As she continued to move in closer she raised her hand and unbeknownst to him she pointed a gun. She pulled the trigger, shooting once, striking him at point blank range. The bullet ripped through his hip as he hit the ground hard.

We were still in the bathroom and heard a very loud sound. Pat swung the door open running out as we followed suit into the living room, coming to my mother's aide. The man was bleeding profusely. My mother furthered her attack by beating him with the gun, while we all added in by hitting and kicking him. My mother dragged the man into the hallway of the building leaving him to tend to his own wounds. She then went back inside the apartment and locked the door.

While on his way out from a hard day of work my father was met by the police. He was arrested for having an unregistered weapon in his home. New York was far from the ways of the South as far as gun laws were concerned. He was set to face the judge that evening. Fortunately, the judge already heard the details of the case and in conclusion gave my father a lecture about possessing a deadly weapon. The judge understood the need for protection and prevention and noted the potential trauma my family would have endured if a weapon were not present. The judge dismissed the case and told my father to go home to his family.

About a year later while in the lobby waiting for the elevator with my mother, I noticed a man that was waiting as well. He entered the elevator behind us and I instinctively hid behind my mother's leg holding on for dear life. She looked down at me asking what was wrong. I looked in the man's direction and she instantaneously became cognizant of my fears. The man in the elevator was the man that she had shot one year prior. I told my mother that I was scared of the man. My mother turned to him and told him to tell me that I didn't have to be afraid of him and that he was sorry for what he did. He apologized and slowly exited the elevator limping with his head hung low, full of shame and remorse.

My father was furious that he wasn't there to protect his family and wanted nothing more than to teach the man a lesson. My mother made it clear to my father that his family needed him to be a free man and that prevented him from retaliating. Besides, she had given the man an injury that he would have to live with for a very long time and that was enough.

The man walked with a cane for the remainder of his life, walking with a limp from a shot to the hip. It was very apparent to everyone in the hood that the Bacote family would protect themselves at all cost. My mother instilled in us that no matter what; we are to fight with and for each other. We are to protect one another or else! And that's what we did.

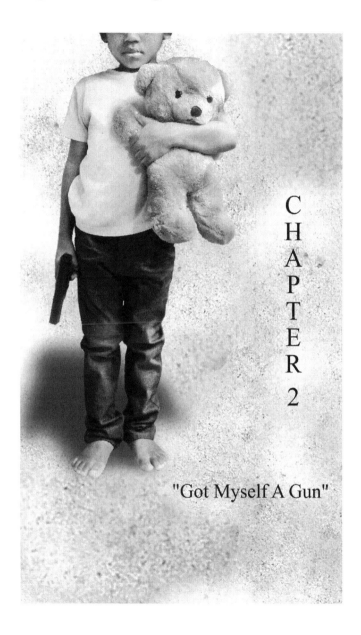

C
H
A
P
T
E
R
2

"Got Myself A Gun"

I was a very curious child. I would frequently visit Ms. Liz's apartment, my mother's friend who lived on the fourteenth floor. Her son Clive who was three years my senior had a souvenir horsewhip and I would always try to play with it. Ms. Liz would put it away whenever I came around, but this day she didn't take notice. Her son Clive had left the whip on the couch. I grabbed the whip, reenacting what I often saw Clive do. I swung the whip forward and when it returned, the tip of the whip hit me square in the eye.

I was immediately rushed to Long Island College Hospital's emergency room and had to have an operation to save my eye. The operation was successful. Both of my eyes had to be covered and I had to stay in the hospital for approximately two and a half months before my vision was restored. The doctors explained to my parents that this was done in order to maintain a proper balance of vision. I went home soon after and my mother monitored my every move, which was an extremely hard task because I was into any and everything. I had to make up for lost time.

Every time I received a brand new toy I would break it apart, thinking I knew how to fix it. That included things around the house as well. My mother would notice the broken items and the first thing I would say was *"Don't worry ma I can fix it."* Both of my parents would obviously be very upset, but the worst they would do was lecture me and laugh it off later.

One day while my mother and our neighbor, Ms. Geneva were out washing laundry, my brother, Nardy and myself played in the hallway as we often did. After a while I began to tire and went inside to rest. I went into my parent's room to get into their bed, but began jumping on it instead. It was my personal trampoline. It wasn't long before I became tired. I jumped down off of their bed and for no apparent reason I felt the urge to check underneath their mattress.

To my surprise, I found what I thought was a toy gun. I grabbed it and proceeded back into the hallway yelling at my brother and Nardy, *"Look, I found a toy gun!"* Waving it in the air, I opened the stairway door and pulled the trigger. It was extremely loud; the sound continuously rang in my ears. I turned back into the hallway, pointing the gun at them; " *Look, it's loud!"* They unanimously screamed out; *"Noooo!"* Being hard headed like every five year-old I pulled the trigger anyway.

The bullet hit Nardy in the leg. Unfortunately, my brother was standing behind him. The bullet went straight through Nardy's flesh, piercing my brother's leg. They both hit the floor hard, screaming holding their gunshot wounds and squirming like fish out of water. I looked at the gun, realizing something bad just happened. Everything became blurry as I stood there in shock.

Black Ray who lived on the floor above us was the first one on the scene. Scared to death, I either gave him the gun or threw it down the incinerator. That detail is still a little blurry to me. I then ran into Nardy's apartment and locked the door. My sister was in the kitchen making a sandwich. I ran past her and went straight into the living room. She yelled out for me to stop running in the house unaware of what just occurred. I began jumping on the couch, pretending to watch television. I knew what I did was really bad and that I was in some serious trouble.

The neighbors darted out of their apartments after hearing all the ruckus. They saw my brother and Nardy on the floor bleeding profusely and ran to their aide. After acquiring the details of the incident and my whereabouts one of the neighbors knocked on the door. My sister answered the door and no one had to say a word she knew something was terribly wrong. She ran out. Seeing all the commotion in the hallway surrounding my brother and Nardy, she bee lined straight downstairs to the laundry room to get our moms. The police arrived before our moms were able to make it upstairs.

A female officer retrieved me from Nardy's apartment and took me into my apartment. She sat me on her lap and proceeded to question me about the whereabouts of the gun. I just shrugged my shoulders up and down. I told her that I wasn't sure and that I think I may have tossed it down the incinerator. My mother came rushing into our apartment and snatched me from the officer. The officer told my mother that BCW (Bureau of Child Welfare) would be coming to our home to further investigate the situation. The Police searched the contents of the incinerator and came up with nothing. The gun was never found.

While at work my father was greeted by the police once again. This was a feeling that was becoming all too familiar. It was a shock to him to receive the news on my brother and Nardy's injury with his gun. To add insult to injury he had to go to jail as a result of it. It was like *"déjà vu"*. My father was fortunate enough to be arraigned that night. The judge acknowledged my father as a hard working parent coming from the south just trying to adjust to the city life.

The record shown that three years prior a weapon was used in an incident where our home was invaded and a rape was attempted on my mom. The judge told my dad, *"Although you are not the shooter in either incident, you do bare responsibility for your household. Now another incident has occurred involving your children."* The judge made it very clear that he would not spare my dad if

33

he ever came into his courtroom again and dismissed the case.

My dad came home tired and overwhelmed, but all the while relieved. Things could have gone much worse. I woke up in the middle of the night to use the bathroom, which was huge within itself. I had a bladder problem and would often wet the bed. This was a problem for me up until my early teenage years. I was about to enter the bathroom, when I was startled by my father sitting in the bathtub. He was laying there in the dark soaking his body after being in those dirty bullpens. I interrupted his deep thought when I came in turning on the light.

When I saw him, I was scared knowing that I was in trouble for what I did. I turned around to leave and he said to me "*If you have to use the bathroom then use it.*" He then seemed to be mumbling to himself, but he was talking to me. He said, "*I'm madder at myself more than I am at you. Do you want to go to the hospital with me to see your brother?*"

I was nervous seeing my brother because I didn't know what condition he was in, plus I knew it was all my fault. Nardy had a flesh wound and he was treated and released. My brother's condition was far greater, the bullet ripped through the bone in his leg. He remained in the hospital for almost six months. He had to go through intense physical therapy and rehabilitation to learn to walk again.

Once my brother came home the slow healing process began. He had to adjust to everyone helping him do pretty much everything until he was able to function on his own. As time passed he regained his strength and was strong enough to walk normally again. We went back to having fun as kids.

One day while playing in the back by the warehouses my brother and our friend Clive found two puppies. They came home with the puppies hoping our parents would let them stay. They lied and said someone had given them the puppies, not wanting to admit they found them. Having no interest in having any pets, our parent's initial response was no. That was until a little more persuasion came from my sister and myself.

They finally agreed on letting us keep one. My mother named the pup Makassa after the song *"Soul Makossa"*. She named Clive's pup Cumo. The pups were brother and sister. It was cool to have them raised within two families that were already close. They were together all the time. That was until Cumo fell ill a year later and eventually passed away.

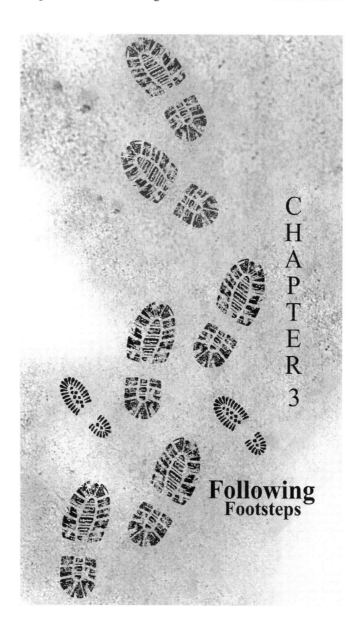

C
H
A
P
T
E
R
3

Following
Footsteps

As an adolescent I was very active and energetic. By the age of twelve I was heavy into skateboarding with my boy Alaric. We'd build our boards from scratch. We would get free pieces of wood from the lumberyard and stencil the shape we wanted onto them. We would then cut and smooth the wood using tools from my father's toolbox. A little paint, wheels, a skid plate and gripping and we were good to go. Our boards were good enough to sell in any shop.

We'd frequent a skating rink in Queens on Roosevelt and Jackson Heights. They had a skateboarding section full of ramps where we could practice our stunts all day. After plenty of practice my confidence was at an all time high. I decided to enter my first tournament in the hood with Alaric. It was a community event held across the street from my building on what we called Smooth St. This was the first of these events and I was beyond excited. I was ready to show and prove and make everyone proud of me. Alaric went before me, but he slipped up and fell. He came back and told me I have to nail this because both of us can't lose. The pressure was on. The competition was steep but I knew I was the best and I had it in the bag.

Unfortunately the worst happened. I missed a trick that I usually landed with ease. I messed up when it really counted. I had to skate quite some distance to reach the ramp. I hit the ramp at top speed gaining height in the air. I flipped the board 360 degrees in flight, but instead of landing with my feet planted on top of the board I landed on my ass. My spirits were crushed. Alaric tried to cheer me up but I wasn't feeling it. As soon as the event ended we went to practice until I got it right and built my confidence back up. Skateboarding had my undivided attention. If only I applied that same work ethic in school I may have been something great.

In school I did things for attention. I was your stereotypical class clown. I was really good at it, but it always got me into trouble. All the trouble I stirred up caused me to be held over twice. I was held over once in the fourth grade and once in the sixth. At that point going to school became frustrating. Not being in the correct grade was very aggravating and I brandished my strife through my actions, causing further trouble.

Despite my struggles with school my parents paid close attention to any extra-curriculum activities that piqued my interest. They showed just as much enthusiasm with their other children. I loved to read and go to the studio with my father while he worked on his album. If my parents saw a glimmer of desire or talent in any area they would support it whole-heartedly in every way possible.

My mom had me taking private piano and bass

guitar lessons. I was not doing too well in school, but I still had to attend my private music classes. I hated it. Instead of playing with my friends after school I had to practice. I picked up on it quick. I had an ear for the music and played better hearing it than reading it off of paper.

For added entertainment at home, my parents would invite family and friends over to watch me perform. I would put on my dark sunglasses and do imitations of Stevie Wonder and Ray Charles on our organ. They found it humorous. After a while I took into it because it was a way to get closer to my parents.

They would work together writing songs and would call me in to voice my opinion. I thought that was cool. They thought highly of my opinion and that made me feel good. I felt even better when it all paid off. One of their songs hit the top 100 Billboard Charts in the 70's. *"Dance All Night (Till' You Get It Right)"* by Kenny Bee. We were ecstatic when we heard the song on the radio for the first time. Things were looking good. We still lived in the hood but things were beginning to look up for us.

My mother worked for the YWCA. She was contracted by the city. She visited all the inner city public schools, teaching the kids a healthy nutritional regimen. My father drove tractor-trailers for the

Teamsters Union. They both had steady jobs and did their best to provide all things possible for us. My father had me alongside him all the time.

I saw many of my friends grow up fatherless and was always afraid that my dad would leave and never come back home. I stayed on him like a pair of pants. My father took the place of the many absent fathers in the neighborhood. He was always active and conscious regarding his health. He'd work out and swim in the pool all day and would bring truck inner tube tires for the kids to play with. He would often jog from Brooklyn to the Bronx and back non-stop. He'd have the entire family running with him.

We did a lot together as a family. Visiting Coney Island was our regular. I would often imitate most of what I saw my father doing. He saw my interest in trucks so he took me on the road with him at an early age. His boss was teaching his nine-year-old son to drive trucks, so my dad took it upon himself to teach me at eleven years old.

The first truck I learned on was a 5-gear Maxidyne Mack Truck. By the age of twelve I was driving on the road, through tollbooths and even through tunnels. I drove Peterbilts, Internationals and Kenworths with the trailer connected. One day he asked me did I want to drive and as always I was happy to do so. I used to jump in between his legs and steer while he changed the gears, but on this day he said I was too big for that. He felt I was ready to drive on my own.

This was my moment. I sat in the seat and pushed my foot on the clutch. I pushed in the emergency button to free the break system. I then put the stick shift in gear. I put my signal light on and drove off. The truck came to a screeching halt. My father looked at me and asked, *'What's wrong'?* I said I was nervous. He told me, *"Take your time, do what you know how to do and nothing more."*

I started over again and this time I pulled it off without a hitch. I pushed the clutch down and pulled the stick out of gear. I pushed the clutch in again and put the stick shift in the next gear. As I went faster my father told me the rules of the road. *"You can't ever beat the road. Don't ever disrespect the road. The road will kill you before you kill the road."*

He always said that. He knew he had taught me well. He showed me how to follow maps. He said, *"Always remember where you came from and where you are going."* He gave me the directions and then to my shock and surprise, he took his hat and put it over his face. He went to sleep. Seeing that made me take everything I was doing serious. He not only believed in me, he trusted me with his life.

A few minutes later, He went into the back of the sleeper and told me to watch the speed limit. He told me to always look up the road at least a quarter mile ahead for the highway patrol. I worked with my father throughout the summer. I did most of the driving when we had long runs, like from New York to Texas.

I had many other duties as well such as keeping the logbooks in order to show how many hours we drove on the road. I also had the responsibility of loading and unloading the truck. That was the best part because I got to drive a forklift. Being on the road with my father allowed me to form a very close bond with him. I remember when he first wanted to talk about the birds and the bees. He asked me if I had sex yet?, at twelve years old! He told me he could help me get right in that area if I needed it. I lied and told him that I had a girlfriend and that we did it already.

My father and I talked about everything. He was teaching me very important facts of life. He taught me the tools that he knew I'd need to survive in my adulthood. For my hard work at the end of the week he once gave me $500.00. That was more than half of what my sister made while working for the Summer Youth Core Program. That was more than what my mother made in a week.

Although my mother saw my hard work and

determination, she had a problem with my father giving me so much money at such a young age. She allowed me to do my own school shopping and get anything I wanted. I had to put the remainder of the money up for my allowance throughout the year. I went to Delancey Street and bought them out.

My first year of junior high school I had a seventeen pair sneaker collection. I had enough clothes to wear a different outfit every day for two months. Even with all that, my sister and mother would buy me things they thought were nice and wanted me to wear. I guess you can say I was a little spoiled.

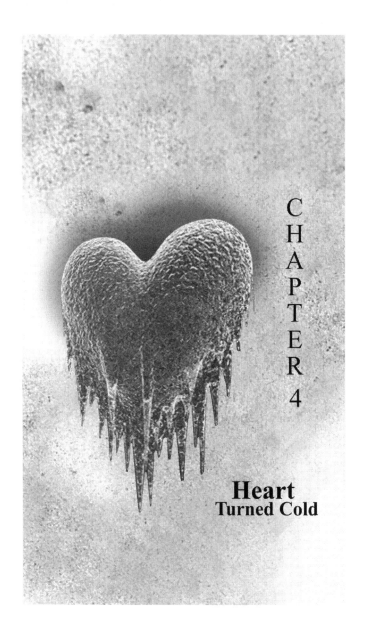

C
H
A
P
T
E
R
4

Heart
Turned Cold

One nice day later that summer, I was playing with a friend Kelly Banks. As it began to get dark, I knew it was time for us to get home. We lived in adjacent buildings. I had a crush on her for a while, but on this day I got up enough heart to ask her to be my girlfriend. She said yes. I was elated. We hugged and I got my first kiss.

We said we would see each other the next day. Oh my God! The next day seemed like a lifetime away. When morning came all I could think about was going outside to play with Kelly again.

Kelly had three older brothers and two were known drug dealers, Curtis Jr. and Artlis known as "8 Ball". Just a week prior they had a major shoot out in the parking lot against their Italian connects. A transaction had gone bad ensuing a war. A few days later both sides came to a resolve, resulting in a ceasefire. The brothers made payment arrangements to settle their debt. The day after I asked Kelly to be my girlfriend, the Italians were scheduled to go to their house to collect.

The brothers needed more time, which they didn't get. One of the Italians grabbed Kelly and began stabbing her multiple times until she was dead. There was a massive commotion for most of the day as spectators huddled outside the apartment. They waited under the building for her body to be brought out. I left my building heading towards Kelly's building unaware of what took place.

I saw the commotion going on under her building. I overheard a spectator saying that something bad had happened in Kelly's apartment, with her being the victim. While all of this was being said the ambulance wheeled her body out on a stretcher. There was a blood stained sheet covering her young beautiful body. As I was forced to take all of this in my body turned as cold as hers. My legs were weakening as I stood there in shock. I never felt so much pain in my young life. The following week tragedy struck Kelly's family again. Her older brother Curtis Jr. was found dead on the roof with a needle in his arm, staged as if he overdosed on heroin.

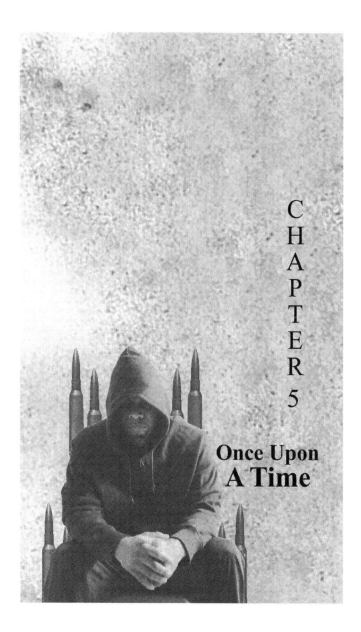

CHAPTER 5

Once Upon A Time

The city was in complete hysteria. Everyone was in panic mode. We were at my aunt's house in East New York in the back yard playing and heard a noise in the bushes. Everyone ran in the house screaming "The Son of Sam is in the bushes. There was a manhunt for him and he had the entire city scared. Fortunately for us, it was just a cat in the bushes.

Not long afterwards there was a blackout and the entire city lost its electrical power. To make matters worse, a transportation strike followed soon after. I had the responsibility of taking my father's car from our parking lot in the projects to a private one about five minutes from our building. I didn't have a license at the time. I was waiting to go back down south to take my test, but my parents believed my driving skills were good enough.

Soon after, my mother started attending night school to get her degree in nursing. If she was running late I would take and pick her up from work and school. I'd sometimes pick up Mia, Ella and Tasha and drive to school. No one could tell me I wasn't on top of the world. That was until I became so cocky that I parked the car in the teachers' parking lot. Damn! One of the teachers saw me. There was no more driving to school for me.

So much was going on in my hood. A gang called the "Ching-A-Lings" aka MC Nomads claimed the hood. They said they were there to protect. The leader of the Brooklyn branch was "Uncle Boze". The Ching-A-Lings were strong in their own right, but one of the most feared was "Possum. He as well as Kevin Busey were my idols in those days and times. They both lived on my block.

There was a drag racing section in the back of the hood. People would race cars and motorcycles for money and the titles to their vehicles. People came from Atlanta, Alabama, Connecticut, New Jersey, Miami and anywhere else imaginable to take part in these events. It was very dangerous back there, but most of us kids would stand right on the sidelines assuming the same risk as the adults.

Summertime was one hell of a time in my hood. I'd find ways to make money. I had a shoeshine box and I set up shop across the street from my building. When my dad's friends came by to hang out I would shine their shoes and hand wash their cars. One day Kevin Busey let me wash both of his cars. He brought out his drop top white Corvette and his yellow Duster Race car. When I finished washing the cars Kevin handed me a hundred dollar bill, which I looked at in amazement. As if it couldn't get any better, my dad let Kevin take me to where they drag raced in the back.

Once we got back there we drove through taking in everything around us. Kevin was greeted with so much respect. I was just riding shotgun taking it all in. Kevin talked about how wild my friends and I were and how he felt I would do big things when I got older. He turned around to drive down the strip, revving up the car, emitting a rough sound from the motor. He then drove off, wheels spinning out, filling the air with the smell of burned rubber.

Ahead of us I saw a lady bending over, butt out, leaning into the car parked on the side. As we drove past her I reached my hand out and smacked her on the butt. Kevin didn't see what I just did and kept driving. He did not realize the car peeled off in pursuit of us. We got to the light on Lorraine St. and made a left when the trailing car began blaring its horn. Kevin pulled over and two guys got out of the car looking very pissed off.

I jumped out the car and started running. When I got to my building I saw Kevin's brother Verdell and "8 Ball". I told them some guys were jumping Kevin down the block. We ran back to where Kevin was, but to my surprise they weren't fighting, they were talking. The lady I smacked on the butt was there as well. All the attention was now on me. Kevin called me over and everyone started laughing. The lady ran her fingers through my hair saying how cute I was. She said, *"That smack on my butt hurt"*. Kevin made me apologize. I hung my head down and told her I was sorry.

When I wasn't with my dad, I was trying to run behind Kenneth. We were very close growing up. We were just three years apart, but around the age of fourteen the temptations of his surroundings had taken over him despite our family being very active in the church. My dad was the lead singer and my mom, brother, sister and myself were all ushers.

One evening my brother decided to take a stand. As dinner was being prepared on the table, he pointed out the pork and refused to eat. He stated that he was now a member of the Five Percent Nation of Islam. He further stated that the black man is God! Of course I began laughing because I knew he was about to get a whooping.

My dad stopped eating his food and began to go in on my brother. He said, *"I worked too hard to have you insult my home with this rhetoric about these beliefs."* My mom intervened, telling my dad to leave him alone. My mom took my brother's plate and removed the pork. She gave it back to him and said," *Welcome into my home God, since you are God I'm sure you will be in church on Sunday."*

My parents may have won that battle, but they didn't win the war. My brother went to church and began recruiting kids his age to become Five Percenters as well. They were stealing out of the collection trays and at lunchtime they would sneak around the corner to buy and smoke marijuana. Seeing them do this didn't make me any better. I stole out of the collection plate once as well and went to the bodega. I bought a little Debbie Dutch apple cake, a bag of Bon Ton potato chips, and a twenty-five cent juice. I felt bad afterward and never did it again.

My brother would soon find trouble everywhere he turned. He carried the name "Savior" and was becoming a very infamous hustler on the streets of Brooklyn. His friends would knock on our door asking for Savior. My mom would say, *"Savior doesn't live here!"* and close the door. My brother asked my mom one day *"Why are you telling people I don't live here?"* and she said, *"You do live here, but Savior doesn't."*

He was sent to The Geller House Group Home for youth under twenty-one in Manhattan. He eventually got locked up a short while after and was sent to Rikers Island to do one year at C-76. When he came home he was sent to The St. Johns Group Home in Far Rockaway. I was beginning to feel the effects of growing up in one of the roughest parts of Brooklyn. The bad part was that my brother was one of the many who held that reputation for roughness. The upside was that no one bothered Savior's little brother.

My brother had his crew from the hood, which consisted of Dorsey, Wise, Shakim, Rakim, Dondy, Crimey and B-Allah. They were all making a strong mark, getting money by any means necessary. BK was known for gunplay and stick up's which my brother and his crew carried out well. They all fed off of each other in one way or another. When you saw them you saw a bunch of young cats doing it big. They represented with dirt bikes, big gold cable chains and the latest trend setting styles.

Dorsey came over to the house to visit my brother one day, wearing a beaver hat, Gazelle glasses, sheep skin coat, jeans, and a fresh pair of Wallabee Clark shoes. My brother stepped out wearing a leather Quarterfield coat, a Stetson hat, Gazelle glasses, jeans and a fresh pair of Wallabee Clark shoes. I wanted to be just like them. They went into their pockets pulling out wads of money and peeled off a few dollars for me. I was overjoyed.

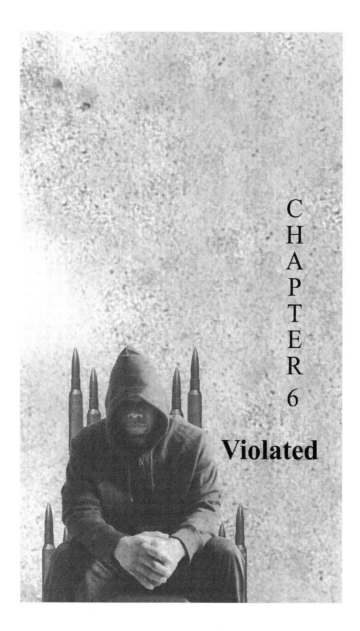

CHAPTER 6

Violated

I went to the P-A-L Athletic center to try out for the basketball team. The Miccio Kangaroos was for youth ages twelve to fifteen. I made the cut and went on to do pretty well throughout the tournament. I was more of a rebounder than a shooter. I played for the Miccio Buzzards soon after. My new coach told me to practice my free throws.

I asked my mom to let me walk our dog late one night, my intentions were to go to the school playground across the street and practice my free throws. I was shooting around for a while when I noticed someone watching me. It was a tall, slim built, dark skin man standing outside the fence. He began to comment on how I was shooting the ball. My dog was barking the whole time, but I didn't think much of it when I tied her to the fence. The man noticed my boom box and said he had a better one if I wanted it. He said we would have to go down the block to his car to get it.

I had been asking my parents for another radio for a while. I thought it to be harmless to go check it out. I took it as someone being nice and generous. The streetlights were out further down the block, so the street began to get darker. Once we got down the block he grabbed me by the collar and reached for the zipper on his pants. He demanded me to get on my knees. I instantaneously went into shock, but then my impulses kicked in.

I punched him in the stomach as hard as I could and ran as fast as my legs could carry me. He chased me and grabbed the collar of my green lumber jacket. I slipped out of it and kept running trying to get to my dog. I finally got to her, grabbing her leash as she began barking loudly trying to get at the man. He turned around and ran in the opposite direction. I hurried upstairs to tell my parents what just went on. Before I could finish my sentence they were out the door. We rushed downstairs finding my jacket in the middle of the street.

My dad was in a vengeful rage. We jumped in the car and circled the whole hood, but didn't see him. Time would pass, but I'd think about that night often. I blamed my hood and my brother for being in that group home. I needed his protection and he was nowhere around.

One day during the summer of 1980, Savior came home on one of his weekend visits. That Saturday the Disco Enforcers had their turntables and speakers out in the park entertaining at least four hundred people. It had been about a year since the incident happened and for the first time I saw the man again! I ran upstairs to tell my dad, but he wasn't home. I was frantic, not wanting the man to get away.

I went in the closet and grabbed a 2x4. I ran out

the door, running downstairs as fast as I could. I saw
my brother and rushed over to him to tell him that I
saw the man. I knew it was going to be on now! My
brother ran up on him and said, *'You bothering my lil'
brother''?* This was not what I expected. I saw no
reason for questioning.

The man was trying to deny it, saying it was a case
of mistaken identity. My anger was building as all of
this was going on. When he turned and looked at me
I exploded. I picked up the stick and swung it as hard
as I could, hitting him in the head. He went down to
the ground hard and my brother, Dorsey, and a few
others began to beat him down. He somehow was
able to get up and run out of the park. I found out
later who he was related to, but I never saw him
again.

Although I never talked about that incident, I held
as much resentment for my brother and his boys as I
did for the man. I felt betrayed by my brother for
being in a group home. It seemed he was never
around when I needed him. I felt he should have
done more to the man when we had him. I
internalized my disappointments building a strong
bitterness towards my brother for many years.

My brother still came home every weekend for his
home visits. I had mixed feelings about his
departures. I often went with my dad to the group

home to visit him. I would tell him to stay out of trouble and come home so we can be a family again.

During one of those visits he told my dad he wanted to get into boxing. He wanted to come home and train with him. My dad saw this as a way to reconnect with his son. He worked it out with the group home and my brother was able to come home and train. My brother signed up at the local gym, "Lunar's Boxing Gym" and went feet first into the boxing world.

Within a matter of months my brother was running with my dad from Brooklyn to the Bronx and back, non-stop. They would swim laps in the local pool, lift weights and do just about anything else to build up his strength and stamina. I would go to the gym with them to hit the heavy bag, speed bag, or jump rope. My attention was mostly on my brother sparring in the ring.

He was working hard and everything was beginning to pay off. He became close to a Cuban boxer named Carlos who was training for the Olympic games. My brother pushed himself to join the games as well. There was a big boxing exhibition going on at the Visitation Center in my neighborhood. It was a showcase for all of the boxers from Brooklyn.

The hype was big in my family because Savior was representing us. We would soon find out that he was in the same weight class as the best amateur boxer in the circuit, Mark Breland. My dad went out and bought all the equipment that my brother needed, mouthpiece, boxing shorts, tank tops and the same tassel shoes that Sugar Ray Leonard wore.

The night of the fight my brother wasn't feeling well and my dad gave him some medicine that made him feel sluggish. When he entered the arena and saw the entire hood in attendance, he quickly snapped out of it. It was him against Mark. He and Mark put on a great performance for the full three rounds. Mark won, but said that my brother was the hardest hitter he had encountered. They would go on to become good friends.

My brother had a few fights after Mark. He went on to the Jr. Olympics and won. He was expecting to go to the Olympic games, but was disappointed when his coach chose another guy on the team to represent them. This was the same guy my brother would often beat in training. Everyone was baffled. *"Why would the coach pick him?"* This move infuriated Sav so much that he quit boxing and went back on the streets harder than ever before.

Mark Breland eventually went pro. He won as many as three title belts in his career. Mark would sometimes see my brother on the streets and try to convince him to come train at the Kronx Gym. My brother turned him down. He was through with boxing. The street was his ring and the hustling game was his title to win.

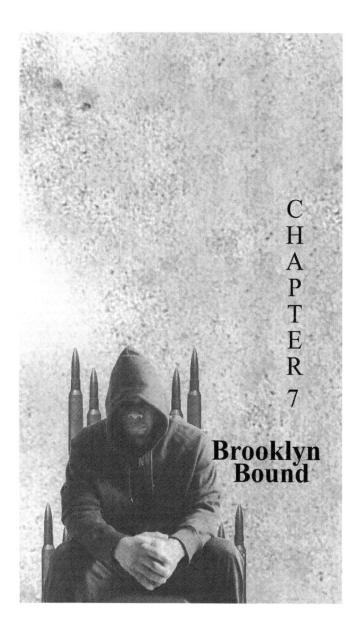

C
H
A
P
T
E
R
7

**Brooklyn
Bound**

On weekends I'd go to 42nd St., where all of New York would be. 43rd and Broadway was where the photo guy "Buck" took classic photos on the famous wall. Brooklyn was strong on the set. Hood stars were in attendance like Bogard, Homicide, Redbug, Iron-Mike Tyson, Chink, Supreme Magnetic, Lil' Jamel, Killer Ben, Born, I-true, Kevin Davis, Bush, Sha-Ru, Rick Martin, True, 50 Cents, Rome, Prescott, Hicks, Scooter, Punch, Bush, JR, Mark Spark, Majesty, Kason, Danny Dan, Unique, Tut, Jesus, Kendu, Lou Hobbs, Rasun, Uzi Delroy, Chief, Kato, Spady, Father Divine, Vance, Haitian Jack and the list goes on.

Girls were strong in their own right too, Cindy, Jackie, Robin, Black Cheryl, Michelle, Jill, Cola, Yoli, Pat, Sharon, Jasmine, Tee, Javette, Mimski, Rena, Black Kathy, Maggie, Malinda, Dottie, Vanessa, Queenie, Natoka, Tasha, Sprucey, Mina, Mimi, Shanell and Damaris made their presence known.

The 43rd St. outings were most lusted after. All the hood stars mingled while the spectators took in the moment. My brother was center stage with his crew. All the gangstas and hustlers acknowledged him. This was my way of befriending these guys as well. I took pride in being Savior's lil' brother.

Along with having just as much heart as Sav, I watched him very well in order to learn the skills he possessed. When I felt like I gained enough knowledge, I went hard. When I was in the city, me, Sav and my crime partner Sha-Ru would network, making names for ourselves. I became really close to 50 cents and that was a concern for my brother. He knew how hard 50 ran the streets.

Truth be told, there was no pressure coming from who I ran with. I put pressure on myself wanting to be just as good as my brother. I didn't want to be Lil' Savior anymore. I had to step it up. One night while chillin' with my boys Bubba, Born, and Everlasting, I saw my brother grouped up with Dorsey and the rest of their crew. We went over to see what they were up to.

They were deep in conversation about a robbery heist they were going to take down the following morning. They had one slight dilemma; they didn't have enough transportation to move their crew and the merchandise. This sounded like a great opportunity for me. I could let my brother see that I had skills.

I pulled my crew away from the others and we started walking across the Gowanas Canal Bridge by Hamilton Ave. Over there was the Bruno's trucking company warehouse. They held tractor-trailers, and cargo vans. Bubba and I climbed over the gate. Once we got on the other side Bubba went to look for the security box, while I jumped in the truck that was blocking the gate.

The keys were in the ashtrays of all the vehicles. There was one problem though; there was no room to drive forward. In order to get out I had to back the truck up and drive through the gate. I started the truck and put it in reverse. I rammed the gate making way too much noise. Born and Everlasting told me to stop, but I had no other choice but to ram it again in order to knock it down. I backed into the gate again and this time I drove through it.

Bubba made his move by running inside. He jumped in a truck and drove off. Born ran inside and did the same, while I jumped out of the truck and ran past Everlasting following the others. I got in the van and cleared the gate, but the dust was clouding my view so bad that I couldn't see Everlasting. I realized something was wrong, so I backed up. Everlasting jumped in and I screamed on him. I told him to get his own truck, but he said he didn't know how to drive.

Once we got back to Hamilton Ave., I told Bubba and Born to follow me. We drove down the avenue that my brother and his crew were hanging on. When they saw us their eyes lit up. I rolled the window down and screamed out to my brother. I told him that we wanted to accompany them on the Delancey

St. heist and then I drove off with my guys following behind me.

We had no license plates and very little gas, but we had leverage to negotiate so we went back to the Ave. Before leaving, we took the keys and put them under the tires of each van because we felt my brother and his boys were going to shake us down. Once we got to the Ave. my brother and his crew circled us and as expected, they shook us down asking for the vans. We kept saying if they let us go with them in the morning then they could have them.

My brother got mad and said that I couldn't go, but Dorsey told him to let me go. Dorsey said, *"Look at what he's doing man. He's already on the streets like you. Let him come and we'll both keep him close to us."* My brother reluctantly agreed. We gave them two of the trucks and it was on in the A.M.

Morning came and everyone met on the Ave. and loaded up in one of the trucks. We got to Delancey St. and parked the truck. I felt the truck was parked too far away and took it upon myself to bring the truck right across from the store. Big mistake. No sooner than me bringing the truck around and double parking, the meter man came and ran the plate. The truck was soon towed away.

Everyone was mad at me, but that didn't stop the

task at hand. My brother, Dorsey, and Rakim went inside. Our cue was them coming out of the dressing rooms. We would then run in and do what we called a "Free For All". That we did. We cleaned them out. We got them for about 60% of their stock. My projects smelled like leather and suede after that. My brother told me, *"This doesn't mean I approve of you doing what I do. I don't want mommy to think I got you running the streets like that."*

To keep me out of trouble my brother gave me a Mo-ped motorbike. He was coming home from the group home more often and I was happy for that. One weekend during one of my brother's weekly visits I decided to stay over at my aunt's house in East New York. Little did I know, my brother had the nephew of the guy that tried to molest me on his radar. My brother threatened and robbed him every chance he could.

The man's nephew Monte was scared to death of my brother. My brother told him that if his uncle got caught back in the hood he wasn't going to make it out alive. Early one morning around 4 a.m. while hanging with Supreme and Abe my brother saw Monte. Monte saw my brother and fearing for his life, he pulled out a gun and started shooting wildly.

One of the bullets hit my brother in the head. Supreme frantically called my parents. They got to my brother before the ambulance and rushed him to Long Island College Hospital's emergency room. He went straight into surgery to remove the bullet as well as a portion of his skull. My dad called me to tell me what happened and to get to the hospital a.s.a.p. My cousin Willie and myself were there by the 9 a.m. visiting time. Luckily the surgery was a success and my brother made it out in stable condition.

One would think this would slow someone down, but my brother was furious that he was caught slipping. He went from the hospital straight to the group home in Far Rockaway. Not long after that, Monte went to Far Rockaway to visit a girl. He didn't know my brother lived out there and could not foresee what was to come. My brother ran up on him putting Monte in a hospital bed fighting for his life.

CHAPTER 8

Kill The Party

One Saturday night, The Disco Enforcers were in the park jammin'. They were knee deep in a DJ battle with some guys from the Lower East Side. As the night grew darker my brother and Dorsey entered the park. My brother knew I was going to be there because I loved watching the DJ's do their thing.

Sav and Dorsey were both wearing Straddler trench coats. They stood out due to the fact that it was summer time. I was real concerned for Sav. He had just gotten out of the hospital from being shot and he still had the bandages around his head. My brother told me to come with him and I did. We walked up to the guys from L.E.S. We stood in front of their equipment and he asked me *"Is this the type of equipment you wanted?"* I said, *"Yeah"*. In a split second he and Dorsey both pulled out sawed off 12 gauge shot guns.

My brother told me to unplug the equipment and take the turntables. As I started doing this he asked, *"Is that all you want?"* I told him I needed the mixer and we took that too. After that night I was DJ Cal Free.

That next weekend, The Battle of The Brooklyn DJ's was going down in the visitation center. It was big talk about the battle and who was going to be there. Names like Leslie Gee, Calvin B, and Clark Kent were heavy in the air. I couldn't miss this for anything and I snuck out of the house.

I saw my brother's boys Shallar and Barkim and I asked them did they see my brother. I slid through the back door with them. While in the back they told me to look out the side door and let them know if I saw anyone coming. They were planning to rob someone.

Barkim opened his Straddler jacket, pulling out a 12 gauge shot gun. It got caught up in his pants and it went off. He accidentally shot off part of his foot. Blood was spilling out of his shoe covering the floor. There was a lot of commotion going on from the sound of the gunshot. Shallar had to carry him out and rush him to the hospital. I couldn't believe what just happened, but I stayed and went inside. The place was jam-packed.

I saw Powerful (Clive) who was like a brother to me. He just came home from jail and I hadn't seen him in a while. As soon as I was going to ask him did he see my brother, mayhem erupted outside and shots were fired. It was crowded at the entrance and people were pushing and shoving trying to get inside and out of harm's way. Someone from Red-Hook was shot, lying dead at the entrance of the venue. Once it was known who the person was all hell broke loose. It was a strong figure from the hood, Greg Degrossa.

The whole hood went on a rampage. Anyone not

from Red-Hook received the repercussions of Greg's demise. Word spread fast on what had occurred and a lot of people got hurt that night. It didn't take long for the hood to find out who was responsible. It was a guy named Chip from Bushwick.

Greg was down with OE (Old English), a well-known crew in the hood. They were on a mission to avenge his death. They went to Bushwick to invade the home of Chip. He was not home, but his mother was. She was viciously beat down in an attempt to find her sons whereabouts. They were unable to catch him before the police did and he was arrested and sentenced for the murder.

After Greg's death it seemed as if the hood came together as one and became a much stronger force. The hood was a fort that held very few hostages. Points were made, if you came to Red-Hook with bad intentions you would receive ten times those intentions.

Late that summer, Madison Square Garden was hosting the Colgate Games. It was a major track and field event and some really good prospects from Red-Hook were competing. There was a well-known trainer named "Speedy" who trained some of the fastest runners in the tournament. It seemed like Red-Hook had a section of our own. I was sitting between my brother and my boy Jus. Both my brother and Jus stepped away to use the restroom. Jus was a lil' dude, but he had on a lot of jewelry. Some boys were scheming on Jus, but that got shut down real fast.

Some dude kept staring at my brother once him and Jus sat back down. My brother had robbed him in the past. The guy was with five other dudes and he was putting them on to who my brother was. They thought they were going to step to him, but my brother quickly jumped up and yelled out "Yo Red-Hook!" The entire section jumped up, females included. Those dudes pulled back and rolled out, never looking back.

That next week, school was in session. Things weren't going so well for me in that area. I was in the seventh grade and I was supposed to be a freshman in high school. The start of the year I attended I.S 88, was transferred to I.S.293, then sent to J.H.S.142. They were all in Brooklyn. At this point the system was so tired of me, they put me in a special education class. This infuriated me. Bad enough I wasn't in my right grade, now I'm in a special-ed class. This move made me rebel far more than I had in the past.

My mom visited the school and had a discussion with my teacher Mr. Chapman. He told her that, if giving the permission of the parent he would use a ruler to physically discipline his students. My mom had given him this permission. Once she left, I warned Chap not to try me.

One day I got out of line and Chap decided to test his ruler out on me. My reflexes were sharp. I picked up a chair and hit Chap with it. He went down pretty hard. Everyone was shocked at what happened next. Chap jumped back up. I saw the expression on his face and knew I was in big trouble.

Chap regained his composure and chased me around the classroom. Before the day was out, I was in the principal's office. Chap refused to press charges on me. He said that despite what took place, I was a good kid. I felt bad because Chap always had our backs and did his best to help us. To make amends with Chap, I agreed to take a psychological test.

Later that week was the test day. They scheduled me for numerous tests on that day. They put a machine in front of me and attached wires to my head and arms. It resembled a lie detector test. As the test began, they put a box with some shapes and a board with the outline of those shapes in front of me. They wanted me to put the shapes in their proper places. I put the triangle in its place, then the rectangle, then the circle, and so forth. I was engulfed in rage because they were studying me like an animal in a cage. In my fit of anger I shoved the board and the box onto the floor, removed the wires and stormed out of the room.

The results of the test concluded that I was mentally stable, but had a bad attitude. My teacher sat with me and asked me what was my problem. He said he couldn't help me if I wouldn't let him know what my issues were. He knew that I was held over twice in public school. I let him know how that affected me. I told him that I wanted to take a placement test and be put in my proper grade.

Chap backed me up and supported me in front of the principal. He arranged for me to take a placement test. Chap stayed after class with me to study everyday. He encouraged me to stay out of trouble and focus. When the day came to take the test, I knew I was ready.

The results came back a few days later. I not only excelled, but my scores showed that I was above an average 10th grader. I showed that I was smart enough to go to my proper grade. The decision in the end was for me to finish out the year in the 7th grade and the following year I would go to the 10th grade. I was ecstatic I was tired of being made to feel like something was wrong with me. I was now able to finish the school year knowing that there was a light at the end of the tunnel.

One day after a school lunch break I was walking through the Ave. with the other kids going back to school. We saw the paramedics attending to a guy named Ross who had apparently been shot. His heart stopped and his cousin Les was pushing for the paramedics to keep trying to revive him. They started hitting him with the defibrillator and after numerous attempts they finally retrieved his heartbeat.

Rumor had it that Ross and Shakim tried to stick up the Pepsi Cola truck deliverer. While attempting to get away Ross got caught in the crossfire and accidentally got hit by a stray bullet. Shakim got away and was on the run for a short time before eventually getting caught. He served up to six years in prison for the crime.

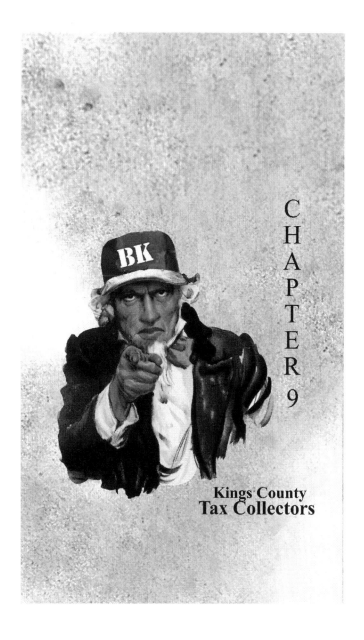

C
H
A
P
T
E
R
9

Kings County
Tax Collectors

Summer time was back around aka get money time. One day while chilling under my building, I saw Sha-Ru. He just came home from Rikers Island's C-76, serving a year bid. We were talking about meeting up in the morning to go get some money. This meant we were going on a robbing spree! We'd go to certain schools in the city and just do us.

We had so much jewelry by the end of the day that we could have opened up a jewelry store. We threw it all on the scale and did what we called "tip the scales". The jewelry was so heavy that the needle went all the way around in a full circle. This was a regular day of events.

We once attained the master key to all the apartments in the hood. We robbed as many cribs as we could in a matter of a few days, then things got too hot. Most days, I'd start out by meeting up with Sha-Ru, Divine and Justice. We all lived in the same building.

I was the youngest and felt I had the most to prove. Every time we'd go out, I'd make a point by scouting and striking our targets first. A few days prior, Sha-Ru and Divine went to Delancey St. and got caught up in a store. They had to make a quick getaway. The owner blocked the entrance while the police were on their way. They only had one option and they took it.

Divine lifted his hands in front of his face and jumped straight through the front window, while Sha-Ru followed right on his heels. They got away, but Divine fell back the next day while we went out to do us. Sha-Ru and I decided to take Lil' Rah with us. Lil' Rah was my homie from my building. Instead of going on a spree we went to Coney Island to visit some girls. Sha-Ru was messing with a girl named Keisha, while I was seeing her sister Trisha.

The girls had two cousins named Tim and Mollock. They had names for themselves out in Coney Island. We linked up with them and did a few robberies. This didn't sit too well with a dude named Macaroni. He was considered the hood's bully. He felt we were stepping on his toes in his hood. This dude did not intimidate us at all. We just kept doing us.

On our way home, Sha-Ru, Lil' Rah and myself got on the F-train at Coney Island Ave. Our stop was about twenty-minutes away at Smith 9th St. The train stopped at 7th Ave. and Young Lovable and a few guys from the hood got on. The train sat there for a few minutes. Lovable was looking around like he was plotting on something or someone. Sha-Ru and I was on point. We stepped to him to see what was good. Lovable had a .45 automatic and said he wanted to rob someone.

He seemed hesitant, so I told him to give me the gun. I pointed the gun in the face of the person closest to me and said out loud, "*This a stick up! Everybody give up all your belongings, your money and jewelry and don't make a robbery a homicide.*"

No one moved on my demand. I guess they were in shock because I was so small. Sha-Ru being much bigger than myself said, "*You heard him, your money and jewelry motherfuckers.*" Sha-Ru punched a man dead in his face because he didn't move. I traveled up and down the train car with my gun pointed towards the passengers, while the others collected all they could.

We went to the next car and replayed the same motions. When the next stop of Smith and 9th St. came up, we calmly exited the train and made sure no one followed us. We walked out of the station cool and collected and headed back to the hood. Once we got to the hood, I backed the gun out on Lovable. I told him he wasn't getting any of the cut and he wasn't getting his gun back. I told him if he didn't want to get shot he'd better keep it moving and he did.

Lovable was mad at us. He went around telling people we were running around acting like cowboys. Soon after that incident, we got our hands on a few more guns. We got a 30 30 Winchester, a .32 and a 12 gauge shot gun. We elevated our style of armed robberies. We kicked in doors, yelling out *"Nobody move this is a stick up!"* That was our calling card.

We weren't the only ones trying to be cowboys in the hood. My boy Tip Toe made a move of his own on the Ave. He decided to stick up the Chinese restaurant. It didn't go as smoothly as he expected. He ended up getting locked up for killing the owner. This didn't seem to slow any of us down, not one bit. We had an adrenaline rush and fed off of our reputations.

We heard the rumor that Tut from East New York had robbed his mom's church. That was too much bravado for me, but I did tip my hat off to him for the courage. He further impressed me when he robbed a MTA bus. These were the actions that would establish street cred and drove us to do more. The borough fed off of each other in one-way or another. BK represented any and everywhere.

Word was out in the hood that another "Free for all" was going down. Someone had gotten a hold of the schedule for 98.7 Kiss FM's summer events. The next date was that weekend at Coney Island. It was at least forty of us from the hood. We hit the boardwalk and in no time went to work strong-arm style. It was almost impossible for the police to catch anyone because it was so crowded.

We set a time that we would all meet back up. We did a head count on all the people who came with us. After a few hours of action, we all met back at the pre-determined location and hit the F-train. We entered the back of the train and robbed everyone. As the train stopped, most of us moved on to the next car and kept going until we got to the front. Once our stop Smith and 9th St. came up, we got off. The next day we made the papers, in an article titled "*The Tax Collectors.*"

We grouped up again a couple weeks later to the Diana Ross concert in Central Park. So many people were out there that day. We didn't travel deep this time. We broke off into small groups. Dondy and Wise were on the move and robbed someone as soon as we got there.

I split off with Jus, Rondo, A-Money, Gina and Lisa. We shut it down for that day and just took in the concert. It was a really good show. Afterwards, we got into a fight with some dudes from the East. After the fight, we decided we had enough for the day and went back to the hood.

The next stop on 98.7 Kiss's schedule was Parsons Blvd. in Queens. I was familiar with Queens since I had family that lived on Jamaica Ave and in Woodside. The plan for Parsons was a little different.

Since we were quite a distance from our hood, we brought along only a few weapons. Once we all got together, we headed to the train station and made our way to Parsons Blvd.

We observed our surroundings, staking out the park. We mapped out the entrances and exits and saw that there were only two. We sealed off both openings and the rest of us spread out inside unnoticed. The group "D Train" was performing live. Wise stood in the center of the park and pulled out the 12 gauge. He let off a few shots in the air. The music came to a screeching halt and we made our rounds. We robbed the entire park. In less than ten minutes we were outta there. Mission accomplished.

Sha-Ru was my partner in crime. There was nothing we didn't do together. Since my brother wasn't around much, I looked at Sha-Ru as an older brother. He was the same age as my brother and the bad part was that he was getting into just as much trouble as him.

Sha-Ru was injured in a car accident when he was a small kid. I was there when he was hit and witnessed the car drive off. Upon impact he flew high up into the air and came down hitting the pavement hard. His leg broke leaving his tibia piercing through his flesh.

The driver kept going, but eventually came back

around the block. He was a white guy who happened to be a lawyer. The lawyer settled out of court for $150,000. Sha-Ru had just turned eighteen and his parents allowed him access to $50,000. He came to get me the morning he gained access to his account. We went to the bank and he pulled out $5,000. He gave me $2,000.

He wanted to stop back in the hood to go see Boe, one of the neighborhood drug dealers. Sha-Ru got some coke and we left the hood heading to the city. When we got there we went on a shopping spree buying leather and suede suits, full length sheep skins, tailor made pants, pony fronts, cardigan sweaters and mock necks. We went crazy on the shoes too, getting Wallabees, British Walkers and Playboys of all colors.

We went home and dropped everything off, then headed back to the bank to get $5,000 more. We split the money the same way $2,000 for me and he took $3,000. This time we went downtown and shopped heavy once more. We went to Albee Square Mall with all of our bags doing it real big. Oh yeah, we had all the attention. Fort Green, Farragut, LG (Lafayette Gardens), Marcy and Red-Hook were heavy in the building. Sha-Ru and I went downstairs to Wendy's where our man Jay worked. We ordered some food and then ordered food for everyone else in there.

We found a spot in the corner and Sha-Ru pulled

out the coke. He put a large amount in a $100 bill. He rolled up a few coke cigarettes, lit them and passed one to me. At this point, I had never gotten high before and I gave him a weird look. He said, *"We're celebrating lil' bro, we're rich!"* When he said that I took the cigarette and smoked it. We then sniffed what seemed like the longest lines of coke I could ever imagine. A few girls wanted to get high with us and we didn't mind sharing.

Everyone was in the mall that day, 50 Cents, Killer Ben, I-True, Spank, Crimey, all the regulars. Cindy, Mimi, Jackie, Loxie and Tasha all had their crews roaming around as well. Sha-Ru and I were shopping and getting high for three days straight. After the third day of getting high, I told Sha that I didn't want to get high anymore. I told him I wasn't feeling good. He said, *"We're still celebrating!"* I persisted, telling him I didn't want anymore and I stopped.

Going downtown to Albee Square Mall to hang out was a regular for Sha-ru, 50 Cents, Supreme from Park Slope, Big Kev from the Fort and myself. One day out of nowhere 50 started calling me Calvin Klein. I guess it was because my name was Calvin and I wore a lot of Calvin Klein gear. He felt that name was fitting. Truth be told, I hated the name. However, since everyone around us heard him call me that, I decided to just make it a brand of my own and that I did.

50 already established a name for himself on the streets by this time. There were many truths and myths to follow him. One encounter that haunted him the most was an incident in '81. It was at the White Castle in Brooklyn off of Atlantic Ave. Two girls were viciously arguing. One of the girls told the other that if she had a gun she would kill her. It's alleged that 50 overheard this and handed the girl a gun. True to her word she shot and killed the other girl.

The girl that was murdered had a few brothers that were locked up. They sought to avenge her death. They wanted 50's head in their crosshairs. 50 got locked up and went to Rikers Island to serve a year bid. He ended up getting stabbed up real bad from an unrelated incident. After his release, his intent was to never go back to jail at any cost. He was fully prepared to hold court out on the streets.

50 had way too many enemies to ever be without his gun. One day 50, Tracy Washington and I decided to hang out in the game room at the mall. We were plotting on a sneaker store a few doors down. We got bored and decided to rob it. Unbeknownst to us, the Rapper/Dj Biz Markie was co-owner. I later became real cool with Biz and assured him that we wouldn't move on his store again.

Tracy was from Farragut Projects. I would meet up with him, then head down to Fort Greene to pick up 50. One morning 50 set up some drug dealers that were hustling in his hood. He distracted them while Tracy and I came around the corner, guns out and stuck them up. To make it look like 50 had nothing to do with it, we stuck him up too. We pulled off a few moves like that. 50 would point dudes out and Tracy and I would move and attack.

One move didn't go too well. It wasn't often that we were unarmed and unprepared. This situation was spontaneous though. It couldn't be ignored because this dude was on our radar. I moved in to strong arm the dude. He was leaving out of Westinghouse H.S. I got up on him. As soon as I pushed up on him he pulled out a butcher knife. His name was Messiah and 50 had him robbed quite a few times in the past.

I had no choice but to retreat and run. 50 and Tracy were laughing so hard while yelling *"Run!,run!"*. I was so mad that I vowed to get him again. We moved on to bigger fish though and I never entertained that thought. We had many targets throughout the borough and wasted no time catching them.

50 ran into Sav and Jus one day. Both my brother and Jus were loaded with jewelry and 50 was on the prowl. My brother was certain that Jus could and

would hold his own. When 50 asked Sav what was up with Jus, my brother told 50 that Jus would hold his own. 50 had plans though, he ran up on Jus and backed him down with his gun. He robbed him, then spun off on my brother and told him, *"Sav, you lucky you my man or I would of got you too."* That didn't sit too well with Jus. He felt my brother set him up because he knew 50 was his man.

After a day of schemes and plots, we often ended up at the mall where everyone in BK hung out. With a sudden twist of events, 50 told me he was enlisting into the army. He signed up under a family member's name. True to his word he went and served. He came back from his assignment, wearing his army suit around the hood for about three days straight with pride. When I saw him wearing his suit that somewhat inspired me.

I was getting into so much trouble out on the streets that the army didn't seem like a bad move. When I signed up to enlist, I put all of my correct info. They denied me because I was only fifteen years old. I tried again the following year and they told me I needed a permission letter from my parents. I went home and addressed my parents. My mom told me, *"You are my baby. If they're not going to force you in, then you can not go."*

During this time, I didn't feel too many options

weighed in my favor. I was sinking more and more into the street life. Although I was running the streets, I still found time to go to school. I was happy to be in my correct grade, but I was still upset that I was in special education classes.

I attended three different high schools by the end of the year. First was Automotive H.S., where I stayed for a few semesters. I hung out with my boys, Boo Ski from my hood and Black Jus from Baisley Queens who were down with the Supreme Team.

I didn't care too much for that school because there were very few girls attending. I requested a transfer to William E. Grady, a school in Brighton Beach, Brooklyn. I chose that school because my cousins Eric and Rhamel went there. As soon as I got there I linked up with my boy Chris Boe who was doing his thing, selling weed. Boe seemed to have a name for himself around the school. He had his own car and seemed to really be getting some good money.

While talking to Chris Boe one day two dudes pulled up. Chris Boe introduced them to me, Trouble and Timbo from Brownsville. We got real cool, since they were into robberies like I was. We'd link up on a regular and rob the students at the school or go a few blocks down to Lincoln H.S. and do the same. Once a teacher got robbed, a lot of heat fell on us and our lil' run together quickly came to an end.

I got transferred to John Jay H.S., the school that everyone in my hood attended. After a while, it was obvious that not much would change. Things even got worse. It got so bad, that most of us from the hood carried guns to school. We were so bold, that we'd take photos in the school hallway with our guns out. Can you imagine seeing guys in school taking photos with sawed off shotguns, 9mms, and .45 autos?

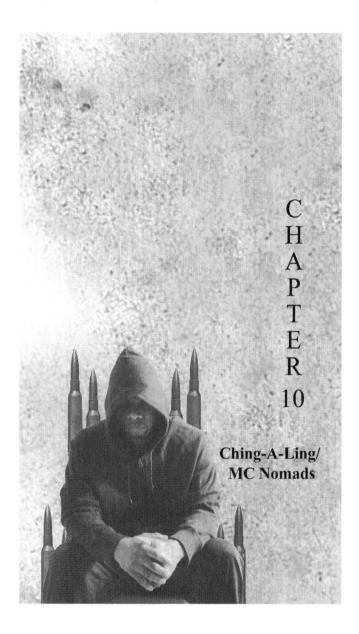

C
H
A
P
T
E
R
10

**Ching-A-Ling/
MC Nomads**

Things were heating up in the hood. Uncle Boze had gotten locked up. He was riding his motorcycle with a young lady from the club when they decided to stop at the White Castle on Atlantic Ave. He pulled into the parking lot along side other bikers who wore the tags from their clubs. Confident of the tags on his back, He walked past the group.

As Boze and the girl got off of his bike, he noticed one of the other bikers arguing with a lady. Boze continued on inside. He placed and received his order, then proceeded to walk out back to his bike. He and his lady friend began to eat their food. Before they could finish, they noticed that the argument between the guy and lady had escalated. The guy began to physically beat on the woman.

Not that it was any of Boze's business, but enough was enough. Boze yelled out to the guy, *"Leave her alone! Try hitting a man like that!"* The man felt he had Boze outnumbered. Him and his boys directed their attention towards Boze. Everyone in the parking lot seemed to react at once. They moved in unison as guns were drawn and a shoot out ensued. Bullets pierced through the air and when the dust settled, the guy that was beating the lady laid on the pavement dead.

Boze was arrested. He faced his fate for an innocent act of self-defense that was reversed in the

the Ching-A-Lings. They were the FTW "Fuck The World" and the FMD crews. Most of the Ching-A-Lings that were in the hood were aware of the relationship Boze had with my family when he was home.

Boze was born and raised in Cuba and was a professional boxer there. When he came to America, he and my parents bonded in friendship. I actually grew up calling him Uncle Boze.

The Ching-A-Lings were out for blood. The clubhouse came to John Jay and sat out front. It looked real crazy outside after school, like a protest or strike was about to ensue. The principal stood in front of the school with damn near the entire precinct alongside him. The police escorted all the students to the train station.

This was around the time that KRS1 from the rap group Boogie Down Production was hanging around my school. This was before he became part of BDP. We eventually met and became really cool with each other, forming a friendship of sorts.

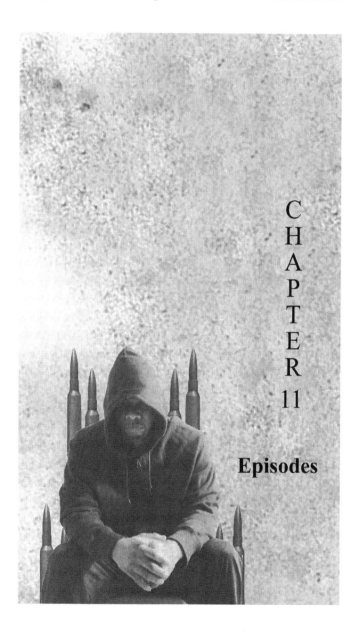

CHAPTER 11

Episodes

The school year ended and summer came back around. My uncle who lived in Maryland came with his family to visit. I was chilling with my lil' cousin Buck when I got into an argument with my brother. My brother got so mad he left the apartment. I told Buck to get ready to go outside. He was excited to go out and hang with me in the city. I told him I was right behind him and to go get the elevator. He had a habit of letting the front door slam. Damn that got on my nerves! As soon as I reached for the door, Buck came running back into the house, right past me.

When I went out in the hallway, I knew something was wrong. The glass part of the elevator door had been completely knocked out for a while now. An older man, who was my next-door neighbor's father, put his head through the empty space to see how far the elevator was. Unfortunately, the elevator was coming down at that moment, leaving him no time to pull his head out. It was too late for him.

The elevator was stuck on our floor and I heard someone in the elevator screaming, *'Yo, stop playing with the elevator!"* I recognized the voice belonging to my brother. I told him not to let the elevator move. I explained what happened, as I ran in our apartment to get my mother. My mom ran out into the hallway to see what happened. She saw the condition the man was in. His hands were straight at his sides. His body was in a stand still position, with a pool of blood beneath him.

The man's daughter came out of her apartment and my mom ran to block her view of her father. The lady, who was around the same age as my mom, went into shock. The police, ambulance and firemen arrived on the scene. They decided to blow the door off with mild explosives. My mom quickly interjected. That wasn't an option, my brother was still in the elevator. They assured my mom that they would only blow the lock off the elevator door. When they did this, the impact made the elevator shake a little.

That was enough to further detach the man's head from his body. His head fell down the elevator shaft and his decapitated body fell into the arms of the firemen. The man's body was placed on a stretcher and his head was retrieved from the bottom of the shaft. My brother got out safely but was overwhelmed by what just happened. That freak accident had a big effect on all of us for a while.

My building seemed to have fallen victim to a series of unfortunate events. Not long after the elevator incident, a Hispanic family that lived next door to us appeared on the news. They robbed a bank near the hood. The father was the mastermind and instructed his oldest sons to go in and stick up the bank. They took a substantial amount of money and initially got away.

By the time they were caught, most of the money was already stashed or spent. This was their sacrifice for the family. They didn't give up the money and settled for the additional time they were facing. Where that seemed to be a good financial move, it was devastating for the family as a whole. The family remained in the projects. They didn't want to make it obvious that they had any of that money stashed away.

It was often I chilled with my boys seeking something to get into, but this night there wasn't anything going on in the hood. I went upstairs to call it a night. As soon as I walked in the door my mom told me to go back downstairs to get my dad. My cousin Willie had a fight with a dude around his way in East New York. I went to my father's usual hangout spot, the parking lot. He was there chilling with his boys.

I told him my mom wanted him and we both went back upstairs. My mom told him that some dudes came to my aunt's house with bats and other weapons. They were banging on the door looking for my cousin, threatening to kill him and my aunt. My dad didn't play when it came to someone messing with his family. At this point my dad knew I was wildin' out in the streets. He told me to round up a few of my boys and meet him back at the parking lot within the next hour. I came back with eleven of my dudes, all armed with guns and ready for war.

This was the first time I ever accompanied my dad to do something of this magnitude, but we felt our cause was probable. We split up into two cars. Once we got to the East, there was no one in sight. We made our rounds in the hood and still no one showed face. Willie guided us to where he thought they could be. We drove past a bodega on Wortman Ave. As we turned the corner, a real big dude was standing there like he owned it. Willie said his name was Pee Wee and that he wasn't there, but the guys were his boys.

I pulled out a 12 gauge, cocked the trigger, and laid the barrel on his chest. At this point he was begging for his life. Over my shoulder, my cousin yelled out, *"He wasn't there!"* Pee Wee knew my cousin. He told Willie to tell me not to shoot him.

My dad pulled me back. We warned Pee Wee that if his boys ever went to my aunt's house again, he wouldn't be so lucky and neither would they. Traveling down the block, we ran into the police. They got out of their car and asked where we were coming from. I stepped up and told them we just came from a basketball game.

My dad spoke to them for a few minutes, then

they got back in their car and left. We felt we had put too much heat on ourselves at that point and we left. For the next few days a few of my boys and myself went out there on our own. We wanted to assure everyone in the East that my cousin was not alone.

CHAPTER 12

Obstruction
Of Justice

While chilling under my building with Sha-Ru and Justice one night, two girls were entering the building, so I held the door open for them. I knew Lona, but the one I didn't know thanked me for holding the door. I don't remember if I responded because I was so mesmerized by her beauty.

As they waited for the elevator the unknown beauty and I exchanged glances. She began talking to Lona, smiling at me as they laughed back and forth amongst each other. Lona said to her, *"Asia you crazy"* and then said, *"Calvin come here."* When I did, they asked me could I escort them across the roof to the next building.

The elevator in their building was broken. I most certainly had no problem escorting them and quickly agreed. As we started speaking, I immediately took notice that the girl Asia was not your average girl from the hood. She spoke too proper. She seemed more mature than what I had assumed her to be. She was the same age as me though. As we talked I was amazed by how attractive she was.

Her skin was a smooth toffee tone. She had sexy eyes, full lips, long straight hair, and her body was proportionate and fully developed. She had the biggest breast I had ever seen on a girl her age. To top it off, she was groomed with class. As we crossed the roof, she held on to my arm really tight, saying,

"Sweetie, don't let me fall."

I assured her that I wouldn't. We got across to the other building, exiting on to the fourteenth floor. We walked towards an apartment I was very familiar with. My parents were close friends with the family that lived there. We spoke a while longer before Asia went inside. I asked could I see her the next day and she agreed.

I walked Lona downstairs to her floor. Before we parted, she assured me that Asia really liked me. Lona called me early the next day to link us back up. Lona was like a sister to me so I knew I was in good hands. She played matchmaker. The following day, I linked up with Asia and not long after, we were inseparable.

As Asia and I became serious I wanted her to meet my parents. When she and my mom met and started talking, she told my mom who her dad was. My mom took a deep look at her and asked, *"What's your mother's name?"* She told her and my mom got up and walked towards her with her arms open. She gave her an affectionate hug. Asia and I looked on in confusion.

My mom told us we were born not too far apart from one another. She told us our families were close until Asia's mom and dad separated many years ago. She said we both played together as babies. Asia's real name was Myasia Mobley. Her nickname was what initially threw my mother off.

Asia's mom had moved to Queens in the suburbs during the mid 70's. Asia very rarely came back to visit when she was younger. Once she became older and was able to travel on her own, she visited more frequently. My mom was more than happy for our relationship and embraced it with open arms. Leave it up to her she would have married us right then and there.

Asia and I were inseparable. We fell in love with each other's heartbeat. We seldom parted, loving each other in every way of the word. It was somewhat hard to adjust to each other's ways because our backgrounds were so different. Her parents expected more in a person than what I possessed. Asia had a hard time at home because of the way they felt about me. She left home and moved in with her grandmother so she could be closer to me.

Asia commuted to school from Brooklyn to Queens each day. At times she fought with me not to pay so much attention to street activities. This would often fall on deaf ears. She hated Sha-Ru and the ground he walked on. She had to blame someone other than myself for my actions. She felt he was a bad influence. I didn't want her to feel in any way that I didn't love her by giving the streets more attention than her. I tried my best to balance it all out.

Her grandmother lived in the same building as her dad and worked the night shift. That was great for us. I went to her crib one night as I often did. She opened the door and stood there in her nightgown. Her massive breasts were protruding through her gown. Her breasts were at least a size 36D. I had an immediate erection. She pulled me into the crib. We kissed passionately her lips so juicy, tasting her tongue. My hands caressing all over her warm body as she began stroking me, telling me how she needed to feel me inside of her.

We went to the room in the back. She began to undress me as I slipped her gown off, letting it fall to the floor. Her breasts were so big, firm and sensitive as I held them in my hand. I began kissing, sucking and biting on her hard nipples as they softened in my mouth. Her body began shaking frantically.

She pulled away from me. She slowly kneeled down in front of me, stroking me and kissing the head of my penis. She began to gyrate my shaft as I went in and out of her mouth. My legs started to give out from under me. Before I was about to cum, she stopped. She got up and laid on the bed with her legs open wide.

I put my hands between her thighs. I put my face

in front of her juicy pussy and put my tongue inside her. She let out a deep moan as she held my head with her hands. She released her delight, filling my mouth with more of her sweet tasty nectar. She pulled me up and I laid on top of her as our eyes locked into one another.

She grabbed my penis and guided it inside of her. When I went in, I went as deep as I could go. I pulled back just enough to hold the head at the entrance of her vagina and then I pushed inside of her again. She held me real tight as she was about to cum and said, *"I love you Calvin"*. As she was climaxing, I exploded at the same time saying, *"I love you too"*. I was still grinding inside of her, touching every crevice of her womb. I turned her on her side, doggie style, then back on her back. We made love through out the night into the morning.

It wouldn't be long before she'd tell me she was pregnant. Although we both were just nearly sixteen years of age, we were very happy. When the time was right, I knew I had to get ready for marriage. I had to be on top of my game now. I was suddenly feeling the pressure regarding what the future held.

I went to my mom's room to talk to her about some things I had on my mind. She had some applications lying across the bed. I noticed the bold lettering on the papers. It was some forms from

Welfare. I looked at them in shock.

"What? Hell No!" My mom walked in the room and I asked her about the papers on her bed. My mom was damn near in tears as she looked down at the welfare papers. She always took pride in having a career. Her and my dad worked hard for what little we did have. Now times had hit hard in our home. She claimed it was only temporary, yet felt ashamed to have to rely on the system to help get our family through hard times. She vowed, that it wouldn't be long before she would find work again.

As a kid, I would always tell my mom, when I got older I was going to buy her a house. I always felt my parents deserved better for their hard work and sacrifice. It hurt to see her suffering like this. I acted like it didn't bother me in front of her. This was even more of an incentive to fuel my demons.

I went downstairs to meet up with Sha-Ru and Reggie. Asia and Lona were sitting on the bench with some friends talking. When Asia saw me, she called me to come to her. I went to her and she asked, *"Where you going?"* Sha-Ru was telling me to hurry up. Asia asked me again, *"Where you going?"* I told her I would be right back.

She kept looking at me and I guess she felt a bad vibe. She became hysterical and broke down, yelling at both me and Sha-Ru. She told him how much she hated him and how I should stay away from him. She was pulling on me, crying and begging me to stay with her. She kept saying, *"I'm pregnant with your baby, don't leave me like this."* I told Lona to come and get her as I was trying to pull away. I started walking away and all I heard her say was, *"I love you, I love you!!"* I said, *"I love you too"* and kept walking.

So much was on my mind. I barely heard Sha-Ru when he asked me was I all right. After all of that I wasn't, but I told him I was good and let's go do what we do. We had plans to go to Marcy Projects to stick up a store and game room on Myrtle and Marcy Aves. Reggie was from Marcy Projects and had some other spots for us to touch once we got there.

When we got there things weren't what we planned, so we changed our direction and caught a cab. We instructed the driver to take us downtown to the Gowanus Projects. Out of nowhere Sha-Ru put the 30 30 Winchester to the driver's head and forced him out of the car. I immediately jumped in the driver's seat and peeled off in the direction of the Brooklyn-Queens Expressway towards Woodside Queens.

When we got there we linked up with my peoples, Shan and T-Quan from Queens Bridge. They had some good spots in mind for us to hit, so we told them to jump in the car. They directed me to some prime locations. We took down a few spots and came up real big. We heard there was a spot in Astoria Projects that had at least $50,000 inside.

Once we got to Astoria, we circled the block to make sure we were good before we made our move. Upon circling the block again, we hit a block called Lover's Lane. We proceeded to cruise through the block until a police car crept up behind us. In a matter of seconds, the cop car hit their sirens and flashed their lights, signaling me to stop.

As soon as I got to the corner of the block, I made a left and floored the pedal to the ground, going up a one-way street. The cop car was in hot pursuit as I made every attempt to shake them. I jumped up on the sidewalk and drove through the projects. Now more cars began to chase us as well. As a last ditch effort, I tried to get to the highway. I knew I could dip in and out of traffic on the highway and get away, if only I could just get there.

I turned on Astoria Blvd., a straight away street and floored the gas. I did close to ninety miles per hour with about six cars behind me. To make matters worse, there were cop cars headed in my direction. It seemed as if the cops were Kamikazes, they wanted me by any means necessary. They were many blocks ahead, but they attempted to get in my lane as a means to stop me.

Stopping was not an option for me. I floored the gas even harder. It seemed we would hit head on. Me and the officer's eyes were locked on one another. I began talking to myself, building up the courage not to turn away. I continued to drive straight ahead. With only seconds to react before a possible collision, the officer turned his wheel. He barely grazed the side of our vehicle, but he lost control and crashed into some parked cars.

I continued ahead and was not far from the highway. We all began planning our getaway. I was a few blocks in front of the officers that were chasing us. We were ready to set our plan in motion. I was going to make a turn off of the main street and stop, so that Shan and T-Quan could jump out with the guns and hide. The others and myself would continue on towards the highway.

We didn't want to get caught with the guns. We attempted a desperate move, Shan told me to make a sudden turn up the block and I followed through. I was going way too fast to make it and I lost control of the car. I slammed into a fire hydrant, three parked cars and a light pole. I made a slow effort to get out and run, but I couldn't move. The others jumped out quickly, running from the scene.

The impact of the crash had caused a great deal of damage on my side of the car. I was pinned in the car and shook up pretty badly. When Sha-Ru saw me still inside he ran back to the car. Seeing that he couldn't pry open my door, he went around to the passenger side to pull me out. I told him to run so he wouldn't get caught. He refused saying that we were going to get away together.

He pulled me out of the car and we went through the backyard of some houses. I couldn't put any pressure on my leg. We didn't know where we were. We were at least trying to get to the next block over. If my leg wasn't hurting so badly, we would of hid out in the back yard until the morning. Sha-Ru wanted to get me back to Brooklyn to get some attention to my injuries.

The police caught Reggie, as the others went their way. The police had the area surrounded. When Sha-Ru and I finally came out onto the next block, the cops rushed down on us. They had guns drawn. They told us to put our hands up, get on our knees and lay down on the ground. They closed in on us. They handcuffed us pulling us up on our feet. We didn't resist.

Little did we know we were in a predominantly white area. We didn't know where we were and had no valid reason for being there. This did not weigh in our favor. The officer that I went head to head with walked up and began shaking me. He said that I had almost killed him. I told him that I wasn't the driver, but he said he would never forget my face. They forcefully put us in the car. They retrieved the 30-30 Winchester a few blocks from the scene, but were unable to find the other two that got away.

We arrived at the precinct. They booked us and charged us with grand larceny, grand larceny-armed robbery, reckless endangerment, and resisting arrest. I was only fifteen years old, but I lied and told them that I was sixteen so that I wouldn't be separated from Sha-Ru and Reggie. My boys told me to tell my real age so that I could go to Spofford Juvenile Center rather than be transferred to Riker's Island. I told them that I wanted to go with them and if I went to Riker's I would get to see my brother as well. He had gotten locked up recently for reasons unknown to me. The precinct did our paperwork and transferred us to Q-Gardens Jail.

The next day, we were arraigned and transferred to Riker's. As we took the ride towards the Island and across the bridge, Sha-Ru felt he had to have a real talk with me. *"Lil' bro, I don't know if they'll keep us together when we get there."* I was like, *"What you mean? All we have to do is tell them to put us in the same unit."* He said, *"It don't work that way"*.

He told me, I should be prepared for what was to come. He said, *"No matter what believe in being able to defend yourself and be confident in your fight game. I don't care how big they are, do not let anyone punk you or take anything from you. Show heart even in a loss and you will get your respect."*

I had on a sheepskin coat and a brand new pair of Nike sneakers. I had a lot to prove if I planned on keeping them. When we got to the receiving room, Sha-Ru was sent to 2-Upper and Reggie and I went to 3-Main. Reggie and I walked into the unit and stood between the "A" and "B" gates. I knew we were being sized up, just the way Sha-Ru said we would be.

He told me that at first impression, people are not always who or what they appear. He said, they'd feed off of and play into my reactions. One dude walked up and said he wanted my sneakers and another followed behind him saying he was taking my sheepskin coat. They walked past Reggie threatening to take his property as well. I was very small in stature, but I had heart. I was going to trust that no matter what. I told the guys that it wasn't going to be that easy. I told them, they needed to figure out who was going to get their ass beat before I got in there.

Reggie on the other hand, was showing every sign of fear. The officer in the bubble assigned us to the same cell and asked did we want to stay locked in. I told him I wanted to take my new admission bedroll to my cell and then go to the day room. Once we got to the cell, Reggie kept saying that his things didn't matter to him. He told the guys that if they wanted his things then they could have it. He chose to stay in his cell. I took my coat off and put all my things on the bed. I told Reg I would be back as the officer locked the cell door.

I went towards the day room and the officer unlocked the door. He looked at me with the expression like, *"Are you sure you're going in there?"* I knew I had to face whatever was to come. Once I got in there, it felt like I walked into a cage full of wild animals.

I did what Sha-Ru told me to do. I went in the middle of the room and put my back up against the wall. He told me not to sit down or leave my back open. He said anyone could come behind me and put me in a headlock that way. All of this info was key to my survival. Most of all, playing the wall didn't make me look like a new jack.

One guy was tall and really dark. They called him Black. He was the initiator and tried to come at me with the tough guy talk. I responded saying *"You still talking?"* They asked me where I was from? I said, *"Brooklyn".* They asked me *"What projects?"* I said, *"Red-Hook".* No sooner than me answering that question another guy got up and said, *"Yo hold up, I know shorty"*.

He asked me did I have a brother that was in the building. I told him, *"Yeah"*. He saw that I wasn't pressed to say who my brother was. I most certainly didn't want to come in here and live off of my brother's name. He asked, *"Is Savior your brother?"* I told him, *"Yeah"*. He extended his hand out to shake mine. I was a little reluctant because I didn't know him to trust him, but I used that to stall for time.

He said he was in the St. John's group home in Far Rockaway with my brother. He asked, *"Do you remember me?"* He said he remembered me and my dad going to visit my brother. I played it off and pretended to remember him. He started telling the other guys that I was official and told them to fall back. This didn't sit too well with one guy named Magnetic. He was talking big about how he didn't care who my brother was. That was my cue. Magnetic was my height, but a little heavier than me.

I told my brother's boy to watch my back so I could go in the corner and fight this dude. Me and Magnetic started going at it. At first we were both getting each other pretty good. We both got the best of each other, until he started to wear down. When his boy Black saw this he jumped in. He told Mag to back up and let him fight me.

At this point, I was tired and I had to fight a much bigger dude. With everything left in me, I stood up and refused to back down. Some dude that was sitting quiet since I got to the unit stepped up. It was obvious that he was the force in the unit. He told Black to fall back and let me finish fighting Mag. I looked at him and nodded my head as a gesture of respect. I went in on Mag to finish him off. We went at it for a while. Once the fight was over my level of respect was sealed and we were cool afterwards.

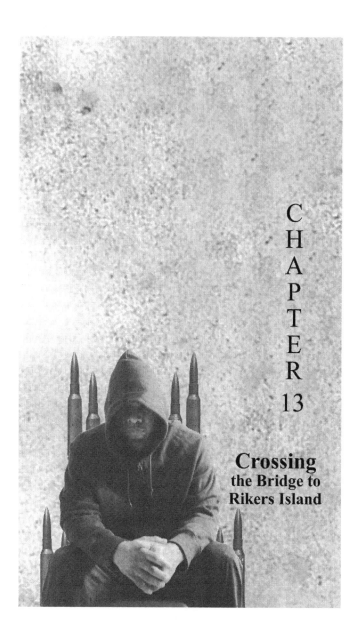

C
H
A
P
T
E
R
13

Crossing
the Bridge to
Rikers Island

My battles had just begun. My next fight was with a dude from Queens Bridge who was much bigger than I was. I did my best, although he got the best of me. He was affected by the punches I was able to land though. We stopped after a while because the officer came to make his rounds. It was time to lock down and get ready to go to the food service.

It was kind of hard to see anyone that was housed on the opposite side of the building. I didn't get to see anyone I knew at this point. I was mad at Reggie because he let them rob him for his bubble goose down coat and sneakers. He kept saying that he didn't want to get hurt and that he was waiting to get bailed out. I knew that was out of the question for me. The past few times that I had gotten into trouble I lied to my mom. I told her that I wasn't like my brother and that those were cases of mistaken identity.

This was one mistake too many, so I wasn't calling home at all. The next day, my brother had an officer he knew escort me to his unit so that he could talk to me. He was housed in unit 6-Upper with his boy Red Bug from Nostrand Ave. They were trying to scare me. They had the officer threaten to beat me up just to see how I would react. I was mad at the whole thing. I saw my brother hiding off to the side so that I couldn't see him.

The officer let us go off to the side and talk for

about an hour. I kept asking my brother to get me transferred to his unit, but he said no. He told me, if you want your own name you have to hold your own where you are and man up. He relayed the same advice Sha-Ru had given. He was mad at me, but even more pissed with Sha-Ru. He always told Sha-Ru that he better not get me into trouble. I told him that I got myself into this, not Sha-Ru.

I went back to my unit. As soon as I walked in, Reggie walked out. His father had bailed him out. We shook hands and he told me to be careful. Now I really felt alone. I saw the dude that let me get a fair one with Mag. His name was Big Russ. Russ told me to be ready for a battle with the kid from QB again.

Russ told QB that he could fight me again, but he wasn't letting him have a weapon without me having one. Russ saw I had heart and that I wasn't going down without a fight. We both were from Brooklyn as well so I guess that was his way of looking out.

As soon as QB walked into the day room he got on his bully talk and told me to play the corner. We went back to the corner and started fighting again. He was hitting me with some good punches, but I ate them. I felt I had taken worse when I fought my brother or Sha-Ru.

I stood toe to toe with dude. I went up under him

and swung a wide punch that caught him right on the chin, he dropped. He went down hard and was in shock. It took him a minute to regain his composure and get up. Although he went down, I didn't want to wrestle with him so I let him get up. We went at it some more and then some of the guys eventually broke us up.

Our unit was called for the mess hall. We had to go into the hall and line up. We walked to food service. Once we got there we were given our trays through a slot and had to find a place to sit. Once seated inside, another unit came in. I didn't expect it to be my brother's. My brother walked in first leading the line. That was a sign of respect. It showed who was the force of the unit. The last man in line was considered the sucker.

My brother had on a sweatshirt, a pair of velour pants, Wallabee shoes and a big gold chain around his neck. Being able to wear jewelry showed that you were respected throughout the entire building. You had to have heart and major status in order to walk around like that and my brother was doing it big. I looked at my brother with respect and admiration, but my mind was on the dude I had a fight with.

When my brother saw me he stopped. Everyone behind him stopped in unison. He looked at me and saw that I had a bruise under my eye. He asked me,

"Are you all right?" I said, *"I'm good."* He kept asking because he saw QB staring at us. He saw that he was much bigger than me and he asked me again, *"Are you all right?"* I said, *"I fought this dude two times already and he's still fucking with me."*

With no hesitation, my brother jumped over the railing that was used as a divider. His boys followed behind him trying to get at the dude. Fortunately for him, the riot squad was right on top of things and grabbed everyone before any major damage occurred. My brother told dude, *"You must not know me, it don't matter where you go in this building, you ain't safe."*

There were two sides to my unit. My brother saw Supreme from The A-Team out in East New York, in the mess hall. He said to him, *"Yo, you not checking on lil' bro and he's in your building?"* Supreme told him he didn't know I was in there. He told him he would get up with me when we got back to the unit. As soon as we got back to the unit I told Supreme that all I needed was a knife.

He knew the dude from QB. He wanted to see if he could interject and squash the beef before it escalated to the next level. He brought us both together. QB said he respected me for not trying to live off of my brother's name. He wanted me to earn my respect. After that conversation the respect was earned. We were cool from that point on.

Tut and Supreme from my projects were in the 5-building. Word got to me that Tut had half of a scissor for me. As time passed I built up a name for myself and held my own. My brother got into trouble and went to the Bing, also known as "The Hole". He wanted me to be on point because he had a beef with a Jamaican dude name Steppa. Steppa was considered dangerous and my brother wanted me to be aware of his enemies.

By this time I got transferred to 2-upper where Sha-Ru was. Officer Scales lived in my hood and was my basketball coach when I was in the P.A.L. center. He got me a job in the receiving room. Bogard, who was like a big brother worked there as well. Bo wore a lot of jewelry and always told me to slow down and stay out of trouble. It was hard to take advice from him when he stayed in trouble. He was in 4-main "The House of Pain". This was the most dangerous unit in the building. Bo was a strong force there as well as Bolo and Big Dee from Brownsville.

One night the new admission bus came to the C-74 building. The busload dropped off the notorious 50 Cents and Rome from Brooklyn. They came in the building with plenty of jewelry on. When 50 saw me he was relieved.

I worked in the receiving room so I had access to a

phone. 50 knew it would be some time before he was able to get to one. He needed me to make some calls for him and Rome. He wanted me to let their people know what their bails were. I made contact with their people and was assured that they were going to be bailed out soon. The only downside was that they had to be assigned to a unit and wait there until they were called for bail.

My shift was up and I had to go back to my unit. I checked to see what unit 50 and Rome were going to. I wanted to give them a heads up so they could be on point. I knew that if they went to population they would not make bail. They would likely have to kill or be killed. 50 and Rome were both being transferred to unit 2-lower. This felt like a set up because they had some major problems with some guys there.

As 50 and Rome walked down the corridor, all eyes were on them. Both the staff and inmates watched them. They didn't check in their jewelry. This would have been considered a weak move in everyone's eyes. They kept everything on, and that was saying a lot. They had two cable chains, two chains with Jesus pieces, a four-finger ring and a watch. They were beyond bold.

I was standing in front of the building when they first got there. I told them both, *"If you want to live turn around and go back to the receiving room."* They were like,

"We got no choice". I told them, *"Turn around and live for another day. Dudes are on the steps waiting for you to come down the stairs"*. I told them, *"The guys that were standing over there grouped up, plan to close in on you when you walk into the building"*. They thanked me, turned around and went back to the receiving room. Their bail had been posted prior to them going to their unit, so my suspicion of a set up was correct.

Not long after the drama with 50 and Rome, I started getting into more trouble and got transferred to 4-main "The House of Pain". The units were split in half by a divider called the C-gate. Bogard came on my side to check on me. He said, *"I guess you're where you want to be now"*. He warned me, *"Do not trust anyone in here, no matter how cool they appear. Everyone in this building will cut your throat for anything."*

One day I was told to pack my property and was moved to 6-upper. Once I got there I linked up with Homicide from Nostrand Ave. We knew each other from the streets so we formed an easy alliance on the inside. He had beef with the Jamaican dude Steppa, the same dude my brother had a beef with.

As soon as I got to the unit I put my property in my cell to get ready for the mess hall. We lined up in a double file line. Homicide and I were first in line. A riot squad escort was on deck to diffuse any major situations between units. They would use as much force as necessary. The riot squad escorted us to and from the mess hall. As our unit was going up the hallway, Steppa and his unit was coming down. Raging bulls were about to collide head on.

As soon as we got close to each other, everyone's instincts kicked in. Both groups' double lines turned single. With everyone's back against the wall; we slowly walked by. Tension was built to the max as we passed. Besides a few death threats, very few words were relayed. The riot squad's presence was very clear and refrained both sides from forming an impulsive blitz on the enemy. Although everyone in the unit was not directly involved in the beef, they were casualties of war. They knew they had to fight to survive just as much as those directly involved.

My stay at 6-upper was short. I got into a fight and was transferred back to 4-main. Things were getting bad, and I was only three months in. My dad and sister came to visit often. My mom was upset and disappointed in my ways and she refused to come see me. Three months later, my mom finally gave in and posted my bail.

When they called my name for bail, I went to Bogard, gave him a hug and told him, *"Love you big bro"*. He had a murder charge and he was going to trial. He was very uncertain of his fate. As a last minute effort to keep me out of jail he said, *"We all seen that program on T.V., Scared Straight. As graphic and hardcore as it was, some of us still rebelled and came behind the same walls they tried to make us fear. Don't come back in here, go home to your family and stay out of here. Do the right thing for yourself".* I assured him that I would.

I left the unit to go see Sha-Ru. Sha gave me a similar speech, but all that advice went in one ear and out the other. Sha told me that he was going to take a plea deal for two to five years. He said he was going to tell them that he forced me to tag along so that I would only get probation. He asked me to look out for him and send some money, food packages and to visit. I told him I would and he hugged me and said, *"Love you lil bro, be careful out there".*

I went to the receiving room to get my discharge papers processed. They had a cell called the "Why me Cell?" You had to sit in this cell while waiting for the bus to come pick you up and transfer you across the bridge. I previously worked in the receiving room so to keep myself busy I talked on the phone and cleaned out the cells until the bus came to get me.

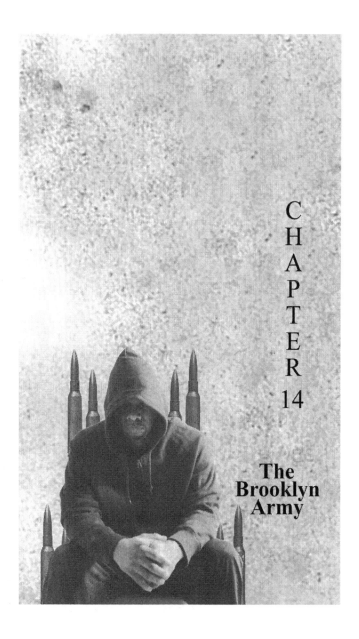

C
H
A
P
T
E
R
14

**The
Brooklyn
Army**

Once I got home I assured my mom that I would do the right thing. The first step was signing up for GED classes. I tried hard to stay out of the streets, but every day I went through withdrawals as if I was an addict. I did all I could to resist the temptations of the streets.

Losing the grip of addiction to the street life, I got closer to my girl Asia. I sought her presence as a source of protection. I didn't want her to feel like some damsel in distress while being pregnant, so I was trying to do right. She practically moved in with my family. At the moment this felt like the best time of my life. Being close to her every day felt good, but the streets were calling and stayed in my head like a disease.

It wasn't long before I lost the battle and the devil won me back over. I started making excuses to go outside. I relapsed back to the activities of the street life. I walked away from the light and further into the darkness. A job was not an option for me at this point. I was slowly getting caught up again.

Once my mind formed an alliance with my body, my soul became one. I was lost and consumed by my environment, like an animal released back into the wild. I was programmed. The streets were tattooed into my brain. I functioned in such a way that I would soon lose control and the game would play itself.

My body became a walking time bomb, destined to self-destruct. I didn't fight it. There was no preventing this crash of my mental. The devils within had plans to cradle me for an early grave. My reality was like sleepwalking through a nightmare. I had to wake before it was too late.

My court date came around. After leaving court I ran into my cousin Will. He was in the army reserve. He was passing out flyers for possible recruits. We haven't seen each other in a while, but he heard that I was getting myself into a lot of trouble. He asked me to come back to the office and sign up. He was aware of my criminal record, but wanted to see if he could figure a way to get around it.

I was excited with at least a little hope. I knew this was my only option besides the streets. My level of adrenaline was at an all-time high. After a short while, Will came out of his supervisor's office. He told me to ask my lawyer about a program that the courts had. A person who had probation or minor legal issues was allowed to serve their time in the service instead of going behind bars or doing community service.

That was the best advice he was able to give me since I had already been arrested. I thanked him and left the office. At that very moment, I felt lost and alone. I hated the person I had become. Though I hated life, I didn't believe in suicide. From that day on, I was on a mission for death.

Not feeling like it was a commitment, I made plans with Sha-Ru's sister to visit him on Rikers Island. Before we left I went to the weed spot to cop a quarter of an ounce. I then went to the store and bought some small balloons. I put small portions of weed in each balloon. I picked up some mini-sized bottles of Bacardi from the liquor store and poured them into a few balloons as well.

Once we got to the Island, we signed in and waited for the bus to transport us to the other side. When we got to the building we put our belongings in a locker. We then had to wait for what seemed like forever for our number to be called. Upon entering the visiting room, visitors had to go through a metal detector. I knew how to beat the detector, so I was able to get through with the contraband I held.

When Sha-Ru walked in, he hugged his sister, then he hugged me and shook my hand. The first transaction was made. I passed him a hand full of balloons when I shook his hand. Before he came out his sister went to the vending machine and got some hot wings, sodas, cakes, and chips. I took most of my jewelry off of my neck and put it around his. I told him that I put $500.00 in his inmate account and then we started talking about what I was into on the streets.

I told him he was missed and it wasn't the same without my partner in crime. As our visit was coming close to an end, Sha-Ru told a kid that just came out to switch time cards with him. That meant that the guy's visitors would have to leave as soon as the officer came back. The guy wasn't reluctant because he knew Sha-Ru was strong on the inside and would cause him big problems. Anyhow, his visitors stood up for him and that's all it took. Sha-Ru and I formed Voltron. Jumping up, we rushed them and a big fight took place.

We put in work before the police came and broke us up. It wasn't a good look for me. The Lieutenant came and he knew that I had just gone home. He witnessed my involvement in the fight and I was about to get arrested. Luckily, Sha-Ru's sister told the Lieutenant that the other guys instigated and we were defending her. They believed her, so they let me go and told me I couldn't come back to their building. Oh well, that was the story of my life. Trouble everywhere I went.

Trouble was my shadow. Taking as big a bite of the big apple as I could, I lived up to the big city of dreams. I played into the hype of the city of sin, wearing a badge of honor along the way. I felt I was on top of the world. I was a known figure, representing the status of a Brooklyn gangsta. I was possessed with the character I had become, Calvin Klein.

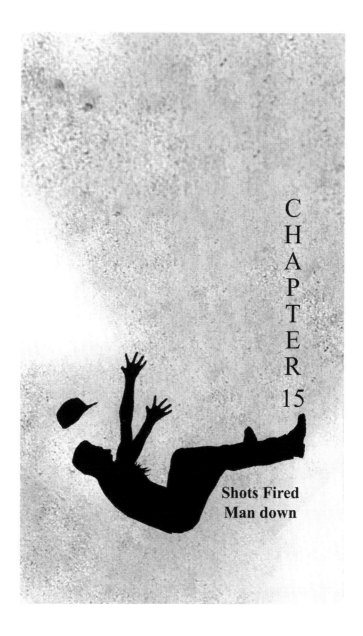

CHAPTER 15

**Shots Fired
Man down**

Since Sha-Ru was gone, I started freelancing with other thieves from BK more frequent than I cared to. It seemed like I was on a schedule to go out on these sprees. I was becoming a serial thief. Either way I looked at it, I was heading down a dead end anyway. I went out one night with Money and Bret from Farragut projects. On a mission, we were armed with our first target in sight. It was the car wash on the corner of Myrtle and Flatbush Aves. This was quick and easy. Bret stayed at the front entrance, while Money and I went inside.

Once inside, I grabbed the guys that were in the office and locked everyone in the bathroom. Money went for the register and emptied it out. While all of this was going on, Bret let a few cars go through the car wash. He didn't want cars being held up on the street attracting attention. This was a smart move on his part. It took us less than four minutes to get in and out. We then proceeded to the city. Before the night was out, we hit about three parking garages. After all of that, we shut it down, went home and called it a good night's work.

The following night, I ran into my boy Kimmie, who lived in the next building from me. He wanted me to go with him to Wyckoff Projects, then to the city. I had a lot of money on me and wanted to have a good time, so I went with him. We stopped at his girlfriend Dena's house. Out of nowhere they started arguing. She asked me to take him home because he had one drink too many.

Once we left her house we went to the city. I ran into my other boys, Star from Fort Greene and Freedom and Kendu from Brownsville. We were taking some flicks when about twenty dirt bikes pulled up. I saw that it was a bunch of Brooklyn niggas. I recognized Prescott and Rome and then I peeped Anna getting off of her bike too.

We all embraced and were taking in the scene when, Iron Mike Tyson and his boys arrived. This was the first time Mike and I had met. We had two mutual acquaintances that were close to both of us, Apple from Brownsville and Homicide from Nostrand Ave. It was so much going on around us that we only talked for a few minutes and then we parted ways.

After a while, Kimmie and I headed back to Brooklyn. As soon as we got off the Smith and 9th St. stop, we saw Shakim. I heard he had just came home. We spoke for a while. Shakim came up with the idea to hit Utica Ave. and do a few lay down robberies. It was getting late, but how could I turn down some money. Kimmie and I went with the move.

As soon as we got there, we strong-armed a few stores and then continued our hunt. By 4 a.m. we shut it down. We decided to stay at Shakim's mom house nearby. We caught a cab. I made it my business not to sit in the middle. It was common knowledge not to sit in the middle. Even with Kimmie being drunk, he still knew better than to sit in the middle. Before we got in, he and I went back and forth. I gave in and just sat in the middle. Shakim was already sitting on the other side. As soon as the driver pulled off Shakim pulled out his gun and sat it on his lap. He nudged me on my side trying to get my attention.

I spoke low so that the driver could not hear me. I said to Shakim, *"We hit a few good licks and we will break the money down once we get to your crib."* Shakim just came home from jail and wanted more. In an instant, he reacted and drew his gun on the driver. He put the gun to his head and told him to keep driving. The driver did as he was told.

The unexpected happened. The driver stopped at a red light and made a move on Shakim. The cabbie was watching Shakim in the rear view mirror. He spun around and grabbed Shakim's hand that held the gun. They began tussling over it waving it in the air. Kimmie froze, He just kept saying, *"Oh shit, oh shit"*. I told him, *"Get out the car!"*. He was so drunk he couldn't move fast enough. I reached over him and pulled the door open, pushing him out.

I was almost out of the car when I felt the barrel

of the gun press against my leg. I couldn't move fast enough and the gun went off, shooting me in the leg. I was still able to get out and run away. Shakim jumped out of the car and ended up dropping the gun. The driver turned around and tried to mow us down. Shakim told me to turn off at the next block while he and Kimmie kept running straight. They did this so that the driver would continue to chase them, allowing me to get away. The plan worked. I kept running, not realizing I ran right past a hospital. I hid in the entrance of a basement brownstone apartment for what seemed to be an eternity. In pain, not knowing how serious it was, I went out onto the street to stop a car.

I was nervous thinking it may be the same cab driver, but luckily it was a different one. I told him that I had been shot and got in the car. He took me down the block to Kings County Hospital, where they wanted to admit me. The bullet went straight through my leg, not hitting any bones. Lucky me. I was reluctant to stay because I knew the police were on their way to question me. I was hooked up to an IV and I was in excruciating pain. I had no choice but to be admitted.

The next day, all hell broke loose in the hood. A week prior, Sav stuck up a Cee-Lo game against Shakim's brother Cooley High. While I was in the hospital my brother ended up having a shootout against Shakim and Cooley because he believed Shakim shot me on purpose. Kimmie came to see me the next day and told me what happened.

Shakim tried to tell him that the shooting was a mistake, but my brother thought he set me up. He believed Shakim was seeking revenge for his brother and wasn't trying to hear anything. My brother knew that Kimmie came to visit me and wondered why Shakim never showed up. Shakim sent a message to my mom expressing how sorry he was and how it wasn't intentional as my brother believed. My mom felt that Shakim's words were genuine. She asked me did I feel it was done intentional and I told her, "No". Then she asked Kimmie the same question and he gave the same answer. It was an accident. That was it, no need for retaliation.

When I got out of the hospital I ran into Shakim on the Ave. He tried to explain what happened. I told him, *"I know what happened my nigga, I was there. I know it was an accident, at least I felt it was"*. He went into his pocket and gave me my share of the money we took that night. We shook hands and he told me to holla at my brother. He wasn't scared but our families were too cool for anything tragic to happen. I told him I would.

The effect of everything going on had taken a physical toll on Asia. For almost a week she wasn't feeling well. One morning she felt very ill and my mom came in the room to check on her. My mom was a nurse's aid at this time and knew pretty much what the problem was. Asia was having a miscarriage. She was under too much stress from worrying about me and my activities out on the streets.

She took the miscarriage very hard, as did I. She couldn't bare being around me for a while, and she moved back to Queens with her mom. This sudden move turned my world upside down even more. I was buried alive. Numb to the consequences, I went on a rampage, robbing everything that moved.

I called my man Tracey from Farragut projects. We planned to link up and then get up with 50 later. Once I reached the projects, my man DC ran up to me. He was the boyfriend of Tracey's sister. He told me that Tracey had just been shot. Someone in the house was playing with a gun a shot him dead by accident. I felt helpless. My man was in the crib dead! There was nothing I could do but turn around and leave.

I didn't want to see him like that. I wanted to remember the last time I was with him. I gave my respects to my lil' brother my way. In honor of Tracey, I hit the block harder than ever before. I didn't drink, so I couldn't pour some out for the homie. I took money in instead.

145

The Brooklyn way was my state of mind. *" Stick up! Hands up, lie down, face down on the ground...don't turn this robbery into a murder"*. I became infamous along the way, building a reputation that would exceed far beyond what I was raised to be. The character I became swallowed all of who I once was. I compromised my morals and principals for an underground tunnel to nowhere. I was rolling with anyone at this point.

It didn't take much for me to react whenever I heard money was involved. I was in the mall one day and I overheard some dudes planning to hit a jewelry store. I was immediately in on it. It was a decent plan. Someone was going to throw a brick through the front window and we were going to do a free-for-all. I wanted to be one of the first hands in, make a grab at what I could get and keep it moving. I made a killing. Soon after this successful stunt, I stepped my pace up and went on an onslaught of robberies. This would finally seal my fate, but I didn't stop until I met the end of my last days of freedom.

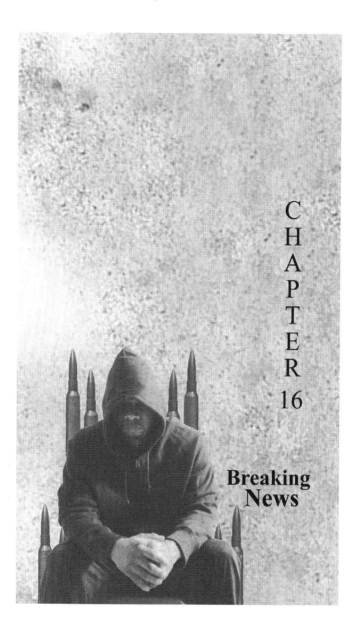

C
H
A
P
T
E
R
16

Breaking News

One day while watching the news with my dad, "BREAKING NEWS" appeared across the screen. They were talking about a string of robberies that happened in Staten and Long Islands. People were scared and in an uproar in regards to their safety. The robbers moved like bandits in the night, getting in and out with ease. They left no trace of evidence to be discovered by forensics. That was until they made two grave mistakes. First, they went to the city on 43rd St. and Broadway Ave. after going on a shopping spree. They celebrated their recent fortune, taking pictures, and partying.

Overnight fortune is easy to detect, especially when you're in the hood. The most common mistake made is pillow talk with your mate. When the so-called person closest to you finds themselves standing outside of your success, they automatically breed jealousy and envy. This was the case with a girlfriend of one of the robbers.

The girlfriend was previously told of the heist they were pulling off. She felt she should enjoy the spoils along with them. Not receiving a piece of the pie left a bitter taste in her mouth. Out of frustration, she tipped off the cops, exposing the robbers' identities. She told authorities of their last whereabouts in the city as well. This led them to investigate the surrounding area of 43rd St. and Broadway.

They found film negatives underneath the grating in the ground. The photographers regularly used this grate as their garbage bin. All of the negatives were collected as evidence and taken back to the forensics lab. This finally gave the officials proof of the identity of the assailants. The second mistake was made during their next heist.

Once inside, they executed their plans as normal. Mask on, guns out, go in hard and fast. They swept the area swiftly and everything was going as scheduled. As they were about to leave, one of the robbers decided to take things to the extreme. The others wanted to leave as planned, but he turned around and demanded the civilians to strip off all of their clothes. They unwillingly complied with his demands and then the robber forced them to have sex with one another.

The rest of the team watched in disgust as these lewd acts were forced upon the victims. The team was infuriated with his careless acts that opposed their intentions. They didn't feel secure enough to leave him behind, so they tolerated it. They assured one another that they will deal with him later. This act really crossed the line and the media turned up the heat for their arrest. People were violated and forced to rape each other, demanding an immediate need for a quick and speedy capture.

I went with my parents to visit some friends that lived in Brownsville's Tilden Projects. They were really under a lot of stress. They were devastated from the negative exposure their oldest son was receiving for his alleged involvement in the string of robberies.

As soon as we walked into the house we felt a black cloud lingering over our heads. Everyone was in mourning. When Ms. Josie, the lady of the house saw my mom they embraced and the tears began to fall. She kept saying that it was all a mistake and her son didn't do this. All I knew was, he was in some serious trouble whether he did it or not.

Ms. Josie's younger son Tray wanted to go outside and get some air. We left the apartment and went downstairs to chill under the building. We put everything that was going on behind us for a while and caught up with each other's activities on the streets. He heard that I had just gotten shot and I told him how that went down. We began exchanging opinions on what would likely happen to his older brother.

Other than the sex acts, I was giving Dru his props. He pulled off all those robberies and was doing his thing. He was quite older than myself and I only been around him a few times. Now that I was out on the streets doing pretty much the same thing as him, I had no place to judge and I didn't. He even used the same line I often used, *"Ma, I didn't do it"*.

When we got back in the crib, Ms. Josie received a call from Dru. He was still in the precinct. He continued to tell her he didn't do it. My mom looked at me through the corner of her eye as if to say, *"Yeah, I heard that before"*. She felt Ms. Josie's pain, knowing that her son was in some major trouble. When it was all said and done, Dru and the others were sentenced to some major prison time. One would think this would be a wakeup call for me, but it wasn't.

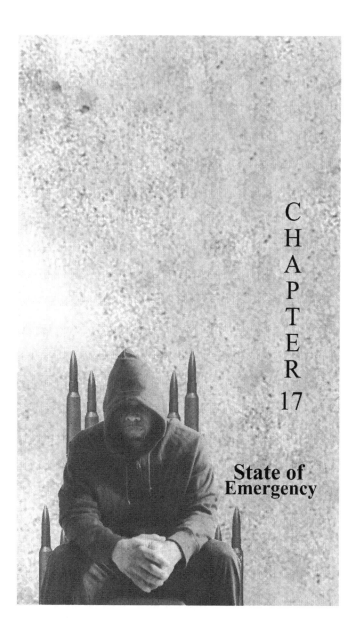

C
H
A
P
T
E
R
17

State of Emergency

Every time I looked out the window, it felt like I was watching a bad horror flick. I felt like I was on a stranded island full of dope fiend zombies, roaming around like the walking dead. They were seeking a fix to ease their urges and to prevent withdrawals. Chasing the ultimate high. *"How ironic is it to be chasing the satisfaction of a high that will be the ultimate cause of one's death?"* This was the view of my everyday reality.

I witnessed the hugest physical being that I have ever encountered, Big Dumar, getting high. He had no regard for anyone. He was shooting dope openly in the park. He strong-armed the other fiends for his fix. He'd wash his clothes at the fire hydrant and hang them to dry on the bench.

This was the summer time and the fiends were lucky to be able to survive these weather conditions. The past winter was very tragic. A friend named Eggie was found in the park under a bench. His family lived in my building. The autopsy showed that he froze to death after an overdose. These were the times that I would visualize myself crying at life and then laughing at death.

My dreams were far from my reality. In order to survive the wilderness of these jungle streets, I had to ask God for the second, not the day. My visions past my teenage years were obsolete. Many kids my age were in gangs. It was normal to see a Ching-A-ling,

Decepticon, Tomahawk, or a member from any other known gang all throughout Brooklyn.

Young blacks and Hispanics were becoming endangered species, genocide a massacre from within. We were all at the bottom of the mountain without the proper tools to climb up and over. We thought we had to follow wrong in order to get right. It was incumbent upon everyone to step our game up. We were brain washed to believe we were obsolete. With those thoughts, we declared war on ourselves. Most youth in the inner city tried to fathom what was certainly a misconception. They were not able to understand the magnitude of their rebellious choices.

Going against the laws of the land, most lived in a fatherless households raised by single mothers. The new normal was welfare or unemployment, declined credit cards, food stamps, hard blocks of cheese and free lunch programs. Many lived in small apartments with too many siblings to count. Wearing hand-me-down clothes to school, to be laughed at and humiliated all the time. Imagine being constantly reminded that, *"You ain't shit and will never be shit."*

Looking for any way out, they would react on impulse. They would move by any means necessary, just to have a little more to put on the table. Contrary to what society thought, the cause was probable in a survivor's state of mind. "The American Dream",

"The Land Of The Free", was farce, to say the least.

What part of the game was this? A State of Emergency should have been called a long time ago where I lived. This was the case for many inner cities in the United States. Needless to say, this was the reality for most young Blacks and Hispanics. Crime was not a choice it was a necessity. The so-called superiors would beg to differ.

Is anyone listening to me? Have you learned who or what I am? I can't see! I'm blinded by New York City's bright lights. I am a kid with a shovel as my only possession. It's the tool to my survival. I better start digging. Digging so far and so long. My body is sore and filled with sweat. Hands full of calluses, rubbed raw from digging far deeper than six feet. Not realizing I'm digging my own grave. In a disillusioned state, I've also dug the foundation for one of the latest developments, a prison. A prison that will confine rebellious bodies like my very own. This development, picturesque is my very own neighborhood.

Let it be to no surprise, this is an example why every hood is called, THA PROJECTS. We are experiments, observed like lab rats to see how many of us can escape the maze. This is one of the many phases of mental destruction. We submit to the devil and allow him to become our personal puppet master.

156

This is a game we'll chase and will never win, but we keep playing because we don't know anything different.

Even with the instructions and rules to the game in hand, we never read the fine print. It states, *"This is a game no one has ever won because it has no ending"*. We are walking through the revolving door of life. The smell of death is always looming in the air, the ghetto's aromatherapy.

There are bits of burnt flesh stuck to the walls from bodies riddled by bullets. Blood stained pavements, spent shell casings, and caution tape surrounding crime scenes. A purge of people fighting an unjustly cause. A decadence of deterioration all around. Loath-full glances, ready to attack at the drop of a pin. Daily funerals and graffiti murals, reading *"In memory of"*. This was what I saw through my eyes of hell.

I couldn't believe that, *"No weapon formed against me shall prosper"*. How could I when the one holding that weapon was filled with a venomous black magic? It's hard to register that only a few were immune and able to repel the poison. Feeling like I wasn't part of the few was a figment of my imagination for a long time to come.

Back on my Brooklyn bull shit. 1984 was to

become the seal of my fate. Before it was completely closed, I intended to wreak havoc. I ran with whatever other lost souls moved around in the darkness of the under world.

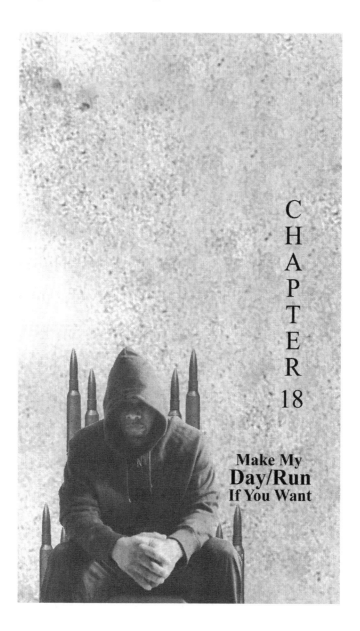

C
H
A
P
T
E
R
18

**Make My
Day/Run
If You Want**

Things with Asia and I were not going too good. She told me, as long as I put the streets over her, she was going to keep her distance. For the moment, that was fine with me. I knew she would always be an option and she would get over it sooner or later.

I started hanging out in Woodside, Queens a lot with my boy Ski Moe who was from Brownsville. His dad lived in Woodside and so did my aunt and uncle. Every time we linked up, we would turn Woodside upside down.

We went on robbery sprees every night. We had everyone scared to come out at night. A lot of areas in Queens's were more pleasant than the hoods in Brooklyn. I got up with Ski Moe one day and he wanted to go to the city so we could dig some pockets. This required very close concentration and precise skills.

After enough practice I became pretty good at it. The easiest place to catch someone was on the train. I got so good that I would bump into someone and hit their front and back pockets, getting away with whatever was inside.

I was on the train one day and stood next to a man who was wearing a trench coat. I hit his pockets, but it took a bit longer than normal because the pockets were so deep. I went a few more stops on the train than I cared to because I was persistent. I was trying to get the wad of money I felt in his pocket, but it kept slipping from my fingers.

I would usually use just two fingers, but I couldn't grip this wad. When I finally got it, I transferred the contents into my pocket and walked away from the man with a smile on my face. I got off the train at the next stop. I stayed there and waited for the train to begin pulling off.

I started waving at the man, saying to myself, *"Bye sucker, I got you"*. The man waved back with a smile on his face. I'm sure that in his mind, he was saying, *"No you didn't sucker"*. Once I got the chance to go into my pocket, I pulled out a wad of fucking tissue! I was so pissed off, but I forced a dry laugh and said, *"Oh well. On to the next one"* I just kept it moving.

Ski Moe wanted me to dig pockets with him one morning, but I had other plans. I was going up to Asia's school, Forest Hills H.S. I told myself I was just going there to see my cousins Quassiem and Samantha that attended that school as well. When I got there, everything was cool for a minute until Quass introduced me to his boys, the Twins. We clicked instantly. They were talking my kind of talk. They wanted to rob a kid from the school.

I saw Asia, but decided to give her the space she

thought she wanted. That was, until she saw me. I was chilling with the boys, when my cousin Sam came and told me Asia wanted to talk to me. It had been a while since we last spoke or saw each other. I knew I was wrong for doing the things I was doing on the streets, but I was respecting the space she asked for.

I walked up to her and gave her a hug and a kiss. We spoke for a few minutes. I told her to call me when she got home and she promised she would. Truthfully, the real reason I went up to her school was because I heard some dude was trying to talk to her. I wanted to kill two birds with one stone. I was going to confront him for talking to my girl and then rob him in front of her. She knew what I was up to. When I saw dude, she grabbed me begging me not to do it. Reluctantly, I fell back and told myself I would get him later.

As everyone got on the train, my mind was still on robbing dude. Asia was up on me trying to distract me until dude got off the train. Quass called me over into a huddle with him and the Twins. He told me he had beef with this other kid on the train and the Twins wanted to set him up. That's all I needed to hear. He was a prime target anyway because he had on a lot of jewelry.

The Twins were down to rob the kid. I told Quass to fall back. I did not want the kid to know he was getting set up. The Twins and I moved in hard on dude. I pulled out my gun and backed him down. I stripped him of all his jewels and the money he had in his pockets.

All was good, until Asia came out of nowhere and grabbed me. She told me, *"Give the guy his shit back. I know him."* I was mad as a motherfucker, but I was not on the greatest terms with her. I didn't want her to completely shut me out, so I passed everything to one of the Twins. I told her, *"See, I ain't got nothing to do with it now, you happy?"* She turned her demands towards the Twin, but he wasn't hearing it. In my mind I was laughing like a motherfucker. I was glad he didn't give it back. She walked away mad at me. Just to be sarcastic I told her to call me. We all got off the train. She transferred to another train as we transferred to the J-train. We were on our way to Brooklyn, Bed-Stuy where we were going to split the takings.

I stayed in Woodside, Queens for a while, still getting into trouble. I started hanging out with my boy HJ, who had two dirt bikes. He gave me one of his bikes. I had the mini 70-Trail dirt bike and he had the XL80. We went everywhere.

I remember I went to Elmhurst, Queens to see this girl I was talking to. Her name was Monica. She was very pretty with a light complexion and short natural red hair. I spent quite a bit of time with her. She was into street thug niggas, so I didn't have a problem being myself around her. I think that she was attracted to me just because I had a name for myself and I hailed from Brooklyn. Brooklyn had a bad boy reputation and most of us wore that as a badge of honor.

One day, while at Monica's house, she received a call that obviously disturbed her. When she got off the phone, she told me that it was some kid she use to talk to. She said he was from Baisley, Queens and was in the area. His name was Supreme and he was stopping by to see her. She asked me did I have my gun on me. I told her, *"Yeah, I'm good"*. I guess she thought something was about to go down. She couldn't do anything other than let the situation play itself out.

He pulled up in his car. I told her to go outside to talk to him and she did. I looked out of the living room window to see how many dudes he was with. I was determining how I was going to play out my position. I wanted see if I could deal with this on my own or if I had to make some calls and have my dudes come through.

He asked her, *"Whose dirt bike is that in the driveway?"* She told him, *"The guy from Brooklyn I told you I used to talk to"*. I could see he only had one dude with him. I looked at his face and I recognized him instantly. It was my man Black Jus from Automotive H.S. Since I saw a familiar face, I went outside to make my presence felt.

I walked out of the side door and headed towards them. Supreme was alerted by my presence instantaneously and watched my every move. Black Jus saw me and was shocked as he walked towards me to shake my hand. I gave a nod to Supreme as to say what's up and he nodded back in return. I made it obvious, that I was carrying a 9mm on my waist. Quite a bit of tension lingered in the air for a few seconds.

Black Jus made it clear that there wasn't going to be any beef over a girl that's obviously fucking everyone. He reminded me and Supreme that we met once before. Supreme came around our school after recruiting Black Jus and Black Jus had introduced us then. Supreme was making a strong name for himself and his crew, The Supreme Team throughout Baisley, Queens around that time.

I remember Black Jus telling me to get down with the Supreme team back then. At that time I wasn't into selling drugs. I was doing my Brooklyn thing, swinging my gun hard and was strongly known for it. Supreme didn't have much trust in me back then knowing 50 was my man. He knew 50 was on it hard, targeting drug dealers and rappers. 50 caught Kool G Rap slipping and stripped him of his jewels. Every dealer and rapper was up on the list and they knew it.

Monica was spoiled. She was the only girl I knew that was sixteen years old with a mink coat and dressed as fly as she did. I was into her; until I saw how she got down. At that point, I told her to go into the house so that I could talk with Black Jus and Supreme alone. Once she got inside, we finished our conversation. We both reassured one another that there were no ill feelings between us over her. It was what it was.

Before they left, Supreme offered me to come over to his team. I told him, *"Thanks, but no thanks. I'm good at what I do, if you have any rivals you need out of the way, have Black Jus give me a call"*. He gave me a smirk and told Black Jus, *"Yo, I like him"*.

Once I got back in the crib, I checked Monica hard. I said, *"You can't be serious yo! Supreme is a grown ass man! If that's your way of doing your thing, and getting the things you want in life, I ain't mad at you, do you"*. She tried to reassure me that it wouldn't go any further, but I knew better than that.

As of late, I was spending less time at Monica's house. My cousin Ill Will called me one evening, wanting to meet up. We hadn't seen each other in a while. He knew I was chilling in Queens and wasn't too far from him. He wanted to introduce me to his girlfriend. He said she had a few sisters I could meet, and I was cool with that. I told him I had to get dressed and then I would meet him on Francis Lewis Blvd.

I took a quick shower. I pulled out a pair of Calvin Klein jeans, a sweatshirt, a suede jacket, and a pair of Wallabees. I put on my jewelry and strapped my gun on my side. I headed out the crib and got to him in no time.

We went to his girl's house, where I met her and her family. As Will described, the sisters were very pretty. I had my eye on one, but she didn't seem to pay much attention to me at first. I just chilled. I didn't want to give off the impression that I was sweating her. Will and his girl asked me to walk up the block to the cleaners with them. We grabbed our coats and went up to the Blvd. We were about to pass the pizza shop when we noticed a few dudes standing outside. They were watching us as we passed. I felt them watching me mostly. I saw that there were more dudes inside.

Will knew I was strapped, but asked just to be certain. I told him I was. His girl told us, *"Y'all don't have to worry about those guys. I know them."* Will and I started laughing and responded in unison saying, *"But they should worry about us"*.

We didn't stay in the cleaners too long. When we got outside, the sidewalk was much more crowded. The dudes came out of the pizza shop to see who we were. As we walked through the crowd, Will's girl said hi to a few of the guys. Their focus stayed on me. All eyes were on my jewelry.

As we passed I heard a few sly remarks that I let slide. I only did this because Will's girl said they knew where she lived. I knew that if I did something to them, they would come to her home on a mission. They continued with the sly remarks. It was but so much I could take. I told my cousin to keep walking ahead with his girl.

I reacted in one motion, spinning off from them. I pulled out my gun and yelled out to the guys, *"Make my day and run if you want"*. It was about six dudes and I told all of them to get up against the wall. They tried to act like they didn't know what was going on, but I had the drop on them waving my 9mm. I searched them, repeating their sly remarks. I told them, *"Instead of talking under my breath about robbing y'all, I'm saying it out loud, I'm robbing you niggas!"*

They were calling to my cousin's girl to stop me, but I wasn't hearing any of that. When we got back to her house, she went hysterical. Will and I remained calm. We weren't even in the house for twenty minutes, when there was a knock at the door. The oldest sister answered it. It was a dude she use to talk to. He told her, *"I just heard about what happened on the Blvd with your sister. I want to talk to the kid that just robbed those dudes on the Blvd. I got beef with those same dudes and I want him to go up there with me to get at them."*

Deb was the oldest sister's name. She asked me adamantly, *"Do you have a gun in my parent's house?"* I replied smugly saying, *"I have one at my parents house too, but if you want me to leave, no disrespect to you or your family, I'll leave"*. She told me to stay in the house because those dudes were down the block and I had to pass them to get home.

The dude that was at the door was persistent and wanted me to come to the door. Deb told me he was good people so I went. He introduced himself as Born Freedom. We shook hands and then he tried to tell me, *"We should go and handle those dudes on the Blvd."* I told him, *"Your beef is not mine. If I have to, I can make one phone call and have half of Brooklyn on that block"*. I turned around and walked away from him, passing Deb. I winked my eye at her, told her thank you and sat back down in the living room.

When she finished talking to dude, she came back in the living room with a brand new perspective of me. She knew I was only sixteen years old and she was twenty-one. At first she thought I was just a kid hanging out with her little sister. She was obviously turned on by all of the drama that went down. She asked me did I really have a gun on me and could she see it. I opened my jacket showing the 9mm on my waistband, flashing a cocky grin.

I didn't even have to pull it out, just seeing the handle got her aroused. She pulled me to the side and we talked for a while. We eventually exchanged phone numbers. It was obvious she was another one like Monica, into street dudes. She was caught up in my rough Brooklyn style and attitude.

I took Deb to meet my mom one day. Being that my mom was still into Asia, she was reluctant to meet anyone new. She hesitantly agreed to meet with Deb. My mom thought she was nice. When my sister Sonya saw her, her reaction was totally different. Her and Deb knew each other from Fashion Industry H.S. At first she thought Deb was there to see my brother. She was furious when she found out she was there with me.

I was feeling myself and didn't see the five-year age difference as much to be getting caught up about. Oh my God, my sister went in on her. Sonya was a firecracker and was no one to mess with. I felt bad, but Deb held her own through the storm of interrogation. It was funny to me that my sister was upset about me dating someone her age.

Deb and I had some good times together, but it was short lived. We eventually parted as friends. Truthfully, I was out of my league dealing with her. The dudes she dated in the past were some real major get money dudes. I was simply on the come up and not on that level just yet. I had to keep practicing my craft. When the time was right to climb up the ladder, I would. Patience was somewhat of a virtue.

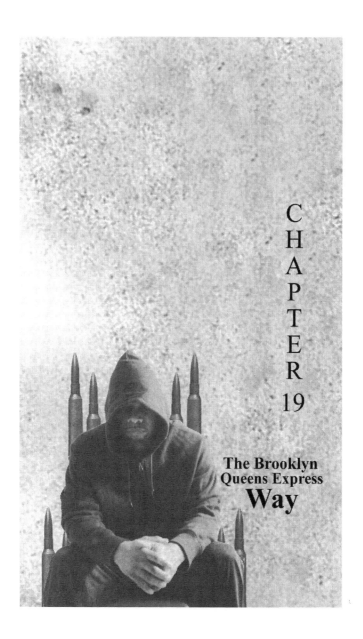

C
H
A
P
T
E
R
19

**The Brooklyn
Queens Express
Way**

Queens became my stumbling grounds just as much as Brooklyn. This was an advantage when I needed it to be. If I had a beef in Brooklyn, I had a team from Queens that would ride out by my side and vice versa. If I was in Brooklyn, my spots were either, the Albee Square Mall or The Empire Skating Ring. If I was in Queens, my hangout spot was the USA Skating Ring, on Roosevelt and Jackson Heights.

They had a BK night at the USA and BK came through deep. Vaughan Mason's *"Bounce, Rock, Skate"* was blasting through the speakers. This night felt awkward because it was well known that Brooklyn had very little respect for Queens. Brooklyn was always on the prowl, ready to rob them at any time. This night would be no different.

The infamous DJ Baby J from Woodside was playing and he knew my cousin Shan very well. He always gave me the Brooklyn Speech. *"No starting trouble on the nights I'm working."* That speech often fell on death ears. My reason for being there was to start trouble.

I went with my boys from Woodside. Once we got there we noticed the line was mad long. I saw a lot of people I knew, but I kept it moving. Baby J always let us in through the side door with out paying or getting searched. My man Big Kev from Fort Greene peeped the side door move. Him and a few other homies

174

from BK wanted to get their guns in too. I told him I already had one on me and to give me two of his. I told him to stash the rest in my stash spot outside. I assured them that it was cool. They reluctantly did it, and then came inside with me.

Once inside, I introduced them to my boys from Queens. I knew niggas would be on their BK shit and I didn't want my Queens boys to get caught up. I passed the homies their burners and told them I was going to make my rounds to see who was in the building. I wound up bumping into a lot of the homies from Bk, Jay, Rob, Panama and Supreme from Park Slope. My African homie Kwado came through as well.

The building was jam-packed and it was boiling over with tension. Brooklyn was walking around scheming, while Queens was playing possum. Everyone was expecting something to go down at any moment. I was standing on top of a speaker when Panama came up to me. I pulled him up onto the speaker with me. Kwado came over as well to let me know that he just saw this kid Farad from Farragut PJ's. He knew we had beef and wanted me to be on point.

No sooner than it being brought to my attention, Farad came over with his mans and extended his hand out to me. He wanted us to be peaceful with the beef we had. I shook his hand and we were good. Panama left and told me he would be back. It wasn't even ten minutes later when Panama came running back to me. He told me to pass him my gun. Screaming over the music he said, *"Yo, we got beef"*. I jumped off the speaker. I knew it was only a matter of time before it came to this.

I told him to point the niggas out that he was talking about. When he did, I was hoping it wasn't my niggas from Queens and it wasn't. It was dark inside but I was still able to see one of the dudes reaching for his waist. I quickly reached for mine and threw Panama behind me. Everyone began scattering, trying to get out of harms way. All the exits opened up and everyone ran out of the building.

Once we got out side, everyone from BK stood behind us. We had our guns out ready to hold each other down. All of a sudden, I heard someone yell. When I looked in that direction I saw the dudes Panama had the beef with. Everyone raised their guns up, and bullets went flying in the air seeking a target. A shoot out ensued for a few minutes.

Seconds later, Supreme noticed one of the security guards raising his gun. He had me in his range, targeting my chest. He squeezed a shot from his .38 revolver. The bullet went zipping through the air. I heard Supreme scream as he pushed me out of the way. The bullet missed me, but Supreme was lifted up off of his feet as the bullet hit him in the back. I heard a long scream, then he gasped saying, *"I'm shot"*. My first instinct was to return shots back in their direction. I spit about eight shots as the security guards retreated back into the building.

A red Camaro with a young, Asian male driver pulled up and stopped at the light. I ran up to him and put my gun in his face. I told him to get out of the car. Big Kev picked Preme up and carried him to the car, placing him in the back seat. Preme kept saying, *"I can't breathe"*. All the girls were screaming, *"Hurry and get him to a hospital!"* The Asian guy said he would take him. With minimal options, that was the best plan. I told the guy, *"I know your license plate number and I will find you if you don't get my boy to a hospital a.s.a.p."* He jumped in his car and burned rubber, running lights, on a mission.

I was going to stay in Queens for the night, but I didn't like what I was hearing on our way to the train station. Some girls were debating whether or not I was the one who shot Supreme. They were proclaiming this with a bit of confidence. I began to second-guess myself. I became disillusioned, damn near loosing my mind. I knew I didn't do it, but I still wondered if he got in my way when I returned fire.

My mind was all over the place. I didn't even pay

attention to who the girls were, not even when Mimi and her crew from East New York sat next to me. They told me I didn't shoot him. I was glad Mimi came and sat with me. She knew I liked her. It was comforting to have her by my side like that. Kev and Panama said they didn't think I did it either. I had to hope Preme didn't die. I needed to hear it from him.

I knew I couldn't go to the hospital, none of us could. Some of the girls from BK stayed at the hospital to support the homie. They filled me in on his progress. I knew he wasn't doing too well. He eventually went from critical to stable condition. He went to surgery and was sent to the intensive care unit. The next few days felt like the worst days of my life. I was praying for my homie to be strong enough to recover from this.

Three days later, I got a call from one of the girls that was at the hospital. I answered and she asked me to hold on. Not knowing what to expect, I was shocked when I heard Supreme trying to speak to me. His voice was very weak, but he was able to tell me that he loved me like a brother. He said, *"I need you to ease your mind in knowing that you weren't the one who shot me. I got hit with a .38."* He said, *"It was better that I got shot, because you would've likely gotten hit in your chest and things would've been worst.*

The girl took the phone from him and told me he

needed to get his rest. She said she'd call me and keep me updated on his condition. I assured her, that I would call every day and would go see him when he got out of the hospital.

Everyday seemed like a lost one. It felt like I was on a runaway train, with no sense of direction or predetermined destination. I knew I wasn't going anywhere good at this rate. It was a matter of time before I would meet the end of the line. Full steam ahead, right into a brick wall.

Back in BK, I often hung out with my boy Jus from my hood. That was a lot of trouble within itself. Jus was a few years younger than me, but like myself he had a lot to prove. He wanted to make a name for himself on the streets and we did it all.

We would go to Lenny's slum jewelry spot around Delancey St., to buy fake gold chains and pieces. We had our own fourteen and twenty-four karat gold stamps. We'd stamp the jewelry to make it look authentic. We visited a lot of factories on payday to get our hustle on. Knowing the jewelry would be able to pass the battery acid test, we challenged any customer who assumed the jewelry wasn't real.

We went through with the acid test a few times. We knew the jewelry would hold its color and not turn on us. We made a $100.00 profit off of every sale. We purchased the chain and piece for only $50.00. We scammed so many people, that we ran out of factories to go to. The customers always thought they were getting the jewelry for a steal. Jus and I pretended to debate over the selling price. He would argue that I should sell it for more. I would act like I was considering it, enticing the customer to accept my initial asking price.

Jus was into selling weed. He would use his profit to cop some product. We would then go back to the hood to Lorraine St. and intercept customers from the Jamaicans. I would have my gun out at my side, while Jus got rid of the bags in front of their spot. We didn't have a whole lot of product so we were in and out before they ever got to us.

The next night was a Saturday. A house party was going down! I was meeting up with Jus that evening. Before I got to his crib, I ran into my brother's boys, Dorsey and B-Allah. My hood was near the piers. Many ships and other aquatic vehicles docked near the hood. Most tourists were naive and would often walk through the projects taking pictures. The hood called them *"Shippies"*. On this night, I saw Dorsey and B-Allah line up one of the Shippies to rob him. I ran into the building they lured him in and joined in the festivities. We dug in all of his pockets and took everything he had. I checked his neck and saw he had on jewelry. I took that too.

Once we got away, Dorsey wanted to see the jewelry I took. He wanted me to put it in his hand. I knew Dorsey's MO (modus operandi) and I wasn't going for that. I let them see it and told them they could come with me in the morning to the jewelry store to sell it. I enticed them by saying that it was real heavy and it would tip the scales. Dorsey had just come home from jail that past week. His case had been all over the news and he was really feeling himself. They called him *"New York's Most Notorious Gold Snatcher"*. Dorsey and Ed, both from my hood, were the top two on the city's most wanted list.

Dorsey told me he would give me $500.00 if I gave him the jewelry. They said they knew a jewelry spot in the city that they could go to that night. They were trying to be slick and wanted to cut me out of the picture. Blinded by greed, they didn't realize that I was even slicker. I agreed to the deal and made the exchange. From there, I went straight to the house party.

It was hard to get inside because it was already extremely crowded. I saw Jus inside as I got to the door. It was Fee Fee's party and she was turning a lot of guys away. If she thought you were there to start trouble, she didn't want you around. She looked at me, Everlasting and Born and said we couldn't come in.

181

Everlasting and Born obviously tried to get in a few times prior to my arrival. They tried to plead their case once more. I told her that I was by myself and would stay cool if she let me in. Fee Fee and I were always tight, so she went against her better judgment and let me in. I laughed as I went inside. I knew that even if I didn't start trouble, trouble would find me someway, somehow.

The party was on the first floor. It was real dark inside and it took a few seconds for my eyes to adjust. Once inside, I caught up with Jus. I told him I was making my rounds to see what familiar faces were in attendance. I saw KP and Juice. We said what's up to each other and I kept it moving through the crowd. Wise, Black, Alvin and Los were inside as well. I don't know what kind of screening Fee Fee was doing. There was nothing but trouble in attendance. It was only a matter of time before things took a turn for the worse.

At least an hour had passed. The DJ began playing slow jams at this time. *"Reasons"* by Earth, Wind and Fire changed the mood. Most of us grabbed a girl and slow grinded it out for the next few songs before the DJ upped the tempo. He started mixing songs like, Cheryl Lynn's *"To Be Real"*, Chic's *"Good Times"* and Cat Steven's *"Was a Dog a Donut"*. I was by the window talking to this chick named Nancy, when all of a sudden things got crazy at the door.

Dorsey and B-Allah were at the door trying to get inside. Trouble was their middle names, so I knew they weren't getting in. They told Fee Fee, if she didn't let them in or kick me out, they would shoot up the place. They pulled their guns out to show that they were serious. Fee Fee had no choice and came looking for me.

She didn't find me fast enough because they were standing outside the window. They pointed their guns inside like they were about to start shooting. Everyone around me parted like the red sea and moved as far away as possible. Fee Fee walked up to me and said I had to leave. Truth be told, I knew I'd have to face them, this was just sooner than I expected.

Things happen for a reason. What better time for a distraction? Some dudes from Roosevelt Projects started shouting out over the music. They screamed out, *"Roosevelt Projects is live and Red-Hook niggas are pussy!"* Wow! They came to the party only seven deep. They were trying to impress the girls that invited them. It was obvious that they didn't know the reputation Red-Hood held. Even the girls that were with them knew they had made a drastic mistake and crossed the line.

The DJ cut the music off and these clown were still shouting out that bullshit. All hell broke loose when one of the dudes bumped into Jus. Words were maliciously exchanged. That was our cue to leave the party and prepare for war. We went outside and devised a plan. If we had to wait all day for them to come out, we were willing. We moved quickly. We ran down the block and ran up to Jus's crib and armed up. As soon as we got back on the block the dudes were coming out of the building.

Dorsey and B-Allah grabbed me and pulled me to the side. I knew they would check my pockets so I put the money in my socks. Dorsey said, *"You think you're slick lil' nigga, you knew that jewelry was fake. Where's our money?"* Laughing inside, I told them I would give it to them the next day because I took it up to my crib. They only let it go for the time being because all eyes were on the dudes that just came out of the building.

Wise pulled out a 12 gauge shot gun and let off a shot in the air. He yelled out to Jus, wanting to know which one of the dudes tried to play him. The dude knew he was in a very bad situation and was out numbered. Even worse, no one in his squad was armed. Fee Fee tried to talk to Jus, but he wasn't trying to hear her, none of us were. We were all on the same page.

As she moved about trying to diffuse the situation, the dudes made a run for it. It was like the entire party was chasing them. Shots rang out, flying through the air looking for a target. The dudes never stood a chance. One of them got shot in the back and he hit the ground hard. His boys stopped for a few seconds and tried to help him. They were pulling and dragging him, but he couldn't get up. They eventually let him go and left him lying there. The rest of them continued running to save their own lives.

Los and me stood over the dude as he begged us not to shoot him again. We didn't shoot him, but we did rob his ass. The only thing that saved him was Fee Fee running to his rescue. She was yelling, *"Leave him alone! Leave him alone! That's my boyfriend, leave him alone!"* She practically laid on top of him, shielding him, crying hysterically. He was later transferred to Long Island College Hospital in critical condition with a bullet lodged in his back.

The following day I took care of my matters with Dorsey and B-Allah. Afterwards, I went to Queens for a few days to lay low. Once back in the hood, I saw Everlasting and Born. They told me, the police were looking for all of us because of what happened the other night. The first thing that came to my mind was, go see Fee Fee. I went to her crib. Unfortunately, Ev and Born came trailing along.

I knocked on her door as Ev and Born stood off to the side hiding by the steps. She and I spoke for a while. She said that her boyfriend's friends bought it upon themselves. She insisted that her boyfriend had nothing to do with it. Acting as if I was really concerned, I asked her his condition. She said he would live. She assured me that no one would press any charges. That was music to my ears. I gave her a hug and thanked her. Ev and Born came from the steps and tried to hug her as well, but she declined their sentiments. She told them, *"Get outta here with that fake shit. I gotta live out here. They were wrong for what they did and that's it, no more drama from that."*

Later that night, Jus, Everlasting and myself went to the neighborhood bar to play some pool. I was good, but Jus played like he was Minnesota Fats at barely fifteen years old. After 9 p.m. on any given night the table was full of gamblers. Sometimes the owner, Ms. Nora would let us go in after regular hours. Just like always, she told us that we only had one hour to play. I moved around the table taking all bets on Jus. Most nights we'd come up big, but for some reason he was way off his game this night. All the money he made from selling weed was already gone. After a few rounds the money I had on me was gone as well.

The old heads at the bar laughed at us. I was mad as a motherfucker. Jus told me to go home and get more money and he would do the same. I've seen him play too many times to doubt him. So I went to my crib and snatched some more money from my stash. I met Jus in front of his building. He had his game face on. We went back inside the bar and didn't even ask Ms. Nora's permission. I looked at her and she gave me a nod, as to say it was okay.

The same guys were there. They were joking around with each other and asked if we had more money to lose. They were shocked when I went back around the table taking bets. They were like, *"Damn, lil' niggas where ya getting all this money from?"* Jus said, *"Don't worry nigga put up or shut up."*

Karma must have had a bone to pick with us. Dude cracked the balls and ran every single one off of the table. He ended the game with the eight ball in the corner pocket. We lost. During the next round dude missed and Jus turned the game around. He was on a roll, but that roll didn't last long and we sank further in the hole. Jus tried to play his way back into the game, but the roller coaster ride wore him out.

With his best poker face on, Jus played into the crowd and started feeling himself. To the surprise of everyone watching, he said, *"Last game all in."* I pulled him to the side and asked, *"Are you sure about this?"* He said, "I'm feeling it, ride with me." I told him, *"Do you. I got you covered"*. The stakes were high. He couldn't make any mistakes.

He cracked the balls. Then, he played his ass off like the true champion he was. Like I said, he couldn't make any mistakes, but he did. He missed what seemed to be an easy shot. He positioned for his next shot and missed again. This left the other guy to run the table dry. The dude offered him a walk (a few dollars for his pocket), but he was so upset with himself and had so much pride that he didn't take it. He exited the bar. I had no problem scooping the money off the table and then I exited behind him. I knew when it was all said and done, those shorts were needed for our next come up.

To be so young, Jus had a bad gambling habit that was out of this world. He was still feeling lucky and thought he could beat dude. He became desperate in his attempts to get more money. He wanted me to give him what was left of my stash at home in exchange for his jewelry. This was a great deal, so I agreed to that.

The exchange was short lived though. After we made the exchange we went to his house. His mom saw me with his jewelry on and had a puzzled look on her face. He told her that he owed me some money and the jewelry was collateral. She paid his debt right then and there and I gave him back the jewelry.

Once we left the crib and got downstairs, he came up with another crazy idea. He offered me the jewelry again for the money his moms just gave me. He told me, *"Don't let my moms see you. I'm going to link up with you tomorrow."* Again, I was cool with that. He had some really nice jewelry.

Around this time, Jus and I started talking to two of the finest girls from around the way, Mia and Cami. Cami was the new girl who recently moved on his block and he was on her hard. As for myself, I had a crush on Mia since second grade. Back in public school I was a little too shy to confront her and tell her how much I really liked her. Anytime she was around I would do all types of things to impress her. I would try to stand out by being the best at sports in school. I would even beat a guy up if he tried to talk to or bother her.

One day while on Mia's block, a girl named Rene tried to play matchmaker. She said me and Mia would make a cute couple. Rene was trying to persuade us to kiss. Mia said no because she was mad at me. I looked at her puzzled and asked why? She said I touched her butt and ran when we were in the second grade. Rene and Yvette were about five years our senior and they started laughing. Yvette said, *"Girl, you need to get over that, you stay talking about him when he's not around. You know you like him".*

189

I'd forgotten all about that second grade incident until she mentioned it. I never thought she was mad at me after all those years. The only way I felt I could salvage things was to apologize and that's what I did. I said, *"I'm sorry if you wanted me to just stand there"*. She tried to hold it back but couldn't and we both started laughing.

It felt good to have some sort of bonding with Mia. I was hoping for much more to come in the future for us. Not only was I making strides at having Mia as my girlfriend, but my brother had put his bid in for me as well. He went as far as to bring Mia to my house and introduce her to my mother as my girlfriend.

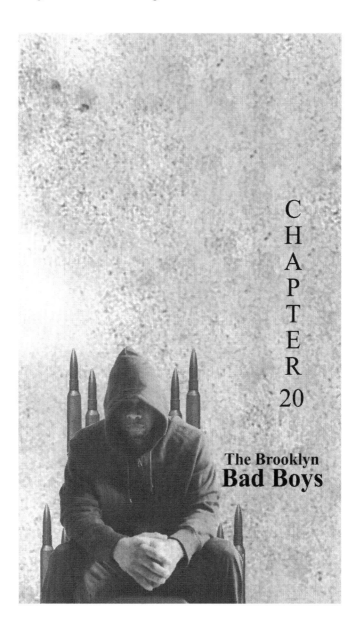

CHAPTER 20

The Brooklyn
Bad Boys

It wasn't long before I started finding myself in trouble again. It seemed as if my brain was programmed to react a certain way. I was immune to any advice that would divert me from my plans. I went way past shallow waters and was at great depths, the bottom of the ocean, a point of no return. All hope was lost. I had succumbed to the violent demons screaming in my head. I was out of control, disruptive and willing to die for a cause I wasn't even certain of. I was truly a menace to society. All of this, just to get a rep. DAMN!

One afternoon, I went to a basketball game at Norman Thomas H.S. in midtown Manhattan, with some of my boys. We went to go see some girls. We met some girls as soon as we got there. When they found out we were from Brooklyn, they started calling us "The Brooklyn Bad Boys". That wasn't our title of choice, but we most certainly represented for the Borough. The girls were telling us that there was another game the following day. They asked us to come through. We were cool with that and exchanged numbers with them.

I woke up the next day with nothing else in mind other than going to the game at Norman Thomas H.S. I spoke with the girl I met named Monique. She was from the Bronx. We spoke the night before for a long while. She called me again while on her lunch break to see if we were still going to the game. I assured her we'd be there and would call her once we got in front of the school.

I called my boy KP and checked to see if he and the others were still going to the game. He told me, everyone was ready and waiting on me. I told him I was on my way to his crib within the hour. When I got there, we rolled out about seven deep towards the Smith and 9th Street train station.

We took the F-Train to Hoyt St. and caught the express A-Train. Once we got on the A-train, I immediately took notice to a guy with a lot of jewelry on. My eyes were locked, lurking on what I called prey. As the doors closed and started moving, I figured out how this was going to play out. My boys already knew what time it was.

My boys crowded around him, as I moved in closer. I walked past him, bumping him to initiate a reaction. We had a stare down for a few seconds, and then I rushed him. We tussled until the train came to a stop at the next station. When the doors opened, I snatched his jewelry. Major mistake! I didn't take notice of the stop. It was the Brooklyn Bridge Station. This station was infested with police. As soon as we got on the platform, I threw the jewelry down.

The dude started screaming, *"Help! Police! I've been robbed."* The police were all over us in no time. Six of

193

us got locked up and were transported to central booking. We were fingerprinted into the system, then went to court to be arraigned. Off to Rikers Island!

All I could think about while crossing over the bridge was being at the basketball game chilling with the girls. Instead I was going to jail. This was when my reality set in. I wish I didn't rob that dude. I only felt this way because I got caught. I knew I was in some real serious trouble that I couldn't get out of this time.

I was already on five years probation in Brooklyn and Queens. The courts made a mistake, giving me probation twice in the same year. Now that I put myself in another situation I knew they would make up for it. My bail was set at $2,000. I knew I couldn't call home for it. My jewelry was confiscated because they said they weren't sure if it was the victim's or mine. I was sick over that because my jewelry would have gotten me out. Now I had to sit in jail until I took a plea or went to trial. I made my bed and knew I had to sleep in it.

We crossed the bridge and the bus took us to the C-74 building. We were brought to the receiving room where officer Williams did the new admissions. He put all of us in the bullpen. There was a line formed inside the bullpen a few feet away from the bars. Quite a few new jacks were on the gate yelling

194

out to the others. They were warned to get off the bars. Some ignored the officers and that's when they caught a bad one. The officers grabbed them by their heads and slammed it against the bars. Many of them had to be transferred to the infirmary.

When Correction Officer Williams saw me, He said, *"Let me find out you like it here"*. There wasn't much I could say. I felt even worse hearing that comment. The admission process didn't take long, but they still made you sit in the bullpen for hours to torment you.

I was housed in building 2-upper. As soon as I got there I realized there were no familiar faces. It was obvious the building turned around with all new dudes. It wouldn't take long before I'd hear the names that rang bells in the building. I heard Chris Boe from Brooklyn a lot. I knew that had to be my boy from high school. I was also hearing Jimmy Ace, now known as Jimmy Henchmen.

I had court the following day so I took a shower early. When I got back to my cell, I realized some one thieved my coat. It was perfect timing for them because I had to lock in. The following morning I went to court. By the time I got back it was late and I had to lock in again.

That next day during lock out, some guys were

packing to transfer upstate. At this point, I still didn't say anything to anyone about my coat. If someone talked about it I was going to do something bad to them. I felt, they must know the person, was somewhat involved or they were just being nosey. They would be the example I needed to show these niggas, I was the wrong one to fuck with. This plan was short lived because that morning a bunch of guys, including myself had to pack up to transfer to another building.

We were told we were going to building C-73. This felt almost like a privilege because women were housed there as well. I got to the C-73 building and went through the new admission process. I was sent to a housing unit called 2-Top. I had court that following morning, and went to bed early that night. I knew I'd be in the bullpens all day the next day.

The next morning, the C-73 bus dropped off all the inmates going to court to the C-74 building. Once I entered the building, I looked to my left and saw there was an inmate in the "Why Me?" cell alone. Most of the time this cell was used for the troublemakers, to separate them from everyone else. As I walked in towards the bullpen, I caught eye contact with the lone inmate in the "Why Me?" cell. He looked at me puzzled. I instantly recognized him and saw he was pressing his mind to remember who I was. I went into the bullpen with Franklin Ave. Big

Jamel, C-God and Wise, some cats from BK.

The troublemaker yelled out to Big Jamel. He told him to tell me to come to the bars. I knew he just wanted to get a better look at my face, so I played into his little game. I went to the bars. He asked me, *"Where I know you from?"* I told him, *"Oh, now you got amnesia. I saved your life and now you don't remember me?"* I walked away after that.

He was fucked up in the head after that. He asked Jamel to ask me my name. I told him, *"Calvin Klein"*. Jamel repeated my name as I went to the bars again. I said, *"You got that many beefs? You still don't remember me? I see you got these niggas in here fooled. You weren't that tough when that 12 gauge was pointed at your chest and you begged me for your life. Remember me now?"* I started laughing and walked away.

Shock waves spread throughout the receiving room. Pee Wee started shaking the bars, screaming that he was going to kill me. He said, *"I run the C-73 building and there's nowhere in the building you can go."* I guess he finally remembered the night I went with my crew to East New York.

Me, Big Jamel and his co-defendants C-God and Wise rode the same bus to Brooklyn criminal court. We got real cool after finding out we knew a lot of the same people on the streets. They told me to be cautious of the kid Pee Wee because he did hold some weight in that building. I asked them a few questions about how things moved in the building. I wanted to know when and where I could carry a shank. I had planned to make one when I got back from court. They told me, if I signed up for school I would be able to see the girls and the kid Pee Wee again.

As soon as I got back from court, I found me a nice piece of steel that I broke off from the radiator. I scraped it on the floor for many hours before I was able to get it really sharp. I then ripped off a piece my towel and wrapped it around the other end to create a handle. I was ready for war now. Whatever! Whenever! Whoever!

I saw Big Jamel again in the food service. I was in front of the line with my man King, from Kings Borough PJ's. He acknowledged me with a smile, a sign of respect. He told me one of my co-defendant's sister Vanessa was in the school asking about me. He told me to sign up tonight so she could talk to me. I told him I'd be there. I knew the Kid Pee Wee would be there so I had to prepare for the unexpected. I had my man King, strap up as well. I had most of my unit sign up for school that night because I wanted a crowd in the hallway when it went down.

As soon as I walked into the school area, Vanessa

came out with her home girl Cola. I instantly took a liking to Cola. I had to focus on the task at hand before I could push up on her. Vanessa told me she needed to talk to me about the beef with Pee Wee. No sooner than her saying this, Pee Wee walked out of one of the classrooms and into the hallway.

Tension was in the air as we locked eyes. He walked with a few of his boys. I was sure he wasn't aware that most of the dudes in the hallway were with me. As he walked in my direction, I told Vanessa to move to the side. I needed a better angle to pull out my shank and do what I had to do.

Vanessa was adamant about not wanting anything to go down. To my surprise, she held a little weight in the building. When she spoke, quite a few people listened. I was impressed. She told me to let her handle this. I trusted her because she was from my hood. I played the move on her call.

She called Pee Wee over to talk. It was obvious to me that they had some intimate dealings with each other. Playing on that, she persuaded him to make peace with me. I told him, *"If I had a problem with you, I would have finished you that night. It's your call to keep this going"*. He told me, he respected my move and was leaving it alone on the strength of Vanessa. *"Oh well, that's cool."* I really felt that was a sucker move and an easy way out, but I was cool with his decision.

The whole building was talking about the night before. When everyone found out what I did to him on the streets as well as how I checked him on the inside, my level of respect went up instantly. The bully had a nemesis in the building. This gave my name a boost big enough to sustain while in jail. I took advantage of it and went even harder. Even the COs had respect for me.

C
H
A
P
T
E
R
21

Prepare For
Battle

Not even one month in and I was told to pack my property to move. Again, my boy King was told to do the same. I was glad my dude was rolling out with me. We along with half the unit were being transferred to Dorm-1.

Soon as I got in the unit, I unpacked my property in my locker. I made up my bed and then I moved around the unit to assess my new environment. Mostly everything was new, so that was a good thing. A few dudes were already there and everyone was trying to find some comfort and settle in. I took notice of two dudes arguing. One dude wanted his boy to sleep next to him. He told the dude that was already sleeping next to him to move to another bed. That was beyond disrespectful. A fight was to be expected.

I recognized one of the dudes that were arguing. It was Born Freedom from Queens. I told my boy King I had to help him with the problem he was having. King didn't ask any questions he said, *"Ready when you are"*. I took my shank from my stash and moved quickly in their direction. King blind sided them and threw a sheet over the other dude's face. He grabbed him and put him in a bear hug while I stabbed him multiple times. The dude screamed for the C.O.s. King swung him on the floor and we both moved swiftly back to our area. The dude never saw it coming. I walked past Born Freedom and told him,

"We even". Then I kept it moving.

The C.O.s were in their office, what we called the bubble. They pressed their body alarms and the riot squad came running into the unit. They took the inmate out and rushed him to the hospital. They then strip-searched every one in the dorm. They came up with nothing and were frustrated. They just opened the dorm and someone got stabbed already! The Captain made it clear that he wasn't going to tolerate any one being stabbed on his watch. He assured everyone that an investigation was pending.

Things calmed down a little and Born Freedom came to my area to talk to me. The dorm was sectioned out by boroughs and it was not easy for some to come into another's area at times. Born Freedom came to pay his respects once he realized who I was. He remembered when I robbed those dudes on Francis Lewis Blvd. I embraced him and told him that I felt I owed him since I turned down his offer that day. At that point we became cool.

We often sat down and plotted future moves to get money when we got out of jail. He would tell me I should consider changing my trade into the drug game, where the real money was. I told him as I told a few other people that were in my ear, that I was open to other options in the future.

It wasn't long before I got caught up in another stabbing in C-73. This time, the C.O. saw me stab the guy and I was immediately transferred out the building. They sent me to C-74, straight to the hole. I was put in a cell across from Tony Rome and Dirty Ron from BK. I knew Tony Rome since I was a kid. He used to be with my brother, so he was like family. Time went by quick. We would be on the gate talking about the streets all night long and would sleep most of the day. I found out Big Jamel, P-Magnetic and lil' Dice were on the other side, but the only time we were able to see each other was at the law library.

One day while at the law library Dice and I began plotting on this kid Sin from Queens. I didn't know anything about him at first. Once Dice showed me the dude, I felt like I hit the jackpot. I guess I was about to get bailed out after all. This looked like it wouldn't be easy to pull off though. He just came down off a writ from upstate. He looked like he was bench-pressing the entire weight pile.

I told Dice I was going to put him in a headlock while he snatched the jewelry. Let's keep in mind I was not big at all and was quite skinny. Despite my size I still did what I said I would do and then Dice snatched the jewelry. Dude shook out of that lock real quick and ran after Dice. He caught him and started to beat the shit out of him. I caught up to them and tried to grab dude. He caught me with a good punch

204

that put me on my ass. I was dazed, but caught my composure really fast. I had to do something. He was tearing Dice's ass up. I grabbed a chair and bust dude in the head twice before he released Dice from this brutal beat down.

When the police came, we were all taken into the hallway. The only person in the hall was Big Jamel's cousin. Dice had beat him once on a robbery move in the past. I'm sure Dice was reluctant, but he had no choice. He had to pass the jewelry off to him and that's what he did. I was so sick about that move. The dude went on a visit that same day and passed the jewelry off to his girl. *"Damn! I was so close to getting bailed out!"*

We formed a double line coming from the law library. Earlier that day, I had some words with this Dominican dude, Roberto. It was left there, or so I thought. As we walked back to the unit, Roberto lined up behind me with a razor in his hand. Tony Rome peeped the move and called for my attention. He told me to let dude in front of me because he wanted to talk to me. He wanted to get me out of harms way and put me on point. I realized it was too late to get a razor from Big Jamel because his group was up front and already went in the hole.

My group got to the top of the steps. Me and Roberto locked eyes on each other. He felt he had the advantage because he had a weapon. He said,*"Wha' giving me the mean mug face."* I didn't waste any time. I rushed him and caught him with a punch that instantly put him down. I don't know why I let him get back up. I grabbed him and put him in a headlock. I felt him weakening. He didn't try to break my grip. Instead he reached up to my face and cut me with the razor. I instantly released him. Once I realized he cut me I rushed him again. The police came soon after and broke us up. I was taken to the hospital where I received fifteen stitches on the left side of my jaw.

I got back to the unit that morning. Tony Rome was waiting for me on the gate. He told me he had to go to court and start trial for Murder-2. He wanted me to be sharp in knowing what I had to do when our cells opened for one-hour recreation. He slid a knife from his cell to mine. He told me, Big Jamel and the others were going to pop it off in the yard as a distraction. That morning Big Jamel, P-magnetic and the others went to the yard. They all took their knives out and had a stand off against the Dominicans and Puerto Ricans aka The Germans.

It was lock out time and the C.O. popped every cell except Roberto's. His man Carlo was standing by his cell asking the C.O. to open it. I had just had beef with Carlo a week prior. This was more than enough for me. I already had my knife out. I came for Carlo and he was unable to move. I stabbed him straight in his head. He was bleeding all over the place. Unfortunately for me, the grip I had on the knife wasn't good. When I stabbed him the knife went right through my thumb. At that point, I was in just as much pain as he was.

I suspected the riot squad would soon be on their way, so I tossed my knife in between the cell doors. Although Carlo was bleeding badly, his boy Lelo passed him a razor. My boy Dirty Ron passed me one and we went at it razor to razor. I was taller than Carlo and had a longer reach. I was getting the best of him. I gave him at least three long, deep gashes on both sides of his face.

After having to deal with the distraction from the yard, two C.O.s rushed to my side. They pressed their body alarms and were waiting for the riot squad to arrive. That didn't deter me. I finished what I set out to do. I eventually lost my weapon in the blood fest. The riot squad arrived and they separated everyone and placed us back in our cells. I felt I accomplished my goal of attack. Mission accomplished.

Carlo went to the hospital to get stitched up. When he returned they sent for me. I got seven stitches in my thumb. Our fight was the talk of the jail. It sparked a racial war throughout the entire C-74 building. I'd been in the Bing for over four months.

As a joke, I asked Captain Torro If I could go to population. He told me I was a "Bing Monster". A Bing Monster was someone who was in the Bing for a long time and would never be able to go to population. I'd either go home or get transferred upstate from there.

One day soon after, the C.O. came to my cell and told me to pack up. I was going to population. Captain Torro was on vacation at this time. At first I thought he was playing, then I felt like it was some kind of set up. I decided to pack up anyway and just play this shit out. Oh man, I was so happy that day. Dragging my property through the corridors felt like a breath of fresh air.

I had on an Adidas short set and a nice sized gold chain with a big piece on it. As I was walking through the corridor of unit 2-lower, a few dudes saw me and stopped the line pointing at me. I dropped my bags and said, *"Fuck you pointing at?* You see something you want?" His man told him, *"Yo fall back that's the kid Calvin Klein."* He looked at me with respect at that point and said, *"My bad yo, you got that."* I picked my bags back up and started dragging them to the 4-building.

They had me going to 4-upper where Jimmy Henchman was housed. We hit it off real good as soon as I got there. He embraced me with open arms and with the upmost respect. He had beef with the same banner (enemy) as I, Carlo.

Jimmy filled me in on how my beef impacted the whole population. He warned me to stay close to him and the Jamaican/Haitian crew he ran with. He made them aware of who I was and told them to look out for me. He also told them to move accordingly if they saw me make a move on anyone. I was grateful to him for stepping out on a limb for me. He told me, he was sure I'd do the same for him.

We strapped up and went to the yard. We had to go through metal detectors, but that wasn't a worry for us. Our knives were made out of plastic, so they weren't going to go off. We cleared the detectors and went in the yard. We mobbed up with a bunch of homies by the basketball court. Most of them heard of me, but didn't have a face to match the name. Respect was acknowledged between us. I finally got to see my boy Chris Boe.

Jimmy, Chris and I grabbed a ball, went on the court and started shooting around. There were four Puerto Ricans sitting in the grass nearby. Jimmy lifted his head up and down as to say, *"I see you."* He explained to me that there was a hit out on me. He told me, *"Stay on point and don't get caught slipping."* I was shooting the basketball as he was speaking, just taking in what he was telling me. I missed a shot and the basketball rolled off a few yards. I went in the direction of the Puerto Ricans to retrieve it. When I got close to the ball the Puerto Ricans jumped up and pulled their knives out of the ground.

Jimmy and the others peeped the move and instantly stood by my side like the militia. The Puerto Ricans had no choice but to stand down and fall back. They were outnumbered and would likely be swimming in a pool of their own blood. They made a smart tactical move and retreated, at least for now. This made me even more focused on what Jimmy advised me of. Every move I made around the building had to be a wise one.

Everything was running smoothly until my boy from junior high school, Big Bob had a beef. I went with him to address it. He had gotten locked up with lil' Pacheco a few years prior. Big Bob and Prince had a beef with two dudes from Brooklyn, Black and Percy. Prince was about to go to trial for allegedly robbing a U.S. senator. As they were fighting, I spit two razors from my mouth and cut both Black and Percy in their faces.

Blood was all over the place. They were immediately rushed to the infirmary to get stitched up. Normally, if someone in population got cut up they were transferred to another unit. For some reason Black and Percy were bought back to the same unit. It was obvious they were going to try to retaliate and they did.

The riot squad escorted our unit to the mess hall and that's when Black made his move. He pulled out a pipe, turned around and rushed after me, Bob and Prince. The riot squad was all over it and jumped on him. They noticed the fresh cut on his face and suspected we were the ones who did it. They lined us up against the wall. They also grabbed a guy named Fleetwood from L.G. PJ's. He had nothing to do with it. He made his plea of innocence, just as the rest of us did.

We knew the "Punishment Squad" was working that night and the repercussions were going to be far greater than what any of us cared to deal with. No matter how tough you were you didn't want to deal with the Punishment Squad. The best of them folded under their brutal attacks.

Bob, Prince, Fleetwood and myself were escorted to the receiving room. We were placed in the very small "Why me?" cell. The only thing on my mind was how we were going to get around this and prevent a beat down. Bob and Prince had their minds made up, they were going to go all out. The C.O. opened the cell and told Prince to step out. This was not standard procedure nor was it legal, but no one played by the book. We were inmate and they were the police, to them we had no human rights. Order was in order and they were about to issue one hell of a beat down.

Prince followed them around the corner, out of site from the cameras. They literally gave him a Rodney King beat down. He didn't go down without a fight though. He did his best to hold up as long as he could, but it was way too much to bear. He blacked out after being hit by one of their nightsticks. They hit him again in his head and then they dragged him by his legs into a nearby cell. They opened the cell motioning for Bob to come out.

Some quick thinking had to go down or it was going to be really bad for me. The only thing I felt I could play on was that my basketball coach was a C.O. in this building and he had just retired. One of the C.O.'s that were orchestrating the beat down was his friend and had given me the job in the receiving room. I kept telling him that I didn't have anything to do with cutting those guys, but he wasn't trying to hear it. Fleetwood began making his plea as well. Still, the C.O. was not trying to hear it and told Bob to come out.

This really felt like a slaughter. Bob left out of the cell. As soon as he went around the corner he made his move. Before it was all said and done, Bob knocked out two C.O.s. They beat him down to a pulp after that. They battered his face real bad, knocked him out and dragged him into the cell with Prince.

The C.O. came back to open the cell and to my surprise told Fleetwood to step out. He stepped out reluctantly, still trying to explain. The C.O. said sarcastically, *"I understand"* and escorted him around the corner. Still trying to explain, Fleetwood turned the corner. That defense was not enough to stop what he got hit with. He was knocked out instantly and dragged to the cell with Prince and Bob.

I was now in the cell alone, bracing myself for what was to come. *"Ok. Here we go."* The C.O. opened the cell and told me to step out. As I stepped out to walk past him, I looked him straight in the eye and said I didn't do it. Right before I was about to turn the corner the C.O. told me to stop and come back towards him. He knew I wouldn't be able to hold up to what they were planning to do to me. The C.O.s felt I was a troublemaker and they couldn't wait to get their hands on me. As a favor to his friend my basketball coach, he gave me a pass and opened the cell with the others and told me to go inside.

I walked into the cell and took a deep breath. I felt a big sigh of relief. I rushed over to Bob who was laid out on the bench to make sure he was still breathing. I checked on both Prince and Fleetwood, then went back to Bob and put his head in my lap. This dude was like a brother to me. We went to school and practically grew up together. He was beaten so bad I almost couldn't identify him. I felt bad because if I didn't cut those dude's faces this wouldn't have occurred.

Bob's face looked like the elephant man's. It was indescribable, bloody and swollen. He lifted his head and asked me, *"What happened?"* He didn't remember much after knocking out those two C.O.s. He let out a dry laugh and said, *"I got mine though."* Trying to fight back the tears, I said *"Yeah big dawg, you did your thing."*

After a long night of bullpen therapy, I was sent back to the unit and the others went to the infirmary. They all came back to the unit a few hours later. Unfortunately, Bob and Prince had to go to court to start the trial for their cases that morning. I'm sure that if the C.O.s knew they were going to court they wouldn't have done what they did. They were now paranoid because an investigation was sure to follow.

Black, one of the dude's that I cut got transferred to the other side of the building. His boy Percy was left alone in the unit. He knew he was in a bad position at that point and he played possum. The unit was under heavy surveillance by the captains and other staff. It wasn't wise to try to do anything at this time.

Later that afternoon, the riot squad escorted our unit to the food service. We lined up in the hallway in a double file. My man Nut from Brownsville and myself were leading the line. Percy was all the way in the back. We entered food service and we all sat down to eat. We only had seven minutes, then we had to get up and leave. I noticed that Percy wasn't eating his food, but I didn't think much on why. I figured he just didn't have an appetite.

Our unit lined up outside the food service, waiting behind the gate to get cleared. The riot squad was escorting us back to our unit. The C.O.s knew that unit 2-Lower was lined up around the corner. They were aware of the beef that I had with the Dominicans. Despite their presence the riot squad knew that there would be an all out war if both units met. They did their best to keep us apart.

Once I heard that 2-Lower was around the corner my attention shifted and that's when Percy took his only shot. I got caught slipping. He rushed straight down the middle of the line. Everyone parted when they saw him pushing full steam ahead. He had a pipe in his hand and hit me in the head with all of his strength. I didn't see it coming. The impact was ferocious and buckled my knees. I was somehow able to keep myself from going down. I tried to gather some sort of composure to at least defend myself from the attack.

Despite the fact that my face was covered in blood, I made an attempt to retrieve the razor that was hidden in my mouth. He was having none of that and raised the pipe to strike me in my head again. I knew I couldn't withstand another blow to the head, so I blocked it with my arm. I instantly felt a massive pain radiate through my forearm and knew it was at least fractured. This was the worst pain that I've ever felt in my entire life.

Sound traveled so fast. Unit 2-lower already heard that I had caught a bad one. I was being escorted to the infirmary by two C.O.s. As I turned the corner the entire 2-lower began clapping their hands. When they saw all the blood they started screaming, *"Yeah Calvin Klein got damaged!"* Trying to peer through the stream of blood flowing down my face, I saw Carlo in front leading the pep rally. All I could say was, *"You didn't do it. The nigga that did this stood up and did his thing. I respect karma."*

My dad and sister came to visit me quite often. They made sure I had all I needed and they were preparing me for my departure upstate. My mom made it clear that she was disappointed in me. Despite her feelings, she said she would do all that she could to make me as comfortable as possible. She said she would not be there if I ever went to jail again. At that point, I had everything I needed to do my time comfortably.

I copped out to two to four years and was on the bus headed upstate. Chris Boe received his sentence around the same time and was on the same bus as myself. I'm sure the same things were going through his mind. I kept telling myself that I was not a kid anymore and I had to man up. I was about to enter one of the most hardcore jails, with some of the most dangerous men that ran the streets of New York.

Within a few hours, the bus pulled up the hill to the Elmira State Prison. It was intimidating to say the least. Besides there being huge walls, there were also two towering statues. The first statue was of a man that looked like a chiseled, bodybuilding gladiator. The other looked like a timid, sensitive homosexual. The statues embodied who to be and who not to be or what could be and what shouldn't be.

The bus stopped between the walls and we stepped off of the bus with our wrists and ankles shackled.

They had us line up along the side of the bus. I looked up at the towers and saw these huge white C.O.s with their shot guns pointed at us. They were daring one of us to run. We were directed through the entrance of the building and straight into the new admissions orientation area.

We had to strip down naked. We then had to lift our arms up and make full circle motions as they sprayed us down with chemicals to de-louse us. Then we were sent to a shower area to wash off the chemicals. Everyone had to get their hair cut bald, even if you were a Rastafarian. If not protected by a court order your dreads had to come off. Anyone who refused went straight to the hole and stayed there until they were ready to obey the rules.

We picked up our bed rolls which consisted of three T-shirts, three pair of underwear, three socks, one pillow, one blanket, one towel, a wash cloth, a pillow case, one cup, one toothbrush, no-brand toothpaste and one pack of top (tobacco). This was all the property you were allowed to have while in orientation. Your new ID number was put on all of your clothes. My number was 84-B-1519. The first number represented the year you were arrested. The letter showed whether you were a boy or an adult and the last number was your list number. You lived with that number the entire time you were in jail. It blew me away when I came in and saw an old timer with a number over twenty years old. He had gotten locked up before I was even born. This was a wake up call.

After a few weeks in orientation my group was transferred to the reception unit. We had to await placement from the system. We would find out if we would go next door to population or if we were going to be transferred to another facility. I wanted to go to Elmira's population because Sha-Ru was there.

He found out that I was in the building and sent me a kite (letter). He overly expressed the need to be careful because there was a hit on me. He said that he heard I did a lot on the Island and that followed me over here. He stressed that he still wanted me to come over, but we needed to keep our knives close to the hip at all times. He said, Brooklyn was strong in the building and was there to hold me down no matter what.

Unlike orientation, reception was loud and out of control. There were four levels of over fifty cells stacked across from one another. When the new jacks walked through reception, the inmates would throw buckets of water off their tier onto them. They would yell out, *"Welcome to hell new jacks!"* You had to be on point walking through there.

Being upstate was a big difference from being on the Island. Some of the C.O.s were huge in stature.

They seemed to have zero liking towards the African American or Hispanic inmates. They expressed their hatred very openly and were just waiting for a justifiable reason to kill you.

It was important to make them aware that you had family on the outside that cared for you. Loved ones that would not hesitate to contact the N.A.A.C.P. or other outlets to expose them. This would at least diffuse their thoughts of sending your out with a toe tag to be buried in Potter's Field.

There were a few young C.O.s that wore short sleeve shirts, proudly exposing their tattooed arms. They wore tattoos of a black baby with a noose tied around its neck. Under it read the words, *"White Pride"*. This was very disturbing. I had to catch myself often, trying not to be filled with the same hatred they displayed.

Even the Aryan Brotherhood, a white clan who had a known hatred towards blacks, weren't as blatant as these C.O.s. I guess that's why there was only one black staff member that worked at Elmira and his name was Mr. Jones. He worked as the barber instructor. He certainly knew his place. He was as close as I had ever been to a house nigga. A *"Yes sir. No sir"*, kind of guy.

I stayed in reception for close to two months

before they transferred me next door to population. How ironic was it that I went to G-block 5-gallery 18-cell, the same unit as Sha-Ru. His cell was above mine. When it came time for lock down, we'd reminisce through the vent all night long. The time went easier being around someone I grew up with.

Sha-Ru worked in the barbershop, so I signed up to work there as well. There was a waiting list so I worked in the masonry program until a spot was available. I also went to the GED program to study and take the test. I felt, I might as well make the best out of being here.

Scheduling my day efficiently also made time go by faster. I woke up at 6 a.m. to start my day. I went to breakfast and would be back to the unit by 7:30 a.m., when the bell rang to announce the start of the day. I then went to the masonry program. From 9:30 a.m. to 11.00 a.m., I attended GED class. I went back to the masonry program until 11:30 a.m. and then prepared for lunch. Lunch break ended around 12:30 p.m.

My afternoons consisted of a rigorous work out. I worked out with my dude Lil' Inf from Fort Greene and two others. We did what we called, "around the world calisthenics". It consisted of twenty sets of twenty pull-ups, push-ups and dips. We did light weight-lifting most of the week and heavy lifting one day of the week to shock the body. We let our bodies rest over the weekend. I imagined I was in military training. This was my form of motivation to push me past my limits, to help me get through my time.

Mostly everyone I knew was in the Five Percent Nation of Islam. Sha-Ru knew I studied my brother's, "Book of Life", on the streets. He wanted me to sharpen my mental sword. He knew I studied different books of religion. The Bible, The Quran and The Nation of Islam Studies were all the books I sought to gain a link with God.

I was an avid reader and would study the "Book of Life" with Sha-Ru through the vent. Within less than a year, I had knowledge of almost 120, along with a handful of plus degrees. One day while in the yard, Sha-Ru saw the Gods (Five Percenters) in a cipher building (talking) and wanted me to step into the circle with him. I knew most of the Gods very well and they knew me as Calvin Klein. When I entered the circle I said, *"Knowledge, Knowledge (Peace God)."* This one God was building. He tried to go in on me being an 85 Percent Build Power (Non Believer). He wondered why I was in the circle. I let him speak his peace. He asked me was I God. I told him, *"Y Equal Knowledge Born"*(yes).

Sha-Ru looked at me, he knew when it was my turn to speak and I sparked the God. What the God didn't

know was, I did have knowledge of self. He asked me
my attribute (name). I told him, *"God"*. He said, I had
to have a name and I told him I did. He asked me
again, and I told him, *"God. I'm the creator of all things,
including your name"*. All the Gods were like, hmmm,
"That's peace God". I exited the cipher saying, *"Salaam"*,
meaning peace in Arabic.

At this time, I was going through a lot of confiding
in Asia. I was trying to make amends. Being that her
mother was still dictating what she could and couldn't
do, she refused to come see me. It was hard to deal
with, but I had to adjust to my reality and move on. I
had to survive through the storm without her. Due to
Asia's lack of support, I reached out to a few girls
from my hood. I did the pen pal thing with Eva, a
pretty looking girl of a mixed ethnicity, with an East
Indian complexion. She was very supportive in
corresponding and I was grateful to her for that.

I received a letter from a friend, Cherry Boss. She
was brown skinned, short and sexy with long natural
jet-black hair down to her waistline. It was cool of her
to take the time out to write me. I spoke with her
once, soon after I received her letter. Not long
afterwards, I received the disturbing from another
friend that Cherry was murdered. She was found in
the park in my hood. It's alleged that she was
pregnant and wanted to keep the baby. This was
against the wishes of whom she was pregnant by. He

was in a bad situation because he was already married with children. Hearing this news broke me down. When I went back to my cell, I cried like a baby.

There was still Mia, light skinned, short hair, with a flawless shine of beauty. Whenever I wanted to talk to her, I'd write my boy Jus a letter in advance. I would give him the date and time I would call. He'd have Mia at his mother's crib, awaiting my call. She made me feel like there was a promising future for us and this made doing my time much easier to bear.

We were allowed to make one fifteen minute phone call per month. You had two chances to get through to the other party. After your second attempt you were marked down on the books as a complete call and had to wait until the following month, no ifs, ands, or buts about it. If there were any grievances, an inmate would take them to the board of committee consisting of inmates that were well respected by everyone in the prison including the staff. The committee would prepare you with all the necessary steps needed to address the staff or the outside court in Chemung County, N.Y.

I stayed in contact with Jus throughout my time. He sent me money for my books, so I was able to get commissary often. Between him, my parents, and my cousins, Eric and Rhamel I lived as comfortable as anyone could.

Eric and Rhamel came to visit me one weekend. They made me feel like I was on top of the world. It had been a while since we saw each other. They drove almost eight hours from the city just to see me. When I went out on the visiting floor, we shook hands then gave each other a hug. They had plenty food, beverages and photo tickets from the vending machines laid out on the table. They filled my account up with about $1,000.

They briefed me on how things changed in the hood, how explosive the new drug *"Crack"* had taken over. The Panamanian's flooded the hood with this drug. They said my dude Jus stepped in as one of the founders, introducing the drug to the hood as well. They said, he was living large, doing it real big.

Jus and I never spoke about any of his doings. He just made sure I had money in my account and had Mia around when I wanted to talk to her. What my cousins were telling me was not a surprise. I was impressed. They said the drug was spreading all though out the city like wildfire. There was pandemonium everywhere.

My cousins were nine to five dudes and they were even tempted to get in the game. So much money was being made, it was hard for anyone to resist. This was a great visit in so many ways. My future and my reality seemed to balance. I knew what I planned on doing when I got home. Get money the fast way.

Soon after the visit with my cousins, my mom and dad came to visit me. I missed my parents. We hugged and then held on to each other for a while. I asked a lot of questions. I wanted an update on my sister and her baby. I missed them so much. Before I went upstate, my sister and niece visited me a lot and I missed seeing them.

Everyone was fine and sent their love. My mom was telling me that my dad won a substantial amount of money from a lawsuit. The family had a chance to make a better life. She started drilling me about getting myself together. She vowed that if I still had a passion to drive tractor-trailers with my dad, they would put down the money to finance our first truck. That sounded promising and to them that was the best option for when I got out.

My parents put $500.00 in my account. Plenty food was laid out on the table. It felt like I was at a picnic. I had concerns for my mom based on how my dad looked. He had on new clothes and a fresh haircut, but he looked tired and lost quite a bit of weight. I know how hurt and responsible he felt about me being locked up. Not only was I locked up, but my brother got locked up again and had two years to serve upstate as well.

My dad placed a lot of pressure on himself and felt like he let us down. My mom always argued with him, saying, "*They made the bed they're sleeping in. They are of age where they have to bare responsibility for their actions*". She always said, "*Life will be good to you if you be good to life*".

When my dad went to the microwave to heat up some hot wings for me, I asked my mom, "*How is he really doing?*" She said, "*Your daddy's fine, he's a grown man who knows right from wrong*". I didn't want to keep pushing the issue to upset her, so I let my thoughts remain puzzled. The visit was now over. I felt happy they came, but sad that they had to leave.

I called Jus soon after so I could talk to Mia. This would be one of the worst calls I could have ever made:

"What's up, you get the money I sent you?"
"Yea, I got it, thanks. (A lot of noise in Jus's background). Did I catch you at a bad time?"

"Kind of, but I can talk. I know you only get one call for fifteen minutes. I don't want you to waste it. Just a lot going on right now."

"Something happened?"

"Sort of. Remember that brand new car I bought?"

228

"The Ninety Eight?"

"Yea, that nigga Rakim just set my shit on fire!"

"Are you for real? Fuck he do that for?"

"It's burning as we speak over that bitch Cami and I don't even fuck wit her like that no more! (Deep sigh). Anyway, I'll buy another tomorrow. We don't have that much time to talk and there's a few things of more importance I wanna talk to you about. I don't wanna have you all upset in there, but you my man and I have to pull you up on something about ya pops."

"My pops? What about him? Something happened to my father?"

"Nah. I know how close you and ya pops are. I can't find any easier way to tell you this, but your pops out here getting high off of "Crack".

(In denial) "Are you sure it's him?"

"You know I know who ya pops is man. Ain't a mistake about it. I saw him come from my spot."

(Taking a deep breath) "Jus, if you do me this favor, I'll never ask you for anything else. You have to promise me you won't let nobody sell that shit to my pops."

"It's only but so much I can do. But, I promise you this. He won't be able to buy at my spot or from any of my people. I can't control anything else outside of that. That's the best I can do. At the end of the day he's a grown man. He makes his own decisions. To be honest, you can't be mad at nobody but him. Almost the whole hood is strung out on this shit."

This really devastated me. It bought me back to when my parents visited and my mom didn't want to talk about why my pops looked the way he did. I told Jus, *"You're my friend and you know how close I am with my dad. Do not let him buy any drugs from you or your crew"*. He promised me, he would do as I wished. From that moment on, he held to his word.

He dropped another bomb on me when he said he had a new girlfriend and it was Mia! I damn near dropped the phone, in shock. I really didn't see that coming.

I asked him was she there. He said, *"Yeah, she's right here"*. I asked, *"Could I speak to her?"* He gave her the phone. I asked her, *"Are you happy?"* She said, *"Yes"*. Although I was hurt, I told her I was happy for her. I asked her to give the phone back to Jus. He got back on. We were quiet for a few seconds, and then he asked, *" You all right?"* I told him, *"Yeah, I'm good"*.

After being incarcerated for two years, I visited the

Board Of Parole. I was in there for less then fifteen minutes, before I was excused. They said I would receive a letter within a few weeks. It was known that if the letter was heavy, you were getting hit with more time. If it had only one or two pages then you would likely receive an early release date.

I was stressed out waiting to receive my parole letter. Within one month I finally received it. It was heavy. I was mad before I even opened it. It said I had nine additional months to serve from the date I received the letter. This meant I was getting hit with as much time as possible.

I would be incarcerated until my conditional release in 1986. To make matters worse, I was being transferred to Coxsackie Prison. Both Sha-Ru and I were depressed the morning of my departure, but we'd both be home soon. We vowed to join forces and be a bigger force to reckon with than in the past.

The following morning I was on the bus being transferred to Coxsakie Prison. It wasn't as big as Elmira, but if it's a prison it's just as dangerous as any other. Being around guys who had life or close to it, you couldn't move around like you only had a short bid. In order to move the right way, I would tell myself, *"One day in here is life in here. I'm sentenced to life until I get back to the free world"*.

After going through orientation, I went to the yard and ran into a few people I knew. Wise from my hood, my boy Big Kev from Fort Greene, P-Magnetic from Franklin Ave. and Boe Sgags from Brownsville, were all there. We met up in the yard to politic. After a while we had to go to our units. It wasn't long before I settled in. I set my schedule, to finish out my time with a peace of mind. I worked in food service with Big Kev and P-Mag, until my release date.

Sgags was usually with his boy Tareek, from Queens. Sgags introduced us. The three of us would often walk the track together. I didn't say too much to Tareek. I didn't really know him, but I embraced him because Sgags vouched for him. We walked the yard pretty much every day for the next eight months. I shared most of what I had planned while walking with these guys. I believed they were my people, but my opinion eventually changed.

Everyone who worked in food service shared the same dorm. One night my boys, P-Mag and Lil' Shan were gambling in the dorm. They went back and forth until Shan lost everything he had. He came and borrowed some items from me and I told him I wanted them back that following week. He was winning and then all of a sudden P-Mag mastered his flow and took him for everything.

They were going back and forth talking shit throughout the game. I didn't pay much attention to them, I was kicking back relaxing and reading a book. Shan asked me for something to eat and for my hot pot. I gave him a few items to make a meal and told him, I wanted my hot pot back the next day.

At 11:45 p.m., the lights went out in the dorm. The night was like any other night. A few people were moving around, but that wasn't unusual. I woke out of my sleep from a very loud scream at around 2:00 a.m. It was P-Mag. Shan used my hot pot to heat up some water. He then put some baby oil in it and threw it on P-Mag. It didn't end there. Shan put two combination locks in a sock and clobbered him. P-Mag was a big dude. He got a grip on Shan and if not for the C.O.s breaking them up, he would have strangled him. P-Mag wiped his face, not realizing he was wiping off his skin. He got it pretty bad and was rushed to the hospital. It took a while, but he was all right.

Time flew and my brother was released from prison in February 1986. He didn't waste any time getting back on his feet. He went back to Red-Hook and adjusted to the new hustle, *"The Crack Game"*. Within a few months of hard hustling, he had two Mercedes Benzs, a boatload of jewelry and all the expensive clothes imaginable. He was on top of his game. Big Kev came and told me, *"Your brother got it going on, he doing big things."* He was getting all this info from his sister Sharon. Kev seemed more excited for me than I was for myself. *"How could I be excited about something I didn't know about?"*

Sharon was close to my brother growing up. I knew that the info coming from her had to have some relevance, but I wanted to hear it from home. I made some phone calls and found out that all of what I was hearing about my brother was true. I got a chance to speak to him and he said he already sent a food package, money, and some pictures to me. He assured me, that I was going to be good when I got home and we'd do big things. This was the same thing Jus assured me. I knew I was going to get it popping one way or another. I couldn't wait.

I had less than thirty days left until my release and I haven't spoken to my cousin Eric in a while. I decided to give him a call. His sister, Sena accepted my call. I heard her crying. I asked her what was wrong. She was so distraught she couldn't get a word out. Eric took the phone from her crying as well. I was like, *"Yo! What happened?"* Between tears, he was able to tell me that Rahmel was in an accident. He was in the hospital, and it wasn't looking good for him.

Eric said, *"Rahmel wanted to be here when you came home and then this happened."* This was the worst thing to hear while in prison. Something happening to a loved one and you're not there to protect them. There was nothing I could do until I got home. I had vengeance in my heart from that day on.

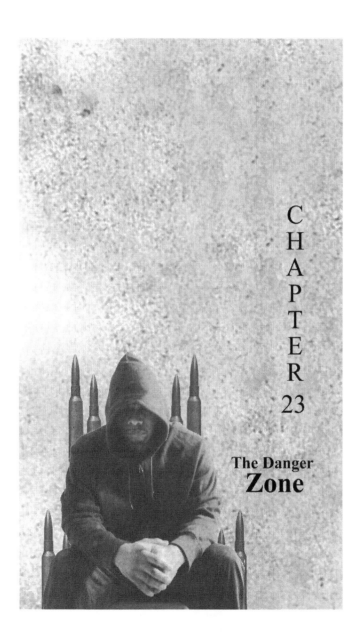

C
H
A
P
T
E
R
23

**The Danger
Zone**

It's June 1986, the day of my release. I left the prison and took a Greyhound bus into the city. I caught the train and got off at Smith and 9th St. Back to the hood! I'm home! As I walked from the train station into the projects, I noticed quite a bit had changed since 1984.

The air was much fresher upstate, but as polluted as the air was it felt good to walk through the hood again. When I was away, Jus, Eric or Rahmel would keep me updated on what was going on in the streets. Seeing was believing. Although, things were much more dangerous, there were no excuses. I couldn't get caught slipping again. I was somewhat prepared due to all the updates, but I knew I had to adjust to the changes immediately.

The stakes had become far greater. I was now older and I had to be wiser as well. Brooklyn stick up kids converted over into the drug trade. It was obvious to the older dudes on the block that their time was up. This was a new day in time, and the new *"BOSSES" were* in town. You either manned up or manned down. Either way, a change had come. You either moved or got moved. The younger generation wanted their turn at the "American Dream" too.

No more standing on the outside trying to peek in. No more being envious of the major hustlers driving fancy cars, wearing expensive jewelry and custom fitted clothes with the prettiest girls on their arms. No more running up on him to get short money while he's asking you, *"How's ya momma doing and where she at?"* Naw... no more lil' nigga shit!

The "Big Nigga" had to step down, get forced into retirement, or get taken down, simple as that. Well, not really that simple, but you get the point. Let's just hope he bows out peacefully and gives respect to the younger G's. Young nigga's stomachs were growling. Their ribs were touching. We all had a point to prove and we were greedy.

Tension in the 80's was at an all time high in the big city. People didn't want a piece of the pie. They wanted the whole pie. Not many could withstand the pressure. When the going got tough, most so-called tough gangsters packed their bags and "relocated". Truth was they got ran out of New York. They had to go OT (out of town) to hustle.

There was a difference between a boss expanding OT and one hustling OT because they had to get the hell out of dodge and had nowhere else to hustle. The hood was too much for most so they had to go. No ifs, ands, or buts about it. Many of those exiled would use the excuse, *"There's more money out of town."*

Transitioning times were often complicated. Everyone had to come out and play in the real

"Hunger Games". Territorial wars ensued often. *"May the best, or better yet, may the strongest be the last one standing.*

The mid 80's turned into *"The Crack Generation".* You went to war to earn your keep. You had to be heartless. You had to follow through with brute force to maintain what you felt was yours. If you were the Man you were gonna pay for it, with your freedom or life on the line. If you weren't, you would likely pay for it with your life.

You had to be on point at all times just in case a gun battle ensued. You had to transcend from luxury to playing the mats (get low) if necessary. If drama went down, you had to know the routine, like a fire drill. If gun shots went off, every man, woman and child knew to get behind something, hit the ground and protect their head, or run as fast as they could in the opposite direction.

For those not directly involved, a gun battle was the greatest show on earth. It was like watching the championship games, but even better. The spectators were thirsty to witness someone gasping for their last breath. They wanted to be up close and personal as the discoloration traveled throughout their body. It was exciting to see them chauffeur the body to the morgue. They enjoyed watching the family members in a fit of hysteria, as they extended their phony sentiments.

I know this sounds horrendous, but this was the norm in my habitat. This was the 80's and not many would beg to differ. The drug use of this era was one of the worst epidemics alongside HIV/AIDS. This wasn't happening only where I was from, but hoods worldwide were affected by this reality. The effects of this destruction were so traumatic they are still evident to this present day. *"Welcome to life in the ghetto."*

I had only a few blocks to go before I got to the back of the projects where I lived. The next block coming up was The Ave. As soon as I hit the The Ave., I couldn't believe my eyes. This had to be smoke and mirrors because the change was just that drastic. It looked like I just stepped onto the set of *Tarzan.* The beasts were lurking everywhere.

I had to take a sudden step back. I saw a guy running in my direction with a gun in his hand. As he got closer, I saw the fear in his eyes. Fortunately for me I wasn't his target, but he was someone else's. He was running from a group of guys. He was running at top speed trying to escape the attackers, but they were heavy on his trail.

He almost ran me over. My instincts kicked in instantly. It almost felt as if I never left. I moved to the side, out of harm's way as the group moved in hot pursuit. As they got closer, I recognized one of the attackers. It was Jus's brother, Rondo. He and his crew were the ones chasing that dude. The dude tried to invade drug related territory in the hood and was now being dealt with.

I've only been a free man for ten hours. I didn't get to see my family yet and couldn't believe what was happening already. This was some kind of welcome home. Everything was happening so fast. Before I knew it, Rondo stopped in front of me and said, *"Welcome home!"* I asked, *"What's going on, why ya' chasing dude?"* He responded, *"Tell you later, right now we gotta catch him."*

Rondo put a 9mm in my hand and said, *"Let's go, we gotta catch this dude".* I was shocked that he did that to say the least. To be honest, if I had been home longer and saw my family already I would've rolled out with them. I said, *"Take this shit back man...I'm good, go do you."* Rondo took the gun back, and said, *"Yea aight...See you around yo."*

I figured Rondo was disappointed. I'm sure he felt a way about it, but I knew what the outcome would be if we caught up with the dude. I didn't want to take that chance. Not today. It was way too soon to be risking my freedom.

For about five minutes it sounded like a firing range. Shots were ringing out like the 4th of July. The

242

sound was deafening, as each bullet spun in the air seeking a drop target location.

All of a sudden, the sun didn't seem so bright on The Ave. An eerie feeling loomed in the air, like a hovering black cloud. A gun battle was going down in the heartland of the hood, no holds barred. When the guns were drawn and the drop was made, you aimed for the top/down. Hit the head and the body was destined to fall.

Not furthering my concern to what was going down. One way or the other, I was keeping it moving. I walked through the park and crossed the parking lot. As soon as I was about to enter the building, my partner in crime Sha-Ru saw me and yelled out...

"Lil' Bro, what's up? Welcome home! Oh yea, it's on now. These motherfuckers got a whole lot of trouble on their hands now.

"Hahaha, you already know bro. Glad to be home yo, you know how we do, crime partners for life!"

"I figured you be coming through around this time, I been waiting on you all day. Ya moms and the rest of the family are waiting for you upstairs. Let's go so you can holla at everybody and get that out the way."

"Yea man, let's go upstairs, that's all I want is to see my moms

and pops. I'm not gonna feel at home until I do."

Sha-Ru and I were walking towards the building and some girl came rushing out. When she saw me, she ran to me and embraced me in a bear hug. She said, *"Welcome home!"* She looked very familiar, but I wasn't sure who she was at first. Then it hit me. It was Tina! Actually, I grew up with her, but within the years I was gone she had taken a very bad turn. She went from looking good to looking like some sort of zombie. I couldn't believe my eyes. I pulled away from her and took a few steps back so I could observe her better. Shocked, I said...

"Tina. Is that really you?" (*Shocked facial expression*)

"Yea. It's me. What you mean? You act like you don't remember me."

"I can't believe how much you've changed. You lost a lot of weight. You look a lot different."

"I lost a few pounds, but I still look good." (Smiling and posing)...

Sha-Ru cut in and said...

"Tina. Stop the bullshit. Tell the truth."

"Mind ya business Sha-Ru. You always trying to start

244

something."

"Com on lil bro, keep it moving. She isn't who she used to be. She's a fucking crack head. Look at her. The bitch looks all skinny like she's dying yo. If she open her shirt, I bet you can see her ribs."

"Fuck you Sha-Ru, you just jealous of me."

"Bitch is you serious! Me jealous of you? Yea ok, come on lil' bro, let's go."

As we walked away, I told her to take care of herself. I didn't know as much as Sha-Ru about this crack thing. I didn't feel as cold hearted towards the people I grew up with as he did, at least not for now. All of that was soon to change.

Sha-Ru came home a few weeks before me. He served almost four years in New York State Prison. He laid low until his other half (myself) came home. Although he didn't have much time on the streets, he felt he needed to school me. He wanted to pass on the game.

We entered the building and there were a few people waiting for the elevator. There was a pretty girl that Sha-Ru instantly began to flirt with. She was real cute with a very shapely figure. He took his attention off of her for a brief moment and got back to telling me about the new hood. He reached in his pocket and pulled out a few capsules. This was the first time I ever saw crack. I said...

"What's that?"

"Lil bro, this here, is the devil in a bottle, hahahaha".

"What is it?"

"This is "Suicide Rocks", better known as "CRACK". If you're the giver, it's the American dream out the hood, but if you're the receiver, then it's like being at the point of no return. Nothing you can't get wit this."

I looked at him with a clear expression of doubt on my face, as if I didn't believe him. I said...

"Yea right. It's hard to believe those little ass rocks in a bottle can be that powerful."

"Oh, you don't believe me. Watch this. You want this bitch right here to suck ya dick?"

I looked at her thinking she was going to curse his ass out, but she didn't. Wow. Ok. I still wasn't completely convinced. I felt like I sort of violating her by looking at her with obvious signs of lust. I knew she had to hear what he just said. If she didn't have a problem with him saying that then I knew me looking at her wasn't an issue at all.

She looked real cute too. Light complexion, mid twenties, very attractive and curvy. She had thick hips and a fat ass. By the looks of her, I wanted more than just my dick sucked. I had to call his bluff. So I told him, *"Hell yea! Make it happen."*

Sha-Ru pulled up next to her and whispered something in her ear. She looked at him, then at me. Then she started to follow him. As they were about to slide off, he yelled over his shoulder and told me, *"I'll be right back lil bro. I'mma line her up for you and get her to suck you off, a lil' welcome home present for you. I got you."* They slid off into the back stairway. He said, *"Hold me down while I talk to her."*

I was surprised when she walked off with him like that. If that's how she got down who was I to complain. Shit, I wasn't mad at all, not when I was about to give her a test ride. No way could I turn down a welcome home present like this. Hahaha.

I figured he was taking too long after about five minutes passed. I missed the elevator twice and was becoming impatient. I wanted to get my nut off with shorty, but I wanted to go upstairs and see my family too. After a few minutes, they came back into the hallway. She was looking at me smiling. I said to Sha...

"What's up bro, she wit it or what?"

"Yea. She wit it, but we gotta see her later. I only had enough to get her to serve one of us."

"Are you fucking serious! You mean to tell me, you had me look out for you while you got ya dick sucked?"

"Hahaha, I would of looked out for you. I meant well bro. I got caught up in the moment. Hahaha, welcome home. Hahaha..."

I couldn't be mad. All I could do was shake my head sideways and laugh that shit off. We laughed all the way up to the tenth floor. We got in front of my parent's apartment and I knocked a few times. *"Knock, knock, knock."* My mom swung the door open. The apartment was filled with the great aroma of my mom's home cooked meal. I so longed for my mother's cooking. My mom pulled me into her arms, giving me the biggest hug. She had the biggest smile on her face and took a deep breath, a sigh of relief. She went into her chants, giving praise, saying...

"Thank God for Jesus! My Sweetness is finally home. Thank you Jesus, for bringing my baby back to me alive and safe. Thank you. Thank you. Thank you Jesus!"

"Glad to be home ma. Being away from the family was the

worse feeling in the world. I'm not ever going back. I promise you that. I'll do the right thing and get myself together."

"I sure hope so Sweetness. I'm praying on it. I see you and Anthony found each other already". (a sarcastic look on her face).

"Yea…. My brother from another mother, hahaha."

"Hi Mrs. Jo-Ann. (giving her a hug and kiss). You know I been waiting for my lil' bro to come home all day." (Smiling)

"I know. You boys are grown now, and I won't try to chastise you, but just remember what we spoke about Anthony before Sweetness came home. He looks up to you and Tyrone. Just give him the chance he deserves. That's all I ask of you. I talk to you like you're my own son, the same way your mother speaks to my baby. We love you boys. When you guys are in jail, you need to know your family is going through the same pain you feel every day you're in there. Don't make this a habit in hurting your family, Ok?"

"OK. Ya know how it is out here, but as I told you before, I promise you we'll do our best in making you more happy than sad Mrs. Jo-Ann."

"OK I'll hold you to that. Now, you can go, so I can finish preparing the food. Do I need to pull out another plate for you Anthony?"

"Yeah, you already know ma! Hahaha..."

Although Savior and Sha-Ru were in the Five Percent Nation of Islam, my mother still called them by their birth names. Sha-Ru and I walked into the living room and my father was sitting there watching TV. When he saw me, he jumped up with excitement and we walked into each other's arms. He said...

"Boy, I'm so glad you're home. It took a lot out of me knowing my boys were in jail. I raised my boys better than that and I know that you can do better than being in jail wasting time like that. You don't need to be..."

"Ok dad. I get your point. I don't need any lectures right now. It's been a long day already and we can talk later if you want, but not right now",

"OK. I hear you. You don't wanna hear what I gotta tell you, just like your brother. You gonna come out here and follow behind him and only the Lord knows the outcome. Just try to be careful out here, and I love you."

"Love you too dad."

My sister, Sonya came out of her room. When she saw me, she ran and gave me a big hug and a kiss. Happy and excited, she said...

"Thank God. My little brother is finally home! It felt like

forever, but I'm so happy you're out of that place. It ain't a place for you to be. I know one thing, you better not go back, you hear me?"

"Yes ma. I hear you. You're something else, you still think you my mother."
"I helped raise your ass too. So you damn right, I'm your mother. I'm just happy you're home. Now, I can get married. I didn't know if your release date would somehow change. I wasn't sure if my wedding date in a few weeks would've been enough time for you to come home and attend the wedding."

"Yea, I heard you told everybody that if I wasn't home for the wedding, you was gonna cancel it until I got out."

"I only plan to have one wedding in my life, and if by God's will, I want all of my family to be there. I held the date off for some time now, but you're home now. That's what matters. Now we can move on."

"Yea. I guess you're right."

I wanted to know where my niece was, so I asked my sister...

"Where my baby at?"

"Oh, Shikia. She's outside with Retta, walking Makassa. They should be coming back upstairs in a little while."

251

My sister and I were talking when my cousin Eric walked out of me and my brother's room. Sav followed behind him. My brother said...

"Bout time you got home. Welcome home lil' bro!"

"Yeah cous, welcome home! We been waiting around all afternoon for you."

"Thanks yo. Glad to be home. I just wanna see where I fit in with everything and do my part. I know a lot has changed, but I have to fit in somewhere. We'll see how it goes...right?"

"Lil bro, I told you, when you was in there. Do ya time and when you get out we gonna sit down and figure shit out. I got a lot going on right now and I'm making my way up the ladder quite fast. You already know, I can hustle with the best of them."

"You already know I know bro. That's one of the things I always admired the most in you. You always told me, that no matter where you are, you have to know how to adjust to where you are and hustle your way through it. I know you doing it big right now. All I want to do is be the one to enforce order and respect around you. If I can do that then I'm doing my part. I don't want to be out here selling drugs."

"I don't want you being out here doing it either. I don't think mommy can handle that. Bad enough I came home doing what I do. It's so much traffic coming in and out of here. It's real

crazy right now. I know mommy not going to take too much of this."

"There's a lot of attention on Savior right now. He's too flashy. All this jewelry and diamond watches. Having two Mercedes Benzes parked in the parking lot is not making it any better for him. A lot of people are jealous. He just came home four months ago. I keep telling him that having those cars is too much and…"

"Yo, E, give him a break man."

"Hahaha. Ok. Yo, ya niggas are crazy."

Noticing my cousin Rahmel wasn't there, I asked…

"Yo, Where's Rha?" Everyone got quiet.

My sister said, "Ya should go in the room and talk."

"About what? All I asked is, where's Rah?"

Eric broke the silence and said, "Yo cous, Rah took a turn for the worse. He's back in the hospital.

"Are you serious! What's going on? Is he ok? No one told me what happened ya'll just said he was in an accident."

"There was a house party out here and some girl from East New York was there. She was pregnant. She got into some

words with someone and they punched her in her stomach. She was rushed to Long Island College Hospital. I don't know if she lost her baby or not, but then her brother and some other dudes came out here after they found out. Not many people were outside due to the police shutting the party down after around 4am.

It was quite a bit of heat in the hood after that. Rha and I was sitting on the bench in front of our building talking, drinking a few Heinekens and taking in the summer breeze. We weren't aware of what happened earlier and before we knew it, five dudes with bats ran down on us.

They made small talk with us, asking if we were at the party and if we knew about the pregnant girl that got punched in her stomach? We told them we knew nothing about it, but for them it didn't even matter who was there or who knew at that point. All they wanted was revenge on anybody. One of the dudes swung his bat at me. I blocked it with my arm and told Rha to run. We ran in different directions. I got away, but Rha didn't.

When Rha never came back to the building, I went on a search for him. Almost one hour later, I found him unconscious. He was at the P.S. 27 schoolyard, lying in a puddle of blood. The doctors said, he was hanging on to his life by a thread and if he was brought to the hospital one second later, he would've died."

"What hospital is he at?"

"He's at Long Island College Hospital. When I went to visit him last week, he convinced me to bring him some clothes and I snuck him out the hospital and took him home. He was home a few days before he turned for the worse. I had to rush him back to the emergency room. He was readmitted at that point. Cous, he's still in bad shape and he's asking for you."

"What's his condition now?"

"He just came out of a slight coma. He can barely remember certain things right now, but he's processing. He has a fractured skull and an enlarged brain. He's asking for you everyday, asking did you get home yet. He keeps saying he got to get home because he gotta help you get on your feet."

This was quite a bit to take in. I just came home. To think there was more bad news to add on top of that. Wow, I started to wonder if it was really a good thing to be home after all. I had less stress and problems on the inside, but I'm home now and this was my reality.

My brother decided to take the floor and lay a few things down on me that was important to know. I had to find out sooner or later, so he said...

"Listen bro, I know this is a lot for you right now, but it's best you get hit with everything at once so we can move on from here. You're twenty-one years old now. Going to jail may have

255

saved you. It may have prevented an early death. Who knows? That really applies to all of us. I'm home. Supreme, Sha-Ru and Powerful are home. Now you're home. It's a good thing for Shamel, that he didn't have to go upstate like all of us did and now all of us are home. A lot has changed."

"I know bro, I can see that."

"Sure you can, but do you see how close the change has been, even in your own household? Do you remember how nice it use to look around here. Now almost nothing is in here anymore? There's a floor model color TV in the living room, with no sound, with a small portable black and white TV, with a hanger as the antenna, sitting on top to give it sound. To top that off, there's almost no furniture in this apartment anymore. Look at daddy bro...Have you not noticed that the king of the castle has fallen from his throne?"

My dad yelled out...

"Don't be telling that boy no damn lies about me. I'm tired of you motherfuckers in here whispering about me in my house! This my house! You don't like it, there's the fucking door! Let it hit you in ya ass on the way out! I'm tired of this shit! I don't wanna hear nobody else talking bout me no more!"

"Ain't nobody talking about you man!"

"Tyrone...you better leave it alone boy! I said what I had to say. You better leave it alone!"

My mom intervened...

"Now, I don't wanna hear anything from neither one of you. I been in this kitchen busting my ass all morning to cook this food for Sweetness and I be damned if ya gonna give me a headache now! End of conversation!"

I guess you already know what happened after that. The Queen had spoken...Hahaha. You damn right. When moms speak, you take heed and listen. Anyway, we went back into our conversation, but spoke much lower this time. My brother continued in saying...

"No need in cutting corners with you lil' bro. It is what it is, daddy out here getting high...He's smoking "CRACK!"

"What? What you talking bout?"

"Are you blind or are you just plain stupid? Ain't no way you gonna tell me you don't notice a change in him. Look at his appearance bro. Nobody wanted to tell you when you were away, but you're home now. This the reality of it..."

When it came to my dad, I loved him the same as my mom. I would've never thought in a million years I'd see him this way. This is a man who never left his family's side, not even at a time when father's left to get groceries and never returned. That couldn't be said about mine. My dad was there my whole life. He genuinely had a good heart.

For many years, he drove tractor-trailers, he was an aspiring singer, he was very athletic and he was my Dad! I couldn't understand, how this could have happened to such a man. I blamed everything and everyone but him. In my eyes, he was the victim.

My brother felt like I should face reality, but truthfully this wasn't my first time hearing this. I guess when I first heard it I didn't really believe it. I brain washed myself into believing anything but the truth. I remember when Jus first dropped that bomb on me. He was the first one to ever tell me my dad was getting high.

I was finally faced with my reality. My mission was set. First up, I was to find out who put my cousin in the hospital and nearly took his life. Then, I planned to wreak havoc on Red-Hook like never before. I felt Red-Hook destroyed my family and I sought revenge against everyone in it. It was war on anyone who'd attempt to stand in my way. My plight began the summer of 1986.

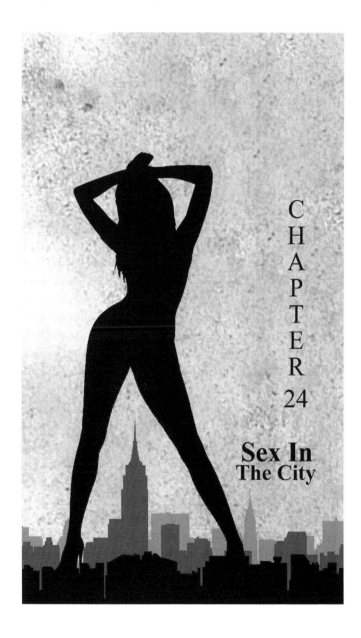

CHAPTER
24

Sex In
The City

After eating dinner with my family, I excused myself so I could go see my friend Eva. One thing I can say about her, she was consistent in corresponding with me the whole time I was gone. I really cared and had feelings for her, believing it to be mutual.

Eva had a radiant beauty about herself. It left you blown away at the sight of her. In my mind, the bond between us had become closer than just friendship. I really had plans on coming home and being with her, but just when I thought I heard enough bad news for one day there was more lurking in the winds.

Eva lived with her mom and sister Rene on the first floor facing The Ave. My defenses were up as soon as I hit the block. I made a conscious decision to stay on point. As soon as I was about to cross the street, I saw Eva sitting at her window. She was taking in the cool summer breeze, when she noticed me as well. She had a genuine glow of happiness on her face and that put a smile on mine.

Her window was low enough for me to pull myself up and give her a kiss. It really felt good to finally see her. Talking to her from her window felt like a reenactment of Romeo and Juliet, but on some hood shit. She made a bunch of excuses about not being able to come outside or go into the hallway. Still, I didn't think much of it.

In her last few letters she said she really had to talk to me. I didn't want to get into it at the moment, so I didn't bring it up. Now that I was home and in front of her, I sensed a slight reluctance on her part. I just went with the flow and continued our conversation. As we were talking, Eva's sister Rene, Jen and Jen's sister Dawn passed by on the opposite side of the street.

It wasn't long before Rene and Jen called me across the street. I told Eva that I'd be right back. She told me not to go, but I still told her, " *I'll be right back.* " I figured they more than likely, wanted to tell me welcome home.

When I got across the street, we all said, *"Hi"* and I gave each of them a hug. It didn't take long, before Rene and Jen jumped down my throat. They overwhelmed me with a barrage of questions about how I felt about Dawn. They were trying to play matchmaker. This kind of threw me off. I was sure they knew I was seeing Eva. Although I was attracted to Dawn, I thought she was still involved with someone else. Not the case. She'd recently broken up with him and now she was single.

What came next was disturbing. Jen asked me, *"Why are you across the street wasting your time talking to someone who's pregnant, when my sister is right here and available?"* Obviously, what I just heard struck a chord. My attention instantly shifted towards Eva. I walked back across the street, with a puzzled expression on my face. She was crying, but I was the least bit sympathetic. At this point, I felt betrayed. I was more disappointed that I had to hear it from someone else's mouth.

Straightforward and direct, I asked her, *"Are you pregnant?"* She confirmed, saying "Yes". She was crying uncontrollably and trying to explain, but I wasn't trying to hear it. I turned my back on her and walked across the street to resume my conversation with the girls. Eva and I were done! At that moment, I was a single man.

Although the opportunity presented itself unexpectedly, I was willing to embrace it wholeheartedly. Dawn was undeniably, a top pick in the hood. She was *"Crème De La Crème"*. She was 5'5 and had a slim svelte figure, with huge breasts to compliment her assets. Her skin tone was honey-coated, golden brown and she sported an Anita Baker haircut. She was fluent in both English and Spanish as well.

I felt bad about what just went down. While speaking to Dawn, my thoughts often drifted to Eva. It seemed as if Dawn read my mind. She broke my thoughts and said...

"I don't wanna keep you over here, if your mind is over there. You can go if you want, I'm not holding you."

"No I'm good. You have my undivided attention. Trust me, you do."

"Now, that's better, that's what I need. I should be all you're thinking about."

Dawn kept my mind occupied. She seduced me with her conversation. We moved off to the side and began to vibe with one another. I told her...

"You know I've been liking you for a long time?"

"Yea, I know, but we both had some one we were seeing at the time. Now that we don't, we can move forward from here if you feel the same."

"Was that a trick question? You already knew from when I use to see you a while back, walking your poodle, how I was feeling about you. No need to look for the best when it's standing right in front of me, right?"

"Oh, that's so sweet."

"I certainly feel the same way you do. Meet me half way and we can go all the way."

"Yea, I guess you right. Did you get half way yet because I'm already there. Waiting on you."

Not much was left to be said after that. Our emotions were already at an all time high. Sparks were flying all around us. I had a burning desire deep down in my loins, yearning for her. Our eyes stayed locked on each other, as I pulled her closer to me. She felt my hardness brush up against her, which turned her on.

I pulled her into my arms. I put my tongue in her mouth, giving her a long passionate kiss. Many hours had passed and it was getting late. I guess time flies when you're having fun. I offered to walk her to her building. Holding hands along the way, we reached her apartment door. Pulling her key out, she opened the door and asked…

"Do you wanna come in?"

(Without hesitation), "You already know I do."

(Smile on her face), "My mother should be sleep by now. Come on, let's go in my room."

"I'm following in your footsteps baby. Take me to the promised land."

"Lol. You so crazy."

Upon entering her room, I kicked my sneakers off and immediately made myself comfortable. She went off into the hallway closet and grabbed a few washcloths and towels. At first I thought we were going to shower together, but she told me to go first. In the Bing on Riker's, I was only allowed a five-minute shower. I swore I would never take another five-minute shower again, but I changed my mind quickly. Like Clark Kent, I was in and out with the quickness.

I came out the shower, wrapped the towel around me and went back into her room. She brushed past me as she went to take a shower herself. I laid back on her bed drifting off, lost in my thoughts thinking about her. Unaware of how much time had passed, I suddenly saw a silhouette in the doorway. The only existing light was coming through the room's window from the outside street night light.

As she entered the room, I stared at her wrapped in her towel. She went to turn on some music, when I stopped her and said...

"Come here baby. The only music I wanna hear right now, is the seductive, erotic sounds coming from you. I want to travel through your body and make you sing to me. I wanna hear how high your octave range is."

"Oh really? If you got me singing lead, I'll most certainly have you as my hype man or maybe singing background."

We gave each other a sly laugh, but the tension was too much to further bare. She dropped the towel from her body. Letting it fall to the floor, she exposed her beautiful voluptuous, sculptural body.

I was mesmerized by her sexy, sensual moves as she walked closer to the bed and climbed in next to me. I was blown away by how small her frame was in comparison to her breast. The moment our bodies met, we got lost in one another's lustful desires. We began passionately kissing and caressing each other all over. It wasn't long before I started feasting on her body. I cupped her huge breasts in my hands and put them in my mouth.

I licked around her areolas and nibbled on her hard nipples. Her body went into a frantic frenzy, jumping from my touch. I possessed total control of her body. I reached down between her legs, rubbing her wet moist pussy. Her juices flowed uncontrollably from her body. The smell of her juices filled the room with a sweet fragrance.

It wasn't long before we changed positions. She started kissing and licking on my chest. Teasing me with her tongue, she nibbled on my nipples while stroking my manhood. My body started trembling and shaking from her eagerness to please.

Without warning, she went down on me. Placing her lips on the tip of my head, she tasted my pre-cum. It felt so good. She started moving her head in a back and forth rhythm, while massaging my balls. I watched my dick disappear in her mouth. She continued masterfully gliding her tongue up and down the sides of my shaft and then back up to the tip. I had to control my eruption, but she wanted me to explode.

Without warning, I turned her around putting her into the 69 position. She lifted her leg over the other side of me, keeping my dick in her mouth and sitting her pussy on my face. I opened my mouth and put my tongue as deep as I could inside of her. Sucking and licking on her clit, I drank all of her honey as it released from her vaginal canal. After what seemed like a lifetime of foreplay, we both were ready for some hardcore loving. She said...

"Baby, I need it bad. I wanna feel you inside of me right now!"

"Come here. You don't have to tell me twice."

I got on top of her, spreading her legs apart. She grabbed my dick and guided me inside of her. The tip of my head touched her pussy lips, spreading them apart. I slowly thrust myself inside. I began pushing in as deep as I could go, until I hit the back of her wall. I wanted her to feel all of me. She started singing right then and there.

"Mmm...Mmm... Ohhh! Mmm... Ohhh Yes! Oooh! Yes baby! You're so deep. Mmm. Mmm. Mmm!

"That's right baby. Sing my song to me. Let me know how good daddy makes you feel."

"Uuugggh.... Uuugggh... You feel so big and strong inside of me! It's too much baby...Ohhh! Ohhh! I'm cummin' already! I'm cummin baby! Baby...Oh baby...I'm cummin' baby.... Uhhh! Uhhh! Owww!

"That's right baby...keep cummin' for me. Keep those legs up, yeah that's right, keep them up. I feel those legs shaking. Damn baby. Your pussy lips are wrapped tight around my dick. Uhhh...damn this pussy feel so good! I'm about to stretch you right on out. Your lips are gonna be swollen when I'm done wit you!"

"That's right baby. Stretch it out. Do whatever you want. It's yours."

"That's right...Talk to me...Talk to me in Spanish. Tell me, daddy you make me feel so good."
"Oh...Oh...Ummm. Papi, papi. Hay Dios mio! Papi me haces sentir tan rico! Hay Dios...Papi me haces sentir tan rico!"

"Yea baby. That's right, you already know. I make it feel so good."

"Baby, let me get on top so I can ride it."

Being that this was the first shot of pussy I got since coming home, I was full of energy. My stamina was at an all time high. Adrenaline on speed, I was ready to go back in. I'm sure Dawn didn't realize what she was up against, but it was too late for all of that. I was going to represent in ways she couldn't imagine and she loved every bit of it.

We changed positions and she was on top of me. This was the perfect view, watching her huge breasts bounce as she straddled down on my manhood. She started riding me, grinding her hips taking all of me inside of her…

"Baby, you feel so good. I feel you all up in my stomach. My pussy is so wet. I can't stop cummin'."

"I don't want you to stop, let it out! That's right, let those big ass titties bounce, I like that. Yeah, just like that babe. I already know. I feel your body shaking. Let it out. Cum on that dick. Baby… I can't hold back no more either, I'm about to cum too. Mmm Mmm, ah yeah. Here I cum baby!"

"Give it to me! Give me that nut baby. Give it to me! I want

that hot nut inside me."

After a well-deserved time out, it wasn't long before we were right back at it. I said...

"I hope you're not tired, cause I still want some more. Now, turn that ass around, and spread those ass cheeks so I can hit it from behind doggie style. Imma stand up in it."

"Damn baby, you still hard!"

"You damn right. I'm about to bring you to your climax. For me, you're a long time overdue baby"

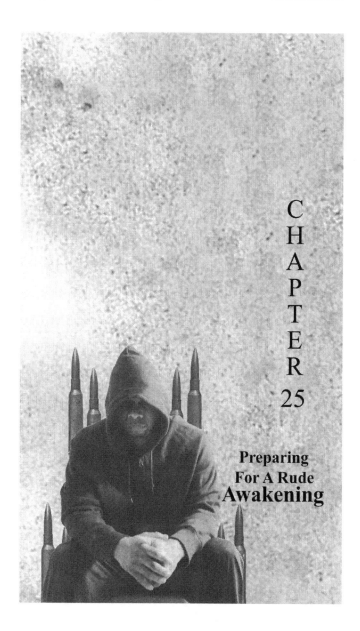

C
H
A
P
T
E
R
25

**Preparing
For A Rude
Awakening**

After a wonderful first night home, I felt like I was on cloud nine. I had a beautiful girlfriend and now all I had to do was get my weight up and get money. I was waiting on my brother Savior. I needed him to get up with me, put me on and assign me to working alongside him. Being his *"Enforcer"* was all I wanted to be.

Before I came home, all I had in mind was to be my brother's shadow. I wanted to be on his ass like a pair of pants. Being a boss was far from my mind. He was the boss, and I was fine with that. All I wanted and needed was a stockpile of weapons and pick of my own crew. He just had to do his thing.

The following day, Sha-Ru arranged for us to get together. We needed to be on the same page as to what our next moves were going to be. The meeting place was in the hood, at *"Dip Park"*. There was a pull up bar and other equipment to work out with. It was about 10:00 a.m. when Supreme, Shamel and P-God met up with us at the park. Fly Ty, Ty's brother T-Rock and Dumar were in the park about to work out when we got there.

With the exception of Shamel and Dumar, everyone else did the *"round tha world"* workout routine. Dumar had a few crackheads carry the weights from his car to the park. He had a long bar, flat bench and dumb bells. He was about to get it in.

Shamel wasn't much into working out and was just chilling in the shade, talking to the girls as they passed by.

Everyone in the park gave acknowledgements with handshakes and head nods and then we got into the work out. It was really hot outside and niggas were on buff after about eight sets in. We were coming out of our T-shirts, drenched with sweat. We went through a rigorous routine, showing off. We were talking shit back and forth, making jokes about who was gonna be the first to break. We challenged each other's conditioning and tested out limits.

If it was considered a show, the star was hands down Dumar. This huge specimen of a man stood well above 6'5 and weighed over three hundred pounds solid. He could bench over five hundred pounds on the long bar with ease. If not for the sun beaming down on us, he wouldn't have broken a sweat.

A few hours passed and the park cleared out once we finished the workout. Sha-Ru, Supreme, Shamel, P-God, and myself stayed to talk. Sha-Ru spoke first. It seemed as if he had everything already mapped out. He just needed my signature of approval to formulate a solid crew. He was clear about the position he wanted to play. He didn't want to sell drugs. He said he was a natural born stick up kid. We were going to rep BK to the fullest, till the casket dropped. Sha-Ru got a little animated saying, *"When my day comes, bury me with my guns in hand"*.

He felt it was much easier to let the dealers make their money and then we'd move in and rob them. They had to reach a certain level to pique our interest though, we weren't trying to rob no broke niggas. He wanted to move throughout the city using females as decoys, setting the dealers up. This was one of the easiest strategies that would likely go undetected, if done correctly. A nigga was a sucker for a bad bitch, all the time.

We'd also shut down any competition that my brother had in his way. It was obvious Sha-Ru was very serious about this. He already started his quest before I came home. He said he had to warm up and practice. He was setting the stage for me to walk on and see the progress in his vision.

He wanted to put a team together such as our Brooklyn cohort's, Tut from East New York and his affiliates *"The A-Team"*. At some point Sha-Ru wanted to form an alliance with Tut. He believed we would be able to not only strong arm New York, but various other states as well.

It was a masterful, well-planned idea to say the least, but there was one problem. Unlike him, not wanting to be a drug dealer wasn't the case for me anymore. I saw a major change in the game since we were away. We never sold drugs before, but I wanted to try my hand at it and see how high I could climb that ladder.

Sha-Ru looked at me with hurt in his eyes. He knew, the only one he could and would trust more than anyone in this world was myself. He pushed further trying to convince me, laying out more of the plan. He named the first targeted area, Queens. The strongest player at the time was Fat Cat Nickolas's crew. Sha-Ru planned to reach out to Red Bug from Nostrand Ave. and Tut to form an alliance with them. We would then go on a round the clock mission and put pressure on Queens.

I told him I would only consider it if my options with Sav, Jus or Rhamel folded. In my mind, that left a slim chance of me being a part of the crew. For the next few days, he was persistent in getting me to reconsider his offer.

I didn't want to go visit Rhamel in the hospital, but I been home almost a week and he was still in there. Sha-Ru and I decided to go visit him. The moment we got to the hospital I caught a bad feeling. I didn't mind putting someone in an ambulance or a casket, but hospitals and funeral homes were two places I didn't like being near. Anyway, I had to go see Rhamel because he was asking for me.

As soon as I walked into his room and saw him, I turned around and walked out. Sha-Ru and Eric ran after me, telling me I had to be strong for Rha and to go back into the room. With every bone in my body, I reluctantly went back in. I went to him and we hugged each other, crying uncontrollably.

I told him I would avenge his pain at any cost. He demanded I stand down and wait for him to get home. Of course I agreed in front of him. Sha-Ru read me like a book and already knew what time it was. He knew I was in my feelings and vulnerable. If this was the only way to get me on board with him and the crew, then so be it. It was on. I was about to get my feet wet and inflict the same pain I felt onto someone else. I strongly believed in Karma. Never retreat and always return fire! Karma's a motherfucker!

We went back to the hood and Sha-Ru came through with a small arsenal of his weapons. The crew, for the first time in a long time reassembled. We strapped up with the Nina (9mm), Four-Fif (45 auto), Uwop (Uzi machine gun) and a 12-gauge shottie (Shot gun). As I grasped my palm around the 9mm, I felt a rush through my body, straight to my heart. I instantly zoned out as we moved in route to East New York on a hunt for the unknown. We really had no idea who we were looking for, but we were going to vent out and look for trouble.

We rolled up to Cypress Projects in Brooklyn. After about twenty minutes in the area, we ran into some familiar faces. What a coincidence. We ran into Tut and the members of the A-Team. This shit felt like it was by design. This happens a lot when you move in similar patterns. The team knew that we were on the prowl.

They were on point in their hood just as we were in ours. Although our gangsta was well respected, we were still on their turf unannounced. Worst off, we were looking suspicious. We were dressed in dark colors with hats pulled down low under our brows. Sha-Ru, Shamel, Supreme and myself got out of the car. We lifted our hats up to show our faces, allowing them to recognize us. Our crews embraced, then Sha-Ru pulled Tut off to the side. He gave reason as to why we were driving through their hood.

Sha-Ru spoke briefly with Tut about the incident involving Rhamel and of course his future endeavors to strong-arm New York. Tut and the team were on board for whatever. Strong-arming was their line of work and what they were already known for. They were certainly not the type of crew to be out of their element. They were seasoned vets at their best.

Now, the only one that needed to be abreast with the movement was, Red Bug. Bug and his crew would likely be a go. We got in the car and Sha-ru told us to head home. He stated that Tut would keep his ear on the street and would either call him or handle the matter on his own. I personally obliged and was sure to return the favor in the near future.

This small hood army that was about to be assembled, was far too much for the city to bear. No one was safe outside. Any target was doomed, to say the least. A lot of funerals were soon to come. NYC's murder rate was about to rise off the charts. There was a war going on outside and I was right in the middle of it, in no-man's land.

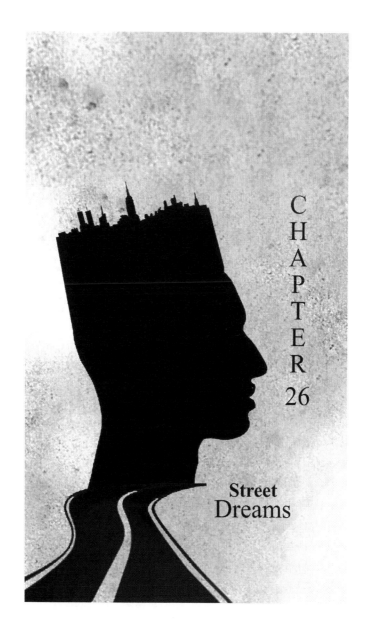

CHAPTER
26

Street
Dreams

Dawn and I had become a very close union, seldom being apart. Other than her having to leave for work, we were inseparable. I hadn't found a job yet and I wasn't looking for one either. There were too many options at hand that brought in far more money than busting my ass working a basic nine to five.

Dawn begged me to get a job and did all she could to prevent me from believing in the illusion of the *"Street Dream"*. Yet to no avail, her words went in one ear and out the other. She insisted that if we worked together, there wasn't anything we couldn't do. She felt like she was protecting me by being with me and keeping me within her eyesight. She had her ways in trying to tame me, but her efforts were slowly slipping away. I was done. All the money I saw within the past few weeks that I've been home was enough for me. The itch was back and I was getting high off of those *"Street Dreams"*.

I was chilling on "The Ave." with Dawn, Jen and Rene. Out of nowhere a beautiful brand new, all white Cadillac Seville pulled up to the curb. A short, slim, light skinned dude got out the car. Everyone was damn near breaking their necks to see who he was. I immediately recognized him. It was my man Booker! We were upstate together at Elmira from 1984 thru part of 1986.

Booker and I worked in the mess hall together. Aside from us both being from Brooklyn, we knew some of the same people and were in the same line of work on the streets. We became real tight while doing our time. Booker and I exchanged information and planned to make some things happen once we both made it out on the other side.

He was released before me and said he'd come check me the third week of June. As a man of his word, he came through. He always said he had it going on and was into big things. He was from the 90's, a very dangerous area in Flatbush, Brooklyn. Mostly Jamaicans claimed that area upon entering into the United States.

Booker was making strong moves on the streets, but he was stepping on some dangerous people's toes. He always joked about how he lived on the edge. This was something we both had in common. Neither one of us could resist the rush that came along with risk and chance.

Booker started coming by everyday to check on me. Everyday felt like an adventure. He gave me a starter kit. He took me shopping and put money in my pocket, making sure I was good. He said he knew I would've done the same for him if it were the other way around. We had each other's back in prison and it was fitting to do the same on the streets.

The bad thing about living on the edge was having to constantly look in the rearview, watching the shadow of death right on your heels, waiting for you to slip. Your mind starts playing tricks on you. You begin to think about all types of shit. You can hear the black hearse following your every move. Everyday felt dangerous in the hood, but his day felt very different.

Most of the day went by and I hadn't seen or heard from my boy Booker. I called a few times, no answer. I didn't want to press him. I figured he was busy and would get at me when he could. A few days passed, still no Booker. Almost a week later, still no Booker. This wasn't like him at all.

By this time, there were a slew of thoughts racing through my mind. I figured at worst, he had to put some work in and was in recluse. I still had to check on him though. So I reached out and called my boy Muddy from the 90's. I figured if anything was wrong, he'd know.

My gut told me something was terribly wrong. Muddy picked up the phone and as soon as Booker's name left my mouth, I heard the worst. He told me Booker got killed earlier in the week and he suffered a gruesome death. Rumor had it, he was beheaded and his head was placed on his mother's doorstep.

It felt like a family member passed away. The maliciousness of his demise was likely revenge from his prior mischiefs. If I was not waiting on my brother or Jus, I would have gotten a little deeper into Booker's movement. Although we hate the outcome, we still try to justify living the fast life. It was now my turn to live as Booker lived, *"Hustle hard and live like a motherfucking gangsta!"*

For a brief moment, I mourned over my boy's loss. One never could have closure over a loss like that. I just picked my heavy heart up, said a silent prayer and kept it moving. Dawn started to see a sudden change in me after Booker's death and not for the better.

I played deaf, not caring to hear anything positive. I was caught up by my surroundings and wanted all of what I saw. That being said, I got swallowed into the myths and pipe dreams of the underground life. I was about to squander my life away and set myself on a course that would eventually bring me down to my knees.

My brother told me to go hustle with Jus and Jus told me to go hustle with my brother. Jus had mostly crack heads working for him and his system was not fitting for me. Anyhow, He knew that he couldn't carry me the way he carried his workers. He knew we came from the same vein. There was no benefit in him helping me because one day he would have to face me head on.

I decided to go back to my brother. One evening, he finally sat me down and told me that he and mom had a talk. She made him promise her that once I came home he wouldn't get me into selling drugs. Upon hearing this, I was infuriated. I didn't care to understand his point of view, not one bit. All I knew was that if we weren't going to be down together, then I was going out on these streets on my own. He could've told me this the day I came home, rather than mislead me for weeks. I wouldn't have wasted so much time waiting.

Once our conversation was over, I felt the vibe between us instantly change. I sought no reasoning from him or my mom. We were raised to stick together and fight together. As brothers, we were supposed to be back to back on those streets. I know his back was up against the wall in honoring my mom's request, but this was the worse thing that could have happened. We would've been much stronger together than apart. At this point, I started plotting on the game looking for a way in.

Although it was unintended, there was a division set between Savior and myself. We were at a fork in the road. We had become competitors in the same game. I set out to prove that I was the strongest man standing in the hood. The thoughts I once had about coming home and getting with my brother or Jus was a distant memory.

Rhamel came home and he was slowly progressing. He went from being partially handicapped to functioning on his own. His situation bothered me a lot because he was trying to recover quickly for my sake. I was humbled by that and grateful for his efforts, but I couldn't wait anymore.

Despite Dawn's numerous protests, I was still bound to the streets. Dawn told me her last boyfriend was a drug dealer. She refused to stand by and watch me slowly kill myself getting involved in the drug game. Not taking her falling tears seriously, I called her bluff and she called mine. Dawn and I were over! Out of my wits and feeling empty inside, I reached out to my crimey Sha-Ru.

The crew was assembled and the mission was in effect. Sha-Ru, Supreme, Shamel, P-God and myself were strapped with heavy weaponry. We were in route to Manhattan our new-targeted area. Queens was a work in progress. We already sent a flock of females into Queens to infiltrate Fat Cat's crew and that required some time. So, we diverted our attention to one of the largest money exchange areas in New York. We were about to strong arm Wall Street!

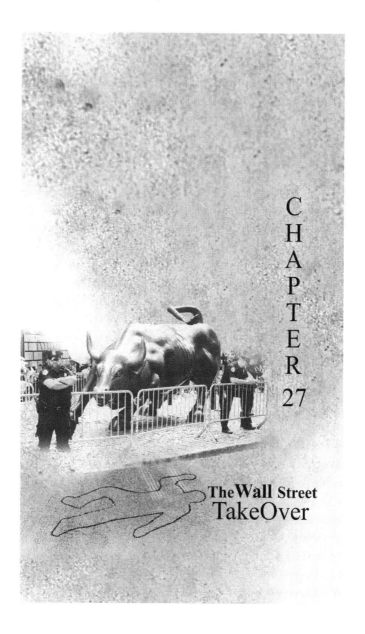

C
H
A
P
T
E
R
27

The Wall Street
TakeOver

The area was mapped out and plotted on some time ago. We did a few drive-bys days prior and felt comfortable with the set up. Now the moment of truth was here. We held a pact to hold court by any and all means necessary. We knew what we were up against. The option to stand down was given before anyone got in either of the two vehicles.

The strike time was 7:30a.m. We had our game faces on the moment we exited the Battery Tunnel. We drove a few blocks down and made a turn on Liberty. Just as we expected, the police were in their normal spot in front of the McDonald's. We drove past the light and circled around Liberty Park. We then circled the area as a precaution to see how many officers were walking their beat.

Knowing we didn't have a lot of time to hit the three areas we planned to hit, we staged an identical scenario. It was an attempt to throw the dispatchers off when the call came in to the NYPD. The escape route was mapped out and the Tunnel was only a few blocks away. We found parking in a secluded area, between the targets. The good thing about Liberty and Wall Streets were that the blocks were very short and narrow.

Once we got out of the cars, we split into two groups. We were to get back to the cars within five minutes flat, no exceptions. Sha-Ru and I went one way and the rest went the other. I walked up the block, passing everyone until I got to the other side. One mind reading the other, Sha-Ru and I drew our weapons simultaneously and closed the block in. We hit them with the element of surprise.

There were customers making purchases of marijuana or cocaine, their early morning fix. They were obviously at the wrong place, at the wrong time. We knew who the dealers were and we gathered them together with ease. We stripped them of all of their possessions, but most of all we planted a seed of fear in them that was sure to grow.

We made it back to the cars in time. The plan was working. We were well aware of the cameras in the area, but we also knew the blind spots where we could draw our weapons undetected. To further our advantage, we had a police scanner. We knew of the call that came in from the dispatcher. We knew that hitting two separate locations simultaneously would confuse the NYPD. This minimized our chances of being apprehended. It gave us ample time to get to and hit the third area on the opposite side of Liberty Park.

The third hit was on Wall Street where the statue of the Bull stood. It was much easier to hit the third mark because the NYPD was on the opposite side of the park. After parking the vehicles, we impulsively went into action, knowing who to get at. We took a much more aggressive approach and pistol-whipped the drug dealers. With not much time to do further, we robbed them and then we were gone with the wind.

Everything went according to plan. We knew not to let up or skip a beat. When you hit someone that hard, you have to maintain the pressure by keeping your foot on their neck. After letting the attack marinate in the opposition's mind for a few days, it was time to address Wall Street once again. We switched our attire to business wear, in order to blend in. We were going to see the Jamaicans this time around.

Jamaican Peter was a smooth operator. He was dark skinned, 5'11, 175 lbs. with a short Caesar hair cut and corporate style of dress. He made a living hustling under the radar for many years, to corporate America. Never in a million years did he expect to be up against this brute force. He never had to deal with such drama. It was definitely, his last days of serenity and peace.

It was very brash and bold of us to go back to this area. We were certainly tethering between jail and freedom. This was a pivotal moment. If we wanted to evolve and persevere in this location, we had to make every move count. With that being said, before early

morning rush hour, we were back in lower
Manhattan.

Walking a few feet apart from one another, we
blended in with the crowd. We went to all the
locations we knew Peter to post up at. He frequented
the McDonald's, the Burger King, and the Kentucky
Fried Chicken. He was a mover, never staying in one
place too long. It took us a while to hunt him down,
but we found his ass.

He was in Burger King drinking coffee and reading
the newspaper. Just to be a little more discreet, only
Sha-Ru and myself went inside while the others stood
posted-up outside. We felt less was best. Sha-Ru as
well as myself was capable of diffusing any situation
that was to come. We didn't want everyone storming
in in mass numbers. It was less distracting this way.

Before leaving the hood, we all switched up our
arsenal. We armed up with weapons one would use
in jail. We carried 007 knives and put single edged
GEM razors in our mouths. We knew that Peter
wouldn't be equipped, so it didn't matter how we
went at him.

The moment we walked inside, he saw us. The aura
in which he held was very unnerving as we stepped
into his cipher and invaded his privacy. Peter's
morning was about to instantly transcend into a

nightmare. To our surprise, he had no force of protection around him, other than maybe a few flunkies and some girls.

He sat there trying to put up a front of candor, by appearing to remain professional and not intimidated. However, it was obvious, his heart was pumping fear. He tried his best to sustain his composure and not expose himself, but he was obviously discombobulated. He was poorly equipped for what was coming at him. If he knew what was best for him, he'd concede to our demands with no further problems.

Once Peter heard our demands, he tried to negotiate. He tried to downplay the level of his organization, saying it was not as lucrative as we believed. We ignored his attempt to mislead us. He was advised him that he could remain valuable to the new movement or he could be replaced. The choice was clearly up to him.

We led him to believe that we knew a few personal things about him including his address. Truth is, that's all we knew. He called our bluff, somewhat doubting our knowledge of knowing his place of residence. That immediately changed the vibe in the room.

We went into action immediately. I jumped up and grabbed Peter, placing him in a headlock. Sha-Ru eyes swiftly swept the area, observing no reaction from his boys. They didn't attempt to make a move to help him. I guess they weren't going to jump into his affairs like that. They posed no threat.

With knife in hand, Sha-Ru pressed it into Peter's chest, barely missing his heart. Sha-Ru searched his pockets and found Peter's wallet. He placed all of his identification on the table, reading everything out loud in front of him.

I didn't place much pressure on his neck. I just wanted to restrain him. I wanted him to witness our doings. He didn't believe we knew his address before, but that disbelief vanished. He was convinced we were beyond the real deal. After the flurry of blows that were thrown within the past few days, Peter felt like it would be best for him to jump on board, at least until he could figure another alternative. Peter's plot in his mind began in that instant.

A few weeks went by with everything running very smoothly. We collected money from Peter, while he collected from all the others in the area. We sustained a slight force in physical presence, so they could be assured that we were not getting comfortable. After a few weeks of collecting Peter's money, we went to Spanish Harlem and purchased our own work (drugs) and dumped everything on him. The man was already broken and knew that he really had no choice but to take what we gave him.

It took some convincing to get Sha-Ru to try a new way of getting money and cop some work. He was hard pressed and stuck in his ways, but he quickly saw the benefits and we were good from there. To look back on things now, our greatest mistake was treating Liberty and Wall Streets like the hood. Our presence on the throne would be short lived.

The wedding day for my sister finally came. Sonya and Conti were getting married! This was most certainly going to be one of the most memorable days in our family's history. My sister was a nervous wreck. We only had enough time for one wedding rehearsal. A lot of people were expected to come to the wedding. What stressed her even more was that just as many people wanted to be in the wedding, even Sha-Ru wanted to be in it. Things had spiraled downhill with Dawn and myself. She was close to both my mom and sister and she too was in the wedding.

My sister had strong concerns. She wondered if the bridesmaids and groomsmen would be able to pull it off, since having had such short practice. Most of them had assured her that they'd been in weddings before. Many of the participant's schedules were not very flexible so it was hard getting any practices in.

They assured her that when they did get together, they would put in extra time to practice and get it right.

Our family thought big, but the reality was we had beer money and with champagne taste. My mom was adamant about my sister having a very nice wedding. My mom laid out her entire life savings and somehow found a way to make that beer money taste like Dom Perignon. The turn out was very big. Three white limousines were parked outside, while a convoy of other vehicles followed suit to the church in Bedford-Stuyvesant.

Bethany Baptist Church is where my siblings and I were baptized and raised as ushers. It was fitting for my sister to want to get married at a place that felt like home to our family. We had Reverend Jones officiate the ceremony. The church was filled to capacity. All of the bride and groom's families and friends were in attendance, as well as damn near half the hood.

Although my dad's physical appearance wasn't at it's best, my sister still wanted him to be the one to walk her down the aisle. At least hat's how it was supposed to be. My dad wasn't as reliable as he once was, due to his drug habit. He meant well, but him getting high came first, even before his own daughter's wedding.

With that being said, the hawk's eyes were on him the moment he woke up that morning. He wasn't able to leave our sight. This had him cranky and on edge all day. He complained about any and everything. His strategy was to get on everyone's nerves, but that didn't work. He fell back and began scheming and plotting alternative ways to get away. When it was all said and done, he did his part and made my sister proud.

After the wedding, then came the reception at The Masonic Temple in Brooklyn. Even more people showed up there. My mom had to have someone at the door to make sure the actual invites got in. The DJ had the crowd hyped and we were all having a real good time. I tried to play into the moment, trying to push back up on Dawn. It seemed like it was working too, until Sha-Ru came.

He told me he had to go. It was kind of unusual that he was leaving so soon, so I asked him what was up. He pulled me to the side so Dawn wouldn't hear us. She didn't like Sha-Ru. She knew that whenever we were together, we were likely up to no good. This case wouldn't be any different. Sha-Ru said...

"If I can come back, I will, but my sister's boyfriend Tray Bag got an issue that needs to be addressed right now and I told him I'd be there for him."

"I feel you, but you can't tell him you'll deal with it tomorrow?"

"Naw. I told him that a few times already, and I don't want him to think I'm not there for him when he got a beef."

"I see. Damn yo, you know I'm not gonna let you go by yourself. Hold on for a minute, I'll meet you out front."

"Ok lil' bro."

Dawn was looking at me, shaking her head in disappointment. I said...

"What's wrong with you?"

"Nothing. You tell me."

"Nothing to tell you. I don't know what's on your mind, but you got it all wrong."

"Whatever you say. I know when you get around Sha-Ru you're up to something. He get on my nerves, you know I don't like him."

"Aw man. You got it all wrong. It's not what you think. (Deep sigh), I need some air right now. I'm going out front. I'll be right back."

"Yeah, ok."

I slipped away from Dawn. I knew it was only a matter of time before her and her girlfriends would find their way outside and notice I wasn't around. To cover myself I went to my brother to get the keys to his car. I told him I had to go to the store for our mother. He went in the trunk and took out a small bag. He told me to hurry back so he could put the bag back in the trunk.

Sha-Ru and I jumped in the car and headed to Fort Greene Projects. Fortunately for me, we were literally five minutes away. I knew I couldn't stay away long and just wanted to do what we came to do. As soon as we got to Tray Bag's crib, Sha-Ru and I armed up. I took a .357 magnum and he took a 9mm from under the mattress.

We didn't have time to change clothes, so we rolled out, as is. I was in a tuxedo and Sha-Ru wore a two-piece suit. Once we got outside, we directed Tray Bag to walk alone in the area he had the beef. We were using him as bait, hoping the guys noticed him. They ran outside the building, drawing their weapons, running towards him. They quickly noticed that Tray Bag was merely a decoy. They stifled our plan of hitting them up in front of their building.

Everyone scattered, getting behind something to

shield themselves, while simultaneously pulling their triggers. Tray Bag motioned us towards a window on the third floor. We saw a dude pointing a 12 gauge shot gun out the window. He let off a round near us. We returned fire, shattering all the windows. Within minutes, the police sirens were all over the place. Before we knew it, we were almost surrounded.

Tray Bag ran towards his building, while Sha-Ru and myself concealed our weapons. With almost no choice, we walked towards the officers that were running towards us. A few things could've happened at that moment, because we were actually trapped. We could surrender, hold court or get lucky. The latter was the case this time.

The police had their weapons drawn and were running full speed ahead. In an instant, Sha-Ru and I played it off and pointed behind us screaming out...

"Officers, they're shooting over there!"

"Yea, hurry!!! Somebody might've got shot too!"

We got back in the car and headed back to the reception. We laughed our asses off at the police. I told Sha-Ru, we should wear suits all the time. We laughed some more knowing that, that was a really close call. I thought about how hurt my sister would've been if I had gotten locked up on her wedding day.

As soon as I got back to the reception, Dawn was on me about where I went. I brushed her off with some lame excuse, saying, "*I didn't go anywhere. I was here the whole time*". It was a pretty good alibi if you ask me. Now, how ironic was it that in less than twenty minutes all hell broke loose. Three dudes walked past the reception hall and recognized my brother. They had beef some time ago. My brother robbed them and they finally crossed paths.

It doesn't take a rocket scientist to figure out what came next. My brother told everyone to go inside the building. He then pulled a sawed off 12 gauge shot gun from the bag he had. Sha-Ru pulled out the 9mm, and I pulled out the 357 Mag. For the most part, it was a stand off with the advantage in our favor. They had no weapons on them, which left them vulnerable. My brother gave them an ultimatum, "*Walk away, or die where you stand. It's your call.*"

Sha-Ru and I wanted to take them around the corner and pistol whip them, but my brother gave them a pass that they were more than happy to take. He didn't want to have anyone come and retaliate while all of our family and friends were around. The worse part was yet to come.

My sister ran outside and couldn't believe what was

happening. She started spazzin' out on us about having guns. She was cursing like a sailor. Everyone told her that the attack came from a random group of guys. They told her if we weren't at her reception, it would've been much worse.

Everyone calmed down for the most part and went back inside the building. The building managers wouldn't let us bring our weapons inside. That was a problem for us. We weren't sure if those dudes were going to come back, but we reluctantly put the guns in the car. We went back inside after being searched. As fate had it, the rest of the evening went by great.

A few months went by and things were going great around Wall Street. All of a sudden, we received some resistance. This kid Shandu ran around on the low, talking about us. He said he didn't see why everyone was so scared of us. He exclaimed how he has been in the area hustling for many years and since we came around he wasn't making any money. He told the others that he was gonna get some work from us and then beat us. He wanted to show everyone how tough we weren't. Bad move on his part.

He did come to me to get some work. I gave it to him. By the end of the day when I was looking to collect, he disappeared. I didn't think much of it and figured I'd see him the next day. When the next day came, he hit the block early, got his grind on and bounced. This continued for a few days and now the streets were talking. I was heated. In his mind, my team's armor had been pierced.

Shandu took my product, re'd up (purchased more drugs) from the profits and bragged about it. The second day I saw him, I gingerly confronted him, not wanting to cause a scene during rush hour. Not wanting to strike expectedly, I gave him a pass. We spoke briefly and I told him he had twenty-four hours to give me double what he made the past few days. He nonchalantly agreed and kept it moving.

Almost two weeks went by and I had yet to see Shandu. He was ducking me. I went to his crib in Brooklyn's Gowanus Projects, only to have his people claim he wasn't there. I could've easily put the team together or ran up in the crib by myself, but I left. I was gonna give it another day or so before I took it to another level.

My patience was wearing out though. The team wasn't aware of the incident for a few days. When they did find out, a meeting was set up in the hood. When it was all said and done, there was a direct hit on Shandu's head. I made it clear that I wanted to deal with dude on my own. I took it very personal. None of my actions were gonna be misconstrued. My motives were clear and my mind was full of depraved intentions.

One morning, Shandu's luck ran out. Today was not his day. I saw him. He was walking towards me with two dudes by his side. I was alone, but no less dangerous. Once I saw him and his boys I sized up the situation. I had my knife cuffed in my hand, concealing it slightly on the side of my hip as I walked towards him. He had a newfound aura of confidence.

He thought I would bow out since I was outnumbered. He felt he could expose me, not knowing he would be opening Pandora's box. His plan was to prove a point in front of his boys. As we closed the gap between us, he tried to create a scene. He started boasting and yelled out, *"Nigga I hear you looking for me! Well...you don't have to look no further, here I am."*

To be honest, I was shocked at this nigga's audacity. When I saw him a few weeks ago, he had none. This dude would have looked intimidating to the average Joe because of his size, but I wasn't your average Joe and I knew he wasn't built like that. My response was in my actions not in words. Once I got within arms reach of him, I swiftly raised my hand up. I dug that knife in him so deep, everything but the handle went in.

He was in shock and froze as I struck him three times. I dug deeper with every thrust turning the knife in his flesh. I was in the zone for the moment. I told him, *"Nigga. You should've stayed ducking me. It was better for your health. Ya blood's not a payment, you still owe me until I say you don't."*

When he hit the ground, I bent down and wiped the blade on his jacket and proceeded to walk away. I glared at his boys with a sly smirk on my face. I walked away until I hit the corner, then I ran my ass off to get away. I found out later that his dudes were decoys. He wanted me to think they were going to ride for him, when he didn't even know them like that.

I felt redeemed when I saw the expression on his face, and the face of everyone around. As far as I was concerned, this was a good look. Truth was, this was the start of my destruction. For one, I put way too much heat on the area and the NYPD turned up their enforcement. They shut down all money-making sources. Next, they put out a bulletin wanting to know who I was and my whereabouts. My days in the area were short lived. I had to stay in the hood and was called on a need be basis. It wasn't long before things went totally left for the team.

This was around the time I shifted gears and rolled out to the Coney Island section of Brooklyn. Mostly Russians lived in this area. Rhamel and I went out there to reopen an area he had a strong hold on prior to his accident. There was a lot to consider at this moment, most importantly his state of mind. He was trying to recover as fast as he could, but he was putting a lot on himself. In doing so, he put both of our lives in jeopardy. Truth be told, it was a real uphill battle for him to remember a lot of things that were once second nature.

At times it scared me, because I was following in his footsteps. He often put us in back alley type of situations with some very ruthless Russians. This was the same backyard that a friend of mine almost met an unfortunate fate. The Brooklyn figure, Mark Spark had recently been kidnapped with another friend of mine named Pep, from Marcy Projects. They were bound, stripped of all their clothing, and gagged. They were tortured individually, for a substantial amount of time. In an instant with no second guessing, Mark saw a thread of opportunity and jumped out of the second floor apartment window. He barely escaped with his life. He was the only one who fortunately survived.

Knowledge of the incident with Mark was widely spread throughout Coney Island and was an example to everyone. If you came on this turf, there was nothing to talk about. The only resolution was death. I called Mark, expressing my intentions going in. He told me, although my cousin was known and respected with some of the Russians, that was only a slight edge. He said for me to move around there with great caution.

He couldn't have explained it better when he said that the Russians were way too strong in the Coney Island and the Brighton Beach areas. The location I was going in was the same block that Mark almost lost his life on. He kept telling me to be careful with strong emphasis. I took everything into consideration, but I was going out there to open up a crack spot and make it big.

Rhamel rented an apartment and then I went to work. I set up inside, while Rhamel went on a mission to steer customers my way. I sat in that apartment for about a half hour when a custie (customer) knocked on the door. I served them and figured a flow of heads would soon follow. After a few hours passed, no one else came. Rhamel came back shortly telling me to pack up and we went home. That was my crack selling debut.

The next day pretty much went the same as before and the next and the next. Almost a week passed and we hadn't even made $500.00 yet. This for me was very disturbing and more so, discouraging. I started complaining about there not being any money out there. Rhamel kept trying to convince me otherwise. His memory was vague and he really was a work in progress. He was still trying to remember certain things and people. He'd say in his defense, that no one knew he was back in the area. He said he was looking for his goldmine, If only he could remember what it was.

After a few weeks, most of the same thing happened, nothing Rhamel and I went outside to do a walkthrough. I started complaining so much that Rhamel told me to go home if I wanted. While we were going back and forth, I noticed a short white girl with a few missing front teeth. She confronted us. She was obviously a crack head. She had the biggest smile on her face. She stood in front of us and I noticed her eyes were glossy, in a daze on cloud nine. She couldn't believe her luck. It was as if God was in front of her and his name was Rhamel.

The weird thing was, Rhamel looked at her as if she was a stranger. He barely remembered her, until she started saying certain things to trigger his memory. This was someone who looked like she got high all day and didn't care about anything else. But guess what? She was an asset. She was Rhamel's goldmine!

Her name was Carol and her trusty partner in crime was Brenda. I lived in the hood all my young life and had been around the worst of them, but these two were the worst snakes I'd ever seen. In an instant, we went from the apartment on Coney Island Ave. to Brenda's raggedy ass crack house on Brighton and

4th Street.

The living conditions were the worst, but with Carol steering the heads to the house, it didn't take long before I knew why she was called a goldmine. She steered in so many heads, that the $500.00 in work I had, was gone within an hour. I had to go get more and sold all of that within a few hours.

After that, I damn near moved into that house. My office was confined to an army cot that I laid on. When someone knocked, I would serve them under the door. I gave both Carol and Brenda four $5.00 pieces of crack daily. This was to get them going and to get the monkey off their backs. Things were going great. Within twelve hours, I was selling up to $1,000 worth of crack.

After a while, Rhamel felt I was working too much in the spot and wanted to shut down after twelve hours. I told him I was fine. I went home from time to time, but I was good. I always started my day with a $5.00 budget. I would go to Dunkin Donuts to buy a tall tea with milk and sugar and two jelly donuts. I had a ways to go, but I knew I had to put my work in and go hard on my grind. Whatever I had to do to get to the top, I was gonna do it until I got all the way up. I was so anxious for the day to begin. I screamed out, *"Look ma, I'm on top of the world."*

The boiling point for Wall Street was nearing pretty quickly since the incident with Shandu and myself. After I left, the team kept the force applied. Supreme and P-God went up there, not anticipating this day to be any different from the others. To our surprise, this morning would prove to be one we would never forget.

Supreme and P-God carried their guns with them, but left them in the car due to all the heat in the area. They parked a few blocks away, got out and walked until they got to the statue of The Bull. They were on edge and cautious a bit. The NYPD had a special task force to clean up the area and our crew was on the top of their list. Moving around had become very difficult since the stabbing. Although he survived, it caused a domino effect. Everything began to fall in the short time we'd been around there. Absolute chaos was expected to follow.

The moment Supreme and P-God hit the block, everything went wrong. Things happened so fast that before they knew it, it was too late. They were caught in the eye of an ambush. It was early in the morning when a barrage of shots rang out through the air. This was from an obviously huge gun. The targets were Supreme and P-God. They tried to get out of harm's way and get back to the car, but P-God got hit! Supreme tried to pull him, but the shots kept zipping through the air.

With nothing to shield them and P-God being too heavy to carry, Supreme decided to try to get back to the car. When he did, he grabbed both his and P-God's guns. He moved as fast as he could to get back to him, but he had to fall back into the shadows of the block. The NYPD swarmed the area within minutes. Supreme had to get outta there. By the time he got back to the hood, the word was already out. Some people who worked on Wall Street, sent word that he didn't make it and P-God was dead!

The moment Supreme heard the news he started feeling guilty and blamed himself for P-God's death. He kept saying that P-God didn't want to go to Wall Street that day. It was too much heat with the NYPD. P-God stated, *"They have extra blue suit and plain-clothes officers in the area and I can't make any money out here"*. Supreme felt that if he didn't push P-God to go, then he would still be alive. Worse than that, Supreme felt like he left P-God to die after he got shot and should've stayed there with him. He felt like he could've done more to help him.

I'm sure the others on the team said the same things to him as I did. I made it clear, that any one of us could've been in his or P-God's situation. If we were, it would've panned out the same as it did. I told him, that I'd rather lose one of them than both of them. He had no reason to feel that he was the blame for anything. At this point, we had to prepare for our brother's wake and funeral. That we did, with heavy hearts to carry.

We were in the crib and I put on a Kenny Gee cd and turned to the song *"Song Bird"*. It had all of us mesmerized. My brother snapped out of the trance and said, *"Turn that shit off!"* There were a lot of emotions boiling up in us and the need to erupt was visible. The only lead we had was that the shooter was a Jamaican male. For us, that's all we needed to know. Enough said.

With that being said, there wasn't too much left to think about. As for Wall Street, it wasn't about getting money anymore. We were way past that. People's denial of any involvement in P-God's murder came from all over the place. A lot of people were in disarray behind this.

Those who knew us knew that a den of lions had reawakened and were hungry for revenge. Some one had to pay the piper for this one. We knew how the game was played. This was the way we all lived and we knew we'd die the way we lived. We read the instructions a long time ago. Death was a part of the game we played.

I assure you this; the NYPD patrolled the area around Wall Street as if the President himself was in town. They assumed everything and ignored nothing. We kept a tab with our insiders on how things were moving around there, so we wouldn't get ambushed. The NYPD were very well aware that one of "The Bullies" got killed. They knew it would be but a matter of time before some sort of retaliation occurred.

P-God's funeral was nothing less than a showing of love throughout Brooklyn. There was a mass of people that came to pay their last respects. All eyes were on Sha-Ru, Supreme, Shamel, Savior and myself. Cameras were flashing like it was some sort of red carpet event.

To see P-God lying in that casket made me realize how special of a crew we had. Being acknowledged and respected, even for underworld activities in the hood, said a lot. Even New York's finest State and Federal Agencies were getting their photography skills on at the wake. We were the center of everyone's attention and we knew it. It didn't matter to us not one bit either.

I don't recall who it was, but someone took a picture of all of us standing in front of P-God's casket, the last photo taken of us as a whole. Although none of us spoke much during the service, it was clear that even in silence we were speaking to each other, reading each other's mind. It's crazy, we stood in front of his casket, talking to the shell of a body that was once P-God. We told him how much any one of us wished to take his place. There were some older people there trying to patronize us; saying how sad it was to see such a young life go so soon. Other's added on saying, *"This should be enough to make you think and change your life."* I commented in saying, *"What life, the way I feel, I wish I was him right now."*

The life we lived made me damn near wish I was dead. Nothing was happy about the life I was living. When you live on the edge of life like I did, the only advantage you have over most is the lack of fear to die. I made myself believe I didn't care about living, which made me think I was invincible, therefore taking more risks than the average person. The only time I came to my senses was when I was barely hanging on to my last breath.

P-God didn't have to worry about being alone. We put our hearts in that casket next to his when it closed. We were literally heartless moving forward. Oh yea, I almost forgot. Jamaican Peter was found dead! I'm just saying…Shit happens"

Neighborhoods Under Siege   Calvin Bacote

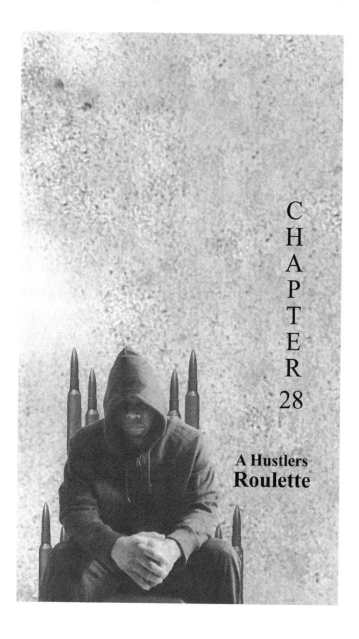

CHAPTER
28

A Hustlers
Roulette

The day of a hustler is never ending. You gotta get ya hustle on from sun up to sun down in order to stay ahead of the competition. There's plenty of money to be made and if you're doing it big, you're making it in your sleep. There was no serenity on the playing field. No subtle approaches to anything, once you unlocked the door of your home and walked out into those streets. I gotta get mine; you gotta get yours. May the best hustler win. That is until the alphabet boys (FEDS) get you and then you lose for real. There's never a peaceful ending to the street madness, just so you know.

After P-God's funeral, Supreme seemed despondent and worn down due to the chaos going on everywhere. He was going through an internal dilemma and still couldn't get over the fact that P-God was gone. P-God's sister Linda was going through it too. At the time, she was addicted to crack. She supported her habit by selling the infamous heroin product known to most as *"Superman"*, but just days before P-God's death, Linda became a pawn between the rival beef of two of the strongest forces in Red Hook. The battle of two titans. Jus vs. King Allah. The Crack King vs. The Heroin King.

At the time, the middle of The Ave. was considered prime real estate for the hustling world of Red Hook. It was like a celebrity prime time event. You had to be on your A-Game to stunt and perform there. The best of the best hustlers came through. Red Hook was a world of its own that many have heard of, but never been for obvious reasons. Being the largest projects in Brooklyn, with a notorious reputation, was more likely the reason it was forbidden. Only true-blooded hustlers and official gangsters came through.

Although the Panamanians are documented as being the first to bring crack into the hood in 84/85, Jus immediately followed suit. He is acknowledged as Red Hook's founder of the crack game. If not for him and his movement, Red Hook would've been in for far more of a rude awakening than it faced under his watch. Many more intruders would've came in and infiltrated the hood. This would've caused a greater deal of mass confusion. They say you don't appreciate something or someone until they're gone.

When the challenge of one's leadership is tested, war ensues. In times of war, people die, go to jail and most importantly lose money. Rules to live by, don't stand in one place too long, be on point with any and everything around you and protect ya neck.

When it came down to Jus and King, both had strong holds on the economics in the hood. Jus had two crack spots in Brooklyn and one in Queens while, King had one heroin spot in the hood. In comparison, it took three of Jus's spots financially to match the one King had. King had a goldmine, making an estimated $50,000 in three hours and that was on a slow morning. Jus had to combine all his spots to match that amount.

Each one had a unique style with an aura of cockiness to match. Jus was much younger and had more of a hood way about himself, while King on the other hand, was much older and had more of a GQ style. Jus would come through in his two toned burgundy and grey Pathfinder or his KLR Kawasaki 650 dirt bike and King would come through in his grey Buick Park Avenue, or his Mercedes Benz with European curtains covering the windows for privacy. These guys were trendsetters in the hood and when they put on a show, they didn't disappoint. If the two would've formed an alliance, then Red Hook could've likely gone down in history as being the strongest hood to take over New York. It was undeniable what they did as individuals as well.

King just came home after serving nearly ten years in state prison. He walked around the hood wearing the same clothes for three weeks, playing possum. He didn't draw any attention to himself, while he plotted on his moves. That was very smart of him.

Just days shy of his death P-God wanted me to go with him to be a mediator between him and Jus. He wanted to address Jus about smacking his sister. I stood on the block making small talk with Jus until P-God got there. Jus gave me my props on how well I was doing in Coney Island. As always, he asked could he team up with me to further expand his movement. Every night that I came back to the hood, I'd go see him and tell him I had a goldmine in Coney Island. I would front like all the money I had on me was mine to keep. The truth was, most of it was Rhamel's. I was just trying to impress Jus and have him think I was getting it like him.

I was telling Jus how I would never hustle where I lived and that's when P-God pulled up. We changed the subject and got to the point of the meeting. Jus was quick and clear with P-God, telling him he had no issues with him. He told him that he forewarned Linda for almost a week to keep her business with King on their side of the block. She didn't listen and crossed the line. He smacked her knowing that it was more disrespectful to King than it was to her or her brother. Jus had no reason to have beef with P-God and he was clear about that.

With that being said, they shook hands and P-God checked his sister in front of Jus. When it was all said and done she was still bitter, but had no choice but to respect their decision. Jus really had his hands full in the hood. He was to most, Public Enemy #1. There were a lot of people trying to come into the hood and attempt to open up shop. Jus jumped on it immediately and shut it down, with his brother Rondo as his most trusted enforcer leading the pack.

When Supreme felt like he wanted to get back into the mix of things, he and Shamel would take their show on the road. They went to Marcy Projects to get money with the God Father of Marcy, "Danny Dan". Danny had recently came home after serving over five years in State prison. He was rising very quickly in the drug trade throughout Brooklyn and abroad. He was the centerpiece of most of what was coming through Brooklyn in the mid 80's. He had the connections and resources, with the wit and heart to match. He was the perfect formula for success.

When Supreme and Shamel teamed up with him they piqued his interest in Red-Hook. The plan was set in motion, but it wouldn't be as easy as Danny had thought. When they came into the projects, Jus sent them back on their heels. Danny was impressed, but not deterred. He regrouped and went back in. The results were the same. Actually, the second time around Danny found a little luck by his side. He got into a shoot out with Rondo and when Rondo returned fire one of the bullets miraculously went straight through Danny's coat, missing him.

Jus called me, and told me to come to his crib. When I got there, it was obvious that he was extremely upset. I really didn't like what I was hearing, because we all grew up together, but for him this shit was much bigger than that. He didn't care if he grew up with them or not. He told me to relay the message to Supreme and Shamel that they were barred from the hood. To make it clear that he was serious about what he said, he had a twenty-four hour, six-man watch in front of both of their parents' buildings. One thing I will say about a fight, it's much easier when you're fighting from inside.

Around this time Danny was trying to recruit me. He knew it would take someone from the hood to match both the mental and physical prowess of Jus. Supreme and Shamel were pitching me to him really hard. They attempted a few times to have us meet. I declined both times. I was still in Coney Island at the time doing pretty well. I had no intentions of hustling in my own hood, plus Jus was my boy.

Days later, I was chilling at my mom's crib when a friend I grew up with called hysterically. He had never been in any kind of trouble and was in no way a part of the street life. He was a working dude. He was downtown Brooklyn working at Burger King. He called and asked for me to come to his job once he finished his shift. He told me some guys were threatening to beat him up. I told him I'd be there. I got dressed and went to the bus stop. I bumped into Sha-Ru waiting for the bus as well.

Sha-Ru was on his way to Fort Greene Projects to visit his grandmother. We hadn't seen each other in a minute, so it was good to see him. I told him to make the stop to the Burger King with me and then I'd go with him to visit his grandmother. Not thinking much would happen when we got there, we walked in. I went to the register where my friend was. He pointed to some guys sitting in a booth. One of the dudes yelled out and said…

"Yea. Over here! He talking bout us!"

"What's up yo. I don't know what he said to you, but is it that bad that someone gotta get hurt?"

"The only one gonna get hurt is that motherfucker right there. We gonna stay here till you get off from work and fuck you up! You wanna act like you can't give up no extra food. If ya people come in here, you gonna look out, right! So when we come through you need to look out too."

"I'm not giving you nothing!"

I intervened…

"Yo, shut the fuck up! Don't make this shit more than what it is. Listen my dude, don't pay him no mind, what if I can get you the extra food you want, will the beef you got with him be squashed?"

"Hell no! Fuck that nigga. We're going to teach his ass a lesson. He said he was going to call his people down here and take care of us; well we're still waiting. Anyway, what you worrying about it for?"

"Cause I'm his peoples!"

With that being said, all hell broke loose. While in conversation with dude, I already slid my knife out and opened it up, preparing for battle if necessary. Well necessary was in full effect. I used that knife like a master chef. I caught dude twice before he tried to get out of the booth. His man tried to swing on me, thinking I was by myself. Sha-Ru came behind him and punched him so hard; he damn near knocked his head off. I jumped out from the booth and stabbed another dude and that's when they saw the odds were against them. They ran for the exit.

Now, can you imagine five dudes rushing to get out of one door? I stabbed them a few more times before they got out the door and ran down the block. You would think they had enough, but they were down the block still talking shit from a distance. They didn't realize that at least three of them had been stabbed, that is until one of them went down. He hit the ground hard and started complaining about his wounds, gasping for air. His lungs had been punctured and he had to be rushed to the hospital with the others.

As for Sha-Ru and myself, we high-fived each other, as to say, *"Job well done, outstanding performance"*. I went back into the Burger King to talk to my boy. I told him to call me and let me know what was being said once the police arrived. I told him to make sure he didn't say he knew us.

Sha-Ru and I assumed that the dudes were from Fort Greene. Sha-Ru's family was real strong out there, with a reputation. We really weren't worried too much about anyone having any advantages over us. We actually saw some of the dudes from a distance when we went to visit his grandmother. I'm sure they saw us and still nothing went down. Charge it to the streets for what it was, just another day in the hood.

Unfortunately for me, two days later, I got a call from Sha-Ru, at the precinct. He'd been locked up for the Burger King stabbing. He told me, that my boy told the police we were there to help him. He thought he was protecting us when he actually hurt us. I couldn't be mad at him because he didn't intend to do any wrong, but now I was on the run. My picture was posted up in all the precincts and the worse thing was, I was on parole!

I couldn't stay at my mom's crib, so I packed some clothes and went to stay with Dumar for about three days. I needed to get my mind right and try to figure out what I was gonna do. I knew Dumar would let me stay there and I needed somewhere to go real quick. I knew he was doing his thing and had a lot of people around him. It would be only a matter of time before the police found out I was hiding out at his crib. That would've been bad for the both of us, if they ran down and searched his crib. I couldn't let that happen, so I told him I was out.

I called my brother and asked him could I stay with him. He had a crib out in Queens Bridge Projects. He was laying low because his girlfriend was pregnant with twin boys. He was reluctant, but he knew I needed somewhere to go so he told me to come through. One would think that my dumb ass would stay low and stay out of the spotlight. Well, I tried, but trying failed quickly.

My brother was cool with everyone out there. He played basketball at the QB center mostly every day. All I did was, move around the hood looking for some homies that I knew. QB was known for being one of the most dangerous places in Queens.

It had been a while since I was in QB to see my dudes T-Quan and Body Guard. I found out T-Quan was still in jail and would be for a while. Body Guard came to the hood from time to time. I used to see MC Shan, who at this point was not as relevant as he once was in the rap world. He would be chilling on the hill outside the QB center, often standing next to his Audi 5000. It would be a bunch of dudes, including Nas, Prodigy and Havoc just to name a few, hanging out off the hill, getting their hustle on.

My brother introduced me to a few dudes, but for the most part, I was laying low and stayed more to myself. I think I was distracting to the hood because of the way I moved. I didn't mingle like my brother did, for obvious reasons. Staying to myself was about to change though. I would be receiving some unwanted attention very soon.

One night I was going to the bodega and bumped into some dudes I knew from Brooklyn. The most I said was *"Hi and bye"*. Before I knew it, the whole fucking projects was looking for me. The Brooklyn dudes ran in The Pub around the corner from the bodega and robbed the joint. Worse off, they killed damn near a hand full of innocent people in the process, a robbery gone wrong!

Just when I thought I had shit for luck, a dude that was born and raised in QB named Butter was at the scene and saw everything. He vouched for me and cleared me of everything I had been accused of. There was already a bad taste in QB's mouth about Brooklyn. They had been infiltrated by the homies from Red Hook one time too many. Jus had a spot out there and was going hard, making examples out of the residents. Brooklyn had a very strong presence in Queens Bridge at this time, and the residents had enough when those innocent people got killed.

I knew my parole meeting was coming up soon. I wanted to test the waters and see if my P.O. had any knowledge of the Burger King incident. I called him. He picked up the phone and I asked if I still had to report in that following week. He told me, *"I need to see you today, right now!"* Oh hell no! I tried to feel him out on what he knew. Surprisingly he was direct about it, he said that a few detectives paid him a visit recently. They had questions concerning an incident I may have been involved in.

I tried to explain my version of the incident, but he told me to come in and do a face to face. That was going to be the only way he would believe anything I may have to say. Now mind you, this was a Friday and he was asking me to come in. No way was I gonna do that. I wasn't gonna be sitting in the bullpens over the weekend, so I asked for a compromise. I gave my word that I'd turn myself in first thing Monday. It took a few seconds before he answered, then he agreed. I guess he figured it wouldn't hurt to give me a few days. He would rather that than have to go out on a manhunt looking for me.

Unfortunately, Monday came quite quickly. As promised, I walked into the parole office and my P.O.

went into action. He had me turn around and put my hands up on the wall. He told me to spread my legs and then he frisked me to be sure I didn't have any weapons or contraband on me. He didn't handcuff me yet, so that was a good thing.

I explained and gave him my version of events. He listened intently to every word, and then responded. He said, *"I'm taking you off of bi-weekly report visits, to weekly visits. No more telling me, you can't find a job. You have to get a job now!"* I couldn't believe what I was hearing. After what went down, his stipulations were only for me to come in once a week. I was more than happy to comply with that. I was prepared to go to jail that day. I thought that no matter what I said, it wasn't gonna be good enough to walk out of his office.

When I went back to Queens and saw my brother and his girlfriend Monie, they were surprised to say the least. They placed bets on me. My brother bet that I wasn't going to turn myself in and Monie said, I would. They had already went to the store to buy a food package. They prepared it for when I would call and tell them I was at Riker's Island. Thanks, but no thanks. I'm still free!

It was about one week after The Pub incident. I was walking with two of Jus' trusted soldiers, Dimpy and Andre. We were walking through the projects when I noticed a dude about thirty years older than us bending down beside a tree. We stopped and the dude came up shooting. Dimpy was the only one with a burner (gun) and he returned fire. No one got hit, but it was a close call.

Later that night Jus came through with his brother and it was deserted. Them niggas knew how it was going to go down and laid low. That was until we saw a dude wearing a white leather 8-ball jacket. He started running when he saw us. Rondo and I were running in front of the pack. We were trying to get as close as we could before letting off any shots.

Dude had a head start from the time he saw us, but we were closing in on him. Dude got to the front of his building. He fumbled with his keys, trying to get in before we got to him. Faith had it that I recognized the dude. With seconds to make a decision, I slowed Rondo down giving dude the time he needed to get into his building. The door locked behind him and we were unable to get inside, dude was safe. If I didn't think better in the moment, dude would've been laid out dead in front of his building. If that had happened, it would've been devastating to the future of the rap industry, because that dude was *"Nas"*.

CHAPTER 29

**One Day
At A Time**

With everything going on around him, Savior stayed far away from everyone. He laid low because he had a phobia of getting locked up again. He feared loosing his freedom or worse case, not be alive to witness the birth of his twin boys. Not that I didn't understand his point, but I felt it was more of a reason to get out and get his hustle on!

My brother and I were shopping at the grocery store when we ran into two Brooklyn legends from Fort Greene Projects, Supreme Magnetic and his brother Rap. They were lying low and away from BK as well and were staying in Elmhurst, Queens. We spoke briefly then kept it moving. I felt the ride home would be a good time to get into my brother's ear about a few things.

The vibe between us was good, until I decided to have a heart to heart with him. I kept pushing him to come out of retirement. I wanted him to get back out on the streets and start hustling again. That didn't sit well with him. It went like this...

"How in the fuck you gonna sit there and criticize me about what the fuck I got and what I'm not doing and what I need to do. You trying to tell me how I need to get my shit together. You act like you're doing it big because you out in Coney Island with Rhamel. Now you think you that nigga! Nigga, you ain't getting no real money!"

"I didn't say I was. Neither of us got shit. I'm just waiting on you to see what you gonna do, so we can..."

"Don't wait on me! All of you motherfuckers waiting on me! I told you, Supreme, Sha-Ru and Shamel, I wasn't doing nothing until my kids were born. If you don't respect that, then fuck all you niggas! I told you before, if I don't ever do anything for my kids, I wanna at least be here to see them come into this world."

"I respect that, but they gonna need things when they get here, and you don't have what you used to have..."

"Yo! Who the fuck you think you talking to! I can turn it up whenever I want! "Sav" gonna be alright! Worry about yourself! You keep talking about what I don't have, Nigga you ain't got shit! You got less than I got and I'm doing bad, so what do that say about you? You in my car, about to go to my crib, in the bed I gave you to sleep in, but I ain't got shit? You better check yourself and stop worrying about me, I'm good!"

My brother and I were quiet for the rest of the ride. By the time we got to the crib, I felt like shit. He broke the silence by telling me he didn't mean to go in on me like that. I cut him off and told him...*"Thanks, I needed that"*. The very next day, I packed my things and went back to Brooklyn to my parents crib. I can honestly say, there were two conversations that triggered me to be the best of the worst and that was one of them. The other was with my cousin Eric. He told me to get out of the game because I would never be as successful as Rhamel. That was all the motivation I needed. By the time I got back to Red Hook the war between Jus and King was turned up full throttle.

I went back and forth from the hood to Coney Island at the time. I was having my own issues with Rhamel though. I guess he must have gotten his memory back because a lot had changed between us by this time. Truth is, I didn't like his style of hustle and the area I was in. It just didn't feel right to me. I told him that I was going to be done within a few weeks and for him to find someone else to replace me. I figured that would be enough time to get a few dollars saved and then start doing my own thing.

I was tired of going up to Manhattan's 140th St and Broadway area where the Dominicans controlled the drug market. It was very chaotic whenever we went to cop work. Buying on this block, you had to give your money to a total stranger and then they'd disappear into a building. You had to hope they came back with your order. This is the chance you took in trusting someone you didn't know. Sometimes you got beat and they ran off with your money. Sometimes you got lucky and were dealt a fair deal with a familiar face.

If you didn't see who you were looking for, you would be directed to the guy's bogus cousin. They all had the same name and claimed to be each other's cousin. The only good thing was that the capsules were oversized. When we brought them back to Brooklyn, we would break them down and make double our money. It was comeback coke (synthetic cut), but it still sold. The whole Brighton Beach vibe made me feel like I was still sitting on the bench and wasn't in the game.

I figured I'd be ready to step my game up once I started doing my own thing. This didn't sit well with Rhamel. Rather than relieve me when I asked him, he chose to do it much sooner. I told him I needed to finish out the few weeks, but he told me that he had someone ready to relieve me now. He said that since we were parting ways, he wanted the $700.00 I owed him. To me, this was just another obstacle in my way preventing my growth in moving up in the game. I wasn't going to let it deter me. More than anything, the negativity and the doubters drove me.

This really was a setback for me. I needed the extra week so I could re-up. He wanted the money I owed him and pressed me about needing it right then and there. I reluctantly gave it to him. I felt that everything was a test, a test I'd planned to pass with flying colors. I'd seen my last days in Coney Island and was now back in the hood.

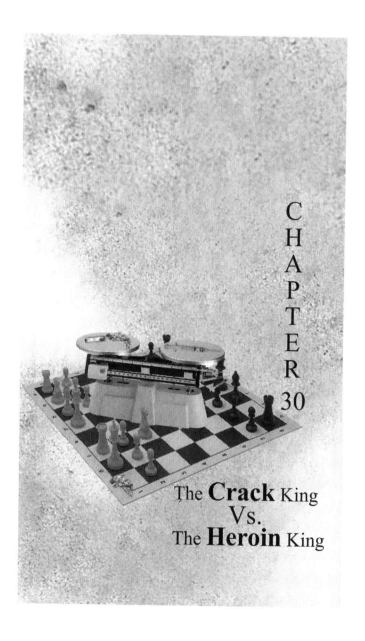

C
H
A
P
T
E
R
30

The **Crack** King
Vs.
The **Heroin** King

The war between Jus and King was historic, to say the least. Red-Hook never saw anything like it before. There were many shootouts and bodies that fell in the past, but this war had no predecessor. This proved to be the case when King delivered a message to Jus he would never forget, nor would he recover from. King's tactics slowly took the wind out of Jus and his crew.

The strongest force Jus had alongside him was his brother Rondo and his cousin A-Money, who were an army by themselves. Rondo literally went to war with King and his crew on his own. A-Money got shot and was disabled. He was sidelined and more or less out of commission. That was a huge blow. The best of what Jus had by his side was getting picked off one by one.

King's brother was shot the same night as Jus's Uncle. Both victims were sent to the Long Island College trauma unit. The clash between crews collided in the hospital. Guns were drawn, but both sides backed down and took precautionary measures. They chose not to hold court in the hospital while both sides' family members were around. Dangerous and all, they respected the rules of war.

Once King's brother got shot, he was ready to turn the heater meter up another notch. Not that more was needed either. The worst blow for Jus was soon to follow and it went right though his heart. His strongest enforcer was apprehended by law enforcement. This loss crippled his entire movement. Rondo got locked up for murder. To be honest, this was when Jus should've waved the white flag, but he wasn't the type to easily bow out or bow down. He battled with what he had, which wasn't much. He mostly had a bunch of inexperienced kids and crack heads by his side.

King, on the other hand, had a crew of older vets that he served jail time with. They stood strong by his side and weren't afraid to go all out and sacrifice. In my opinion, King Allah changed the game forever in Red-Hook. He set very high standards when it came to war. The things he had in his arsenal were above and beyond the hood's imagination.

Jus's spot was on the first floor on The Ave. and was better known as flagpole. King went up to the window and told whoever was in the apartment that they had thirty seconds to get out. He then tossed a small object through the window. Everyone's hearts dropped from fear of what they saw. It was a grenade! The explosion shook and vibrated the block and was heard throughout the whole hood. Everyone got out safely, but the entire living room was completely destroyed. This brought life to the saying, "There's a war going on outside". This was a whole new level of war that neither Jus nor anyone in the hood had ever seen.

If ever there was a message to be made, this was it. No one died, but everyone was overwhelmed. Most went to the apartment to see the after effects of the damage. The windows were knocked out, the walls were knocked down and it was dark with rubble everywhere. No one wanted to work in any of Jus' spots. It wasn't safe for them anymore. King's goal was to shut Jus's spots down and limit his means of getting money. Stopping all financial resources was a definite knockout. It's hard to maintain money when you're at war.

Interesting enough, one would think King had enough on his plate, certainly not the case. It was alleged that he staged a plan to kidnap the wife of one of New York's biggest king pins, Fat Cat Nicholas. Cat's wife had been preyed and plotted on for some time. Her every move had been stalked for months. Suddenly she was grabbed, bound and gagged, then put up for ransom. In exchange for her life they wanted two kilos of heroin and $500,000 cash. She had forty-eight hours to live.

Fat Cat's wife was released the day after her apprehension. Not long after the exchange, every agency imaginable to man crashed in and raided Red-Hook. Someone made a deal with the police to turn in the crew involved in the kidnapping for a lesser sentence. He walked through the projects pointing up at the windows of the alleged people involved. The FBI put a mask over the informants face, but everyone knew who it was.

The van used in the kidnapping, was found in the hood and towed away. A lot of doors got kicked in that day. They were closing in on who they felt were the masterminds. King was running out of time and was very close to seeing his last days as a free man. Yet, he still had unfinished business to tend to. By all means, he intended to close out like a King was supposed to.

Before his final curtain call, King had done almost the impossible. He ran Jus out of the projects. Jus later claimed that his departure was a strategic move. Jus had a crib out in Elmhurst, Queens and was laying low. He was like a wounded animal, trying to find a way to redeem himself. King knew he had Jus on the ropes and was going for the knock out with his next move. Jus's tenure would soon be over.

King went to the home of one of Jus's most trusted soldiers, Shorty. His crew was standing outside of Shorty's crib, surrounding all of his windows. He unfortunately lived on the first floor. It was known that Shorty held the crew's arsenal. King knew this move would defeat Jus. Jus had no choice but to concede to defeat. This would be the final blow. King had Shorty's back up against the wall, with no way out. The fear in his family's voices rang out loud as they begged for their lives. King screamed out his demands to Shorty...

"I want every weapon you have in your house on your front door in less than five minutes.

"Yo King! Don't do this man! My moms and my whole family in here! I don't have anything to do with Jus no more man!"

"I'm sure you don't, but you got less than five minutes now. I'm sure you and your family see what you're up against and in less than three minutes they gonna be flying through your windows if you don't open your door and give those guns up. Your family's blood is on your hands! Is your loyalty with Jus or your own family? Just give the guns up and we good."

Shorty knew what he had to do, but he feared they were going to kill his family anyway. King and his crew were members of the Five Percent Nation of Islam and so was Shorty and his family. King had given his "Word is Bond" that he wouldn't do anything to him or his family as long as he complied with his demands.

Shorty had seconds to unlock his door. He agreed to King's demands. In doing so, he felt great relief. He no longer had to endure the grinding task of a battle he wasn't built for. Without further hesitation, Shorty opened his door and handed over a duffle bag full of high-powered weapons. He disarmed himself of every gun Jus had. Jus was done. He had no choice but to disappear for a while, regroup and live to fight another day.

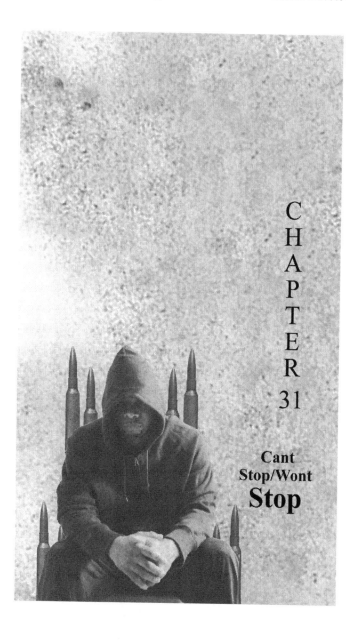

C
H
A
P
T
E
R
31

Cant
Stop/Wont
Stop

"Now lets back up a bit. I hope you didn't think I was just a fly on the wall while Red-Hook was under siege! This was the perfect time for me to finally get my feet wet and branch out on my own."

I left Coney Island and was now back in the hood with nothing to show for, to no fault but my own. I was determined more than ever to get mine. I went around in circles for a while. I was trying to figure my way through all the madness. I had to get off the sidelines and straight onto the playing fields. My odds were the same as all others no more and no less. I was right in the middle of a war between two elite hustlers on the block.

I plotted for a while, analyzing from a distance. I felt if I could make it in my own hood, I could make it anywhere. There was a lot of pressure coming up under the notoriety of my brother. I knew my debut on the block would make me or break me.

I knew I had the heart to go up against anyone on the block, but I lacked the hustling skills and experience. I was motivated by those who doubted me. I wanted to prove them wrong. I wanted to do it better than those they compared me to. I guess I was gonna learn along the way because I was going all in. Having a reputation as a gunslinger and a robber didn't fit well in my resume. Many people didn't want to recruit me, so I was best off going the independent way.

I left Rhamel's crib with my confidence matching my doubts. My debut was only minutes away. I walked towards prime real estate in the hood, The Ave! Since Jus and King were at war, the territory was now open for the taking. They were at each other's head so much, they didn't see the birth of a new boss in the hood.

Supreme and Shamel slowly started working their way back into the hood, attempting to catch Jus by surprise. Supreme previously told me to open up on flagpole. He told me I needed to be careful though. With that in mind, I walked on the block and went in front of the building. I opened up and within an hour I had a steady a flow of crack heads coming in. There were so many of them coming at me. I was so overwhelmed I didn't take notice of what was happening around me.

I was on my own, without a look out and I got caught slipping. Two dudes threw the drop on me. They backed me down with a .38 revolver. They forced me in the building and robbed me! When they ran off, I ran out of the building and around the corner. I went to Shorty's crib and banged on his door. I wanted to get a gun so I could look for the dudes who were more than likely still in the hood. When he opened his door, I felt the worst vibe ever.

I instantly felt he had something to do with lining me up to get robbed. The expression on his face when he opened his door told it all. I told him I just got robbed and needed a gun. He told me he didn't have one. I knew this was a bold-faced lie and backed out of his hallway on my heels. I assumed the dudes were in his crib. I spun off and started running.

I had no wins right then, but vowed to initiate payback down the line. I was frustrated that I got caught slipping. I took a loss for about $400.00 worth of cash and work. All I had to my name was about $380.00 worth of crack. My back was up against the wall, but I refused to shut it down.

I went to my mom's crib and went in the kitchen draw. I pulled out a knife and went back to the block with fire in my eyes. I was hitting the block on point this time. I needed a look out. I saw Everlasting and told him to hold me down while I sold the rest of what I had. The flow came back in no time. I was like a hawk, watching everyone. In my mind, if the dudes came back, things would go down much differently. Although I was bringing a knife to a gunfight, I was ready to go all out to protect my earnings. They had to kill me to get to this package.

It didn't take long before bullshit came at me again. Since I was a new face on the block, a crack head tried to play me. Everlasting was directing traffic my way and a cheese line (long line) began to form outside the building. I was serving as fast as I could, but they just kept coming. Shit was popping now! All of a sudden, a real tall slim dude came and asked for five and then another dude asked for the same.

I served them simultaneously. The second guy gave me $25.00 and walked off with his purchase, while the first one was still fumbling with the work and his money. He was inspecting the vials and told me some had less than the others. He was trying to make a switch on me. He was trying to swap his old vials that held chips of soap with my vials filled with crack. I peeped the move and tried to spare him. I didn't want his money and told him to give me my vials back. Then, the worse thing that could've happened; happened.

He tried to press up on me and talk over me. I looked at the line of crack heads and then back at him. I made my move. I pulled out my knife and introduced it to him. I stabbed this dude at least a dozen times. Him and all the other crack heads standing in the hallway were begging me not to kill him. As I was stabbing him, I spoke out loud for all to hear. I said, *"If any of you motherfuckers think you can beat me for $5.00, "I'mma kill you!"*

I knew I had crossed the line and may have gone

too far that night. Before I left the scene of the crime, I gave Everlasting a few dollars and kept it moving. As soon as I turned the corner, heading to my parents crib, Supreme, Shamel and their man Danny, ran towards me with their guns out. I had on a Suede coat, with blood all over me. They were asking me what happened? I told them, *"Some crack head tried to beat me for five cracks, so I stabbed him up".* Danny started laughing, and said, *"I like this dude already".* He was impressed with what I was saying. He said to me…

"Go to ya crib, put everything you got on in a garbage bag, then throw everything in the incinerator."

"Man, I'm putting this shit in the washer and dryer, then I'm out. I'm on parole. If dude dies, I'm done! If he lives, I'm done!"

"Check this out. Throw everything away and meet us in twenty minutes in front of Supreme mother's building. We gonna go around the corner and check ya work out, see how much damage you did, then we'll go from there."

I did what he told me to do, and then I went downstairs to meet up with them. We got straight to the point. He said…

"Very impressive work. I like that. Fortunately for him, he looks like he's gonna survive. Now, this is how we gonna do

this. I'll go to the hospital first thing in the morning and pay him a visit. Whatever is needed to make this go away, we'll do whatever it takes. I've wanted to get up with you for a while. All Supreme and Shamel talked about was you. They said you were the next up and coming boss in Red-Hook. I'm sure you already know I have interest in doing business out here and I'm told you're the man to get with?"

"Man, I don't know about all of that. I'm just trying to do my thing out here without having to work for anyone. I got a long way to go, but in due time I'll get there. The only way I'm interested is if you give me half on consignment for what I buy and keep me consistent with work at all times. That's what I'm wiling to partner up with. Anything else other than that, I'm good."

"Ain't nothing I can't do for you. I don't know why you wanna go that route and get what you buy when you can keep your money and I'll give you everything and more than what you can buy right now."

"That sounds like I'm about to work for you. Again, like I just said, I'm not working for anybody. I'll grind my way up and get where I need to be in no time. I got two lil' homies that I'll put up against any crew or spot when it comes to selling that work."

"I hear you, well if that's how you wanna do it, we can get started now. How much you got?"

"Right now, I got $500.00."

When I told Danny I had $500.00, I really didn't have it. I went upstairs to my mom's crib, having to think fast. This dude was waiting for me downstairs, to go pick up my purchase and my money was short. I knew my mom was fed up with me and disappointed at the choices I was making. The only good thing in my favor was that she didn't have an ear to the streets to know all of what I was into.

No time to waste, I went to my mom and begged her for $300.00. Obviously, she told me, *"No!"* I went to my sister and asked her for the money. She looked at me like I asked her for a million dollars and said, *"No!"* I couldn't take no for an answer, so I pressed and begged my mom again. I told her that I'd give it back within a few days. After about twenty minutes of wearing her down, she gave in and gave it to me. I ran downstairs so damn fast. I thought I took too long and they left, but they were still there waiting.

We got in the car and jumped on the Brooklyn-Queens Expressway (BQE) on our way to Marcy Projects. Danny Diamonds aka The Godfather, was from Marcy Projects and based his lucrative business there. He ran a multi-million dollar drug enterprise. He turned the hood into a Brooklyn landmark, due to its resources of supplying drugs to the underworld. A blind man could see that he ran a very impressive, tight knit organization.

We went to one of his stash spots that held a substantial amount of drugs. In that moment, history was made between him and I. To be honest, he was sort of surprised at the lack of knowledge I had in selling drugs. Prior to our linking up, I would get my work in capsules and then break them down to double my money. Now, I was getting it cooked up in crack form and would buy my own capsules and break it down myself. The deal went down as I requested. He gave me one ounce on consignment and I paid for the other. He threw in a few packs of capsule, tops and razors. He then took me back to my hood. I went in my building to the third floor to meet up with my two lil' homies.

When they saw the work, they acted like we hit the lotto. It took us less than a half hour to bag everything up and then we went straight to business. Lil' Ra and Black aka Domanit, were two of Red-Hook's best kept secrets. Lil' Ra was short in stature, with the heart of a giant. He stayed with the latest fresh gear. Ra's right hand man, Domanit, was tall, slim and a mirror of his partner. He too stayed rocking the freshest gear.

Oh yea I almost forgot, they stayed tree'd up (high off of weed) from the time they woke up to the time they went to sleep, if they ever slept. Weed was an energy booster for them, to my surprise. I was able to get the best out of them when they were high. They had no apprehensions once they hit the block.

When we left Domanit's crib, all they kept saying was, "We're gonna make you rich." I said, *"Make us rich"*. They worked on one accord, knowing the other's moves without having to say anything. Ra left us for about fifteen minutes to sweep the hood and direct traffic to the back. I looked out for Domanit as he pumped (sold) the work under our building.

The crack heads were more than happy to get out of harm's way while Jus and King were still going at each other. All the crack heads wanted to make a purchase somewhere safe. We were very careful in detecting danger because we were treading on the grounds of others who fought to claim this area. I knew Jus was dealing with a dilemma and couldn't focus on any further invasions, even if he wanted to. My timing to make my move into the hood couldn't have been better.

The old saying was, when it rains it pours. Well, there was a hurricane over Jus and his crew. No one saw me coming. My rise came by surprise. There was a plethora of deterrents around me and my crew, but we stayed on point. When we were about halfway through the package, I called Danny and told him I was almost done. He told me to come back to his hood, so I jumped in a cab.

When I got there I gave him the money I owed. Then I told him I needed to buy an ounce with another on consignment. He corrected me and told me he was giving me 62 grams. From my calculations, I added up two ounces to be 56 grams, so that's what I wanted. I thought he was trying to give me a hand out. I told him, I didn't want the extras. He looked at me like I was crazy and gave me what I asked for.

I went back to the hood and went through the same routine as before. Rather than finishing the whole two ounces and hitting the block, I bagged up the first $500.00 and hit off Ra and Domanit. They went back under the building to get their serve on. I chopped the rocks and bagged up as fast as I could. When I finished each $500.00 pack I tossed it out the third floor window to Domanit. I couldn't bag up fast enough. The flow was crazy!

Before we knew it, we had almost $4,000.00 to re-up with. I took the first $3,500 and went back to Marcy Projects to meet with Danny. I paid him what I owed and told him I needed 112 grams (4 ounces/a big 8th). Normally, he'd give 125 grams, but again I felt like he was giving me a hand out and I turned down the extras.

I told him, I had $3,500 and would put the $500.00

on the back end of the next trip. He saw how fast I was moving and was cool with it. He gave me my package. I guess he didn't want to slow me down. So he said, if I came short we could tally everything up and even any debts that following day.

I jetted back to the hood and went through the same process. I chopped the rocks and bagged up as fast as I could. This went on throughout the night, into the morning. We broke day! The block was bubbling with a non-stop flow of crack heads. The last time I went to see Danny, I picked up 224 grams, a quarter of a kilo (key). Again, he said I was supposed to get 250 grams, but gave me what I'd asked for. That was the last time I heard from him that day.

I called Danny around six in the morning. No answer. I called every half hour after, no answer. We tried to stall the crack heads and told them we were about to open back up soon. It was frustrating to turn money away because we had no more drugs to sell. Me and my two-man crew were embarking on a major production and now our assembly line was stalled.

I called Danny again around 11a.m. The phone rang a few times before he picked up! He said...

"Yo, what up?"

"You tell me? I've been calling you for a few hours now. Yo I need to get up with you, like right now, I need..."

"Not on the phone. I'm about to get up and make my rounds now. I'll come see you first. I'll be there in about forty-five minutes."

"You can't make it sooner?"

"That's the best I can do, I'll see you in a few."

I waited impatiently like a motherfucker, but I was on his time. I waited under my building with my crew. After about a half hour, Danny called me and told me to meet him in front of Supreme's building. Moments later I heard loud music, LL Cool J banging through the speakers. Danny was turning the corner in a brand new BMW with chrome BBS rims. The car was a thing of beauty. Danny got out the car with the swag of a dude who felt like the world was his. He knew that all eyes were on him and he was the man. He embraced me like we were best friends for years.

This dude had an aura about him that drenched with confidence. He got straight to it and started breaking things down to me. He wanted to know where I was selling my drugs at and how many people I had working for me. I gave him the run down on my system, which was impressive for a small network. He said…

"What's going on with you?"

"I'm good. You around now? You got that?"
Damn yo, you real straight to the point. I like that. How much you need?

"I got enough to buy a half a key, plus the half you got for me on consignment, so that means you got 896 grams for me, that's close to a whole one right?"

"Are you serious? You finished the last package I gave you already?"

"That's what I was trying to tell you when I was calling you, I finished that over five hours ago."

"Wow, OK. Where you set up at and how many you got in your crew?"

"I'm right there under my building, and I got two of my lil' homies."

"What! You gotta be bullshitting me! I hope you know what you got here. You got a fucking treasure trove on your hands. A fucking goldmine!"

"Oh word! That's what's up! I knew we had a good flow going on last night. We stayed out and broke day. We could've done

better if we had more work. I thought you said you could keep me with a consistent flow yo?"

"I can and I will. I got you. Come take a ride with me, I wanna show you something."

"Man, I don't have time to go nowhere if we not gonna go get that work. I gotta get back to the table, bag up and get my homies back on the block.'

"I told you I got you just take a ride with me. It'll be worth your while, trust me. You need this right now."

I got in the car with Danny. In all honesty this was the first time I'd ever been in a car with a car phone. I didn't give him the benefit of the doubt either. I didn't think the phone worked. He must've been reading my mind, because he asked me did I want to use it. Man, I got on that phone and called my ex-girlfriend Asia. I showed my ass off. All it took was for me to be on a car phone to feel like I was on top of the world. I thought I was the man. At that moment, no one could tell me anything.

Of course, she didn't believe I was calling her. Oh well, I tried to tell her. I screamed in her ear. The music was on and I thought I had to talk over it, not knowing better at the time. When I got off the phone, Danny started schooling me on the many facets of the drug game. We drove all over Brooklyn, going to all of his crack spots, making his pick up rounds. His actions displayed all of what he was telling me. There was no doubting this guy, not for one second. He was the real deal.

I lost track of how many spots we visited after a while. I guess since he had a fast car and utilized that speed as much as he could. He drove with such recklessness that it was unexplainable. He was pushing that car to the limit. After a few hours, we were back in Bed-Stuy. He pulled over and called a girl over. He told her we were coming up to her crib in a few minutes to see her and her girlfriend. We got in front of her building and got out of the car. We finished up on the conversation we were having. He said...

"I'll be honest with you. I know a lot about you, more than you think I know. I been trying to get up with you and in on the action in Red-Hook for a while. You proved my theory to be correct when you did what you did in one day. With the right person in control of the market for your hood, Red- Hook is a treasure trove, a fucking goldmine! I'm playing your hand the way you'd play it, but I have to pull your coat on some things. Between your first purchase and now, you could've had more money in your pocket. The extras you didn't want, I added up and put to the side for you. That's yours. I tallied up what you owed me. If I break down everything in the weight I got for you, you're even with your debt and I still owe you! I'm saying this because I don't need to beat you for anything. If you want,

I'll walk you through the process, so you'll know. Then you'll be able to know how to play your hand much better. I'll take care of what I owe you when I get that next package to you later."

"Damn yo. Thanks for breaking it down to me like that. That's what's up. I'm sure you already know why I was reluctant to get up with you in the beginning. I didn't wanna feel like I was gonna be pulling you in my hood and stamping your entry, when Jus and his crew was pushing you out.

"I know that's your man. I told you, I know more than you think I know, but I also know that if Jus wanted you down with him, he had the opportunity when you first came home and he didn't take it."

"You right, but he still my man. One thing I won't do is go to war with him when there's no benefit in it for me. That doesn't make sense for me as far as I'm concerned, but I still won't do anything to go against him either."

"How you think he's gonna feel when he's done with his beef with King, that is, if he survives and you're doing it big like you're doing?"

"I'm sure he's gonna be happy for me. I guess when it's all said and done, I'll have money to match him and that's when we can make Red-Hook that much stronger."

"That's very naïve of you, but I understand. When it happens,

don't say I didn't tell you so. You don't even have a clue to the level you just reached in less than twenty-four hours. You're officially in the game playing with the big dogs. You're that dude in ya hood already. Jus ain't gonna like that. What you think him and King is going to war for right now? They don't sell the same product and they both got plenty money. They're going to war because of their egos. Nothing more, trust me on that."

Before we went upstairs to see the girls, Danny went into his glove compartment. He pulled out a bag and then went under the front seat. He pulled out some plastic bags and then popped the trunk where he had a few more bags. He started opening the bags and spilling everything out into the trunk. He then started putting the stacks of money into one big bag. I tell you at that time, I never saw that much money in my entire life. This dude was doing this shit in broad daylight like it was nothing. He closed the trunk and walked away from the car and told me...

"Let's go, the girls been waiting on us for a while."

"Go where? You can't be serious."

"What you mean?"

"Yo, how much is that in the trunk?"

"Close to half a mill."

"What and you about to walk away from it and go see some girls! Man, tell them to come downstairs! Fuck that! I ain't leaving this car!"

"Ha ha ha. Listen man. If somebody steals the car, guess what? They hit lotto! Anyway, I'm good over here. Everybody knows who the car belongs too. Don't worry about it, let's go."

I reluctantly went with him into the building and upstairs to the girls' apartment. When we got inside, he introduced me to the girls then pulled the one he was dealing with off to the side. I was talking to her friend for a while, when I asked her if she would accompanying me outside to catch the breeze. She was cool with it.

After being outside for about a half hour with girlfriend, Danny came downstairs with his shorty. The moment he saw me he started laughing. I knew what he was laughing at. There was no way I was going to connect with this girl, when all I could think about was the money in the trunk. So, I asked her to come downstairs with me. Without her knowing, I was watching the car while getting to know her. It was all good as far as I was concerned.

Danny and I went to Marcy Projects to pick up my package. He gave me half a kilo already bagged up and the other half of the brick. That was a good look.

It would've taken a while to hit the block if I had to bag all that work up by myself. When Ra and Domanit saw all that work, they swore we were rich! We were on the rise to the major leagues.

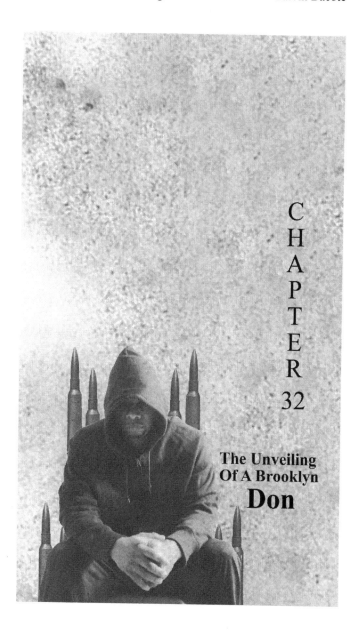

CHAPTER 32

The Unveiling
Of A Brooklyn
Don

The next few weeks were very crucial for me. I had to make some tough decisions for the movement. I let Ra and Domanit hand pick their own crew to work with, while I focused on other things. Since the day Danny and I linked up, he came to the hood and picked me up everyday. I was cool with this because I knew the crew had things under control. Being that I was so close to Danny, I was soaking up every move he made like a sponge.

Being so close to this man, I had no choice but to embrace his greatness and work ethic. I applied it to the mold of who I already was. I studied him like a book. He was a facilitator, but most of all a great Zen master. With a substantial amount of knowledge for the game, he often appeared to be way ahead of his adversaries. He'd often say…

"If you're playing the game, you have to understand the instructions. Have a plan. Go in and devise your plan and most of all, have a blueprint that you believe will win. If you don't believe in it, it won't work. Don't make an example out of the little people. Make one out of the giants on the block. Break them down to the ground. Outside of yourself, your strength comes from the people you know. You're only as strong as the connections you have. If you have the best connect around, that makes you the best around."

When I first got into the drug trade, I was a little unorthodox. I was coming into myself quite well under Danny's tutelage. It seemed as if he was training me for a reason and actually, he was. He had a lot of interest in showing me what I needed to see and the magnitude of what I needed to know. When he felt I was ready, the proposal he'd present to me would be monumental in our movement going forward.

My style was redefined from what it once was as a stick up kid. Danny lived the same way I did coming up on the streets. He was a stick up kid and his gun game was strong. With his help, my transition into the drug game was a lot smoother than it was alongside Rhamel. I converted my style to maximize my greatest potential and my gun was my greatest asset.

When I looked back on how my brother handled his business, I saw he didn't have many, if any guns around him. He was more of a manipulator and could talk his way in or out of any situation. I on the other hand, wanted to use my gun skills as the differentiator between my brother and myself. If there was any doubt, I would turn my gun game up any and everywhere I went. I didn't come in the game to play games. I wanted to get in, do big things and put my stamp on it. My brother once told me...

"You won't have any longevity in this game, let alone be a free man if you take on the style and emulate those guerilla tactics all the time. I'd rather be like the Italian gangster Charlie

'Lucky' Luciano because he was a thinker. He had a stretch of success, lasting long in his reign. Unlike the hardcore gangster style of Alfonse "Al" Capone hat you've taken. Your aggressive style will never last longer than a thinker in my opinion. Combine them into a formula that will apply you to lead better. Maybe then will you be able to last another day alive and free. Maybe you could fulfill what you set out to do on these streets and that's to get it and watch ya money pile up."

Although I knew my brother was right about everything he said, I rebelled against his advice. When I needed or wanted to stand by his side, he rejected me so his advice fell on deaf ears. The tides had turned and it was my turn to be the man of power and I was gonna do it my way. I had Danny by my side and was willing to take my chances and go up against the world if I had to. In all fairness, I knew my brother was just as skilled in hustling in the drug trade as Danny. I just never told him that.

Whatever Danny heard about my gun game, it proved to be true ten times over. The heater meter on my gun was all the way up. I had a vicious point to prove. I played no games and held no hostages. It didn't matter who was in the way. When it came to my gun, I didn't need any advice from Danny or anyone else. I showed my ass off and held my own and he was thoroughly impressed with that.

When it came to swagger, Danny and my style complimented each other very well. In my mind, we had become one of Brooklyn's best tag teams. We gelled well as we gracefully moved around the city, becoming each other's third eye. There was a major problem that lingered in his mind. He tried to, but couldn't shake it as easily as he'd thought he could.

We both had some quick decisions to make. I felt like I was way ahead of where I would have been. Danny kept me with a consistent flow as promised. I had to install a twenty-four hour shift for the crew. Lil' Ra and Domanit, who were now my main lieutenants brought in their boys as workers to get their hustle on too. I was cool with it, but I made it clear to them, *"Do not have any one person on a shift past sixteen hours. I need everyone to stay on point at all times. I don't need police sneaking up through the back door because someone is tired and not on point."*

In order to stay ahead of the 76th precinct that patrolled my hood, I'd take Lil' Ra with me. We would drive by or walk through the precinct block. We had their shifts down pact. We went three times in twenty-four hours to scope out the precinct. We would go during the 8 a.m. to 4 p.m. shift, the 4p.m. to 12-midnight shift and then the 12 a.m. to 8 a.m. graveyard shift. We wanted to be on top of the cars the detectives drove as well. The hood nicknamed them *"The Silver Bullet"* and *"The Burgundy Boys"*. We wanted to see how many cars went out on patrol at all times. They monitored us and we returned the favor.

The 76th patrolled the Red-Hook and Gowanus Projects. We would sometimes call our dudes from Gowanus to stage a smoke screened shoot out as a decoy. The precinct would take the call from out there and we would do what we had to do in Red-Hook. There were some detectives that had a reputation just as ruthless as ours. They loved shootouts and would often hold court on their own terms. A bunch of gangsters with a badge is what we called them.

The most ruthless of them all was Skinner-9 millimeter and Kato. They shook shit down in the hood for real. They would raid our spots, log in the guns and drugs, but pocket most of our money. They were out of control and played by a different set of rules. Red-Hook held the largest murder rate in New York City and Skinner and Kato had their share in many of those murders.

So much was going on, but by this time I had my money and my weight up. I was feeling good about almost everything. Danny told me he was about to set up a meeting with his partners and he had a serious decision to make. He told me he spoke to them about me and wanted me to meet them. Truthfully, I told him I didn't want to meet anyone and I told him why.

I wanted to stay anonymous just in case he needed me to put any work in. This applied to partners, co-partners or whoever. I told him, *"I don't get close to or gain feelings for anyone."* When I said that, he felt how genuine I was with it. He knew he had someone who would go all out and was willing to die for the cause. He responded by telling me, *"These are people you need to know. They already know you. I just never told you who they are and I wasn't until the meeting this evening."*

Lately, Danny was sort of talking out loud to himself and was throwing subliminals at me. He kept saying he needed to bring a partner to the table. He would throw a few names up in the air, but he always dismissed them because of a flaw in their character, either they were a gunman and not a drug dealer or vice versa.

When he spoke like that, it made me that much more conscious to the difference between the drug dealers and the gunmen. I had to distinguish the two and make sure I put people where they belonged. Don't force the drug dealer to be a gunman because he didn't have the heart for it. Don't put drugs in a gunman's hands if he's not a thinker. Don't put them in the position to fuck up. If someone did both, then great you had a well-rounded hustler able to hold their own around the board. All I did was listen. When Danny spoke, you listened. He always taught you something, even in basic conversation.

One thing played heavy in my mind though. I'd recently bumped into Jus when I was in Fort Greene Projects at the barbershop. Jus was with his girl Mia. He was driving a white Cadillac Cimarron with a black ragtop. I'd just bought a charcoal colored Audi 5000 turbo. I was parking when I noticed him pulling over. He got out of the car and walked towards me. We embraced and went into conversation. It was awkward to say the least. Our egos clashed. I felt a bad vibe coming from him. I told him...

"What's up with you man? Good to see you!"

"Yea I hear you, what's up with you?"

"I'm good, doing my thing, making it happen."

"Yeah, I hear you out in the hood?"

"Yeah, I got the back of the hood locked down. I can't wait for you to come back man, so we can sit down, talk and make some moves together."

"Oh Jus coming back, and I'mma take back all of what belongs to me. I thought you said you never was gonna hustle where you live? What happened to Coney Island?"

"You make it sound like I gotta explain what I'm doing to

you? I tell you like this, there's more than enough money in the hood for both of us. I look forward to seeing you back in the hood and on the block, let's get money yo."

"Oh Jus will be back. You better believe that. Real soon."

"Well, real soon remains to be seen right? I'll be there when you get there."

That conversation didn't go well. It didn't sit well with me either. I was trying to embrace my dude. I was hoping we could eat at the same table. I felt he was trying to be real cocky and arrogant towards me. This is what I hoped wouldn't be the case. Danny made a prediction that Jus would never see things my way. He just wasn't accustomed to sharing with anyone.

When most of his peers got locked up, he went to war on his own. He built the projects the way he wanted it and now I was invading his turf. That's why he was happy to hear that I wasn't interested in hustling in the hood when I first came home. Now we had a major problem. The hood wasn't going to be big enough for the both of us.

I've been pondering a power move for a while now. I felt that it would be in my best interest if I made it, so I did. I made a proposal to Danny that I was sure he wouldn't resist. Instead of him being my connect, I would partner up with him. Checkmate! By making this pact of partnership, he had to agree to two conditions immediately.

I offered him half of my proceeds. I vowed that I would take over and expand deeper into Red-Hook and would bring in more money. In return I wanted half the proceeds he made from Marcy Projects, along with a stockpile of weapons. I knew he would be able to provide those on the spot. My money was my power, but I knew well enough that my guns were my respect. If I had any chance at protecting what I was claiming, I'd better be ready for war at anytime, anywhere and with anyone.

Danny tried to debate with me for a while, but it was really non-negotiable. For one, I knew how bad he wanted into Red-Hook. For two, Red-Hook made more money than Marcy Projects did. Danny knew this was a no brainer and he was all in with my offer. On this day Red-Hook and Marcy bonded in blood. Both teams together were a force to reckon with. Danny still had some issues in the back of his mind that he had to clear up before moving forward.

Danny knew how close Jus and I once were, and that was a major concern for him. This set in Danny's thoughts deeply. He didn't want to feel like he was wasting his time or helping me too much. He needed some assurance in knowing where my loyalty lied.

I proved myself to Danny on any level. Whatever he threw at me or came my way with, I mastered. Yet and still, he felt a way about Jus. We got into a real deep conversation about Jus one night and I felt he crossed the line. He actually did it on purpose to see how I'd react. He asked me to set Jus up and to have him killed. I said...

"What the fuck you think I am man! I ain't no motherfucking snake! I done did everything under the sun with you. I showed my respect and loyalty, but you got me fucked up if you think I'm gonna set my man up for you or anybody else. If I have beef with him when he come back to the hood, then that's one beef I don't want or need you by my side with."

"All I'm saying is that, he's gonna be a major problem. He got bad intentions for you. He's plotting right now as we speak on how he's gonna come back in. He heard the word on the street about how strong you're getting in the hood. He ain't coming no other way, but the hard way knowing how you are. He's been through too much to be second to anyone. All I'm saying is, I can take care of it for you."

"You can't take care of shit for me! I don't fuck with him and I never will. He had his chance when I came home to put me down on his team. You my partner and my loyalty is with you. I prove that everyday I set foot on these streets. Jus ain't no sucker, I can call him right now and he'll meet you wherever you want, but I'm telling you to leave that alone! You want in,

I got you in. I got this and that's that."

"Ok, whatever you say. Don't say I didn't tell you so when he sell you out."

Danny and I moved on after that conversation. It was back to business as usual. I figured he was skeptical and optimistic, but there was no more I could say or do that I hadn't already. My loyalty was in tact, so I was at peace with that. He feared that if Jus were to survive his beef with King Allah, he'd come back to the hood. He felt he'd convince me to form an alliance with him, which would push Danny out.

I remember when Danny took me to a cabstand on Atlantic Avenue near the White Castle. He said this was where he copped our drugs. He staged this entire scene. He parked the car at an angle. He thought it was a blind spot. He didn't want me to see him go around the corner, but I did. He jumped in a cab and disappeared for about twenty minutes. He then returned with a package full of drugs. I had no reason to question anything, so I didn't.

Then one day, we were going to pick up another package. Once in the area, Danny passed by the cabstand. I told him he passed the spot. That's when he told me, he'd been misleading me the past few weeks. He wasn't sure if he could trust me all the way, without hesitation.

He confessed to me that while I sat in the car at the cabstand he went around the corner and took a cab to his mother's house. He handled his business and then came back to get me. He was very tactical. He suspected he was being followed all the time, so he always created diversions. He would either speed up, circle a few blocks or run a red light before going to his destination. Running the light was one of my specialties as well. I would take a ticket over being followed any day.

He still felt a way, regarding my closeness with Jus. Danny wasn't big on taking leaps of faith. This move was a trump move. It was make or break for him. Danny had a decision to make and he couldn't keep pausing. He wasn't sure if there was a worse case scenario. In a defining moment, him and Jus face to face, who would I side with?

Danny went on to say, that he was taking a chance bringing me to his mother's house, but he needed me to meet her. This was his final test. If his mother felt a good vibe from me then everything was a go in his eyes. If his family was the last determining factor of my fate, then I had no worries. My heart was genuine from the day I linked up with him.

When I walked into the house, I instantly felt like

family. I was not expecting their reception to be any different. I was never known for biting the hand that fed me. Most of all, I wasn't a snake type of dude, so I knew it would go well and it did.

Danny's mom was in her room resting. Danny entered her room, giving her a hug and a kiss. He gestured for me to come in and introduced me to her. She just came home from the hospital and was bedridden, for reasons unknown to me. I just as well went to her bed and gave her a hug and a kiss as if I were her own son. I told her it was my pleasure to meet her. My approach was nothing less than genuine. Danny met my mother previously and he embraced my mom the same as he did his own. He even called my mother Mom.

My sentiments were the same. His mother was Mom to me from that day on. After leaving Mom's room, we went into the kitchen. A few of Danny's trusted soldiers from Marcy Pj's were sitting at the table. I already knew everyone that was there and I took a seat next to Ty Ty's oldest brother Telo. I proceeded in taking care of business. Although everyone knew who I was, they were very surprised that I reached this level of Danny's trust. They couldn't believe he brought me to his mom's house. I guess at the time, I may have been the only one outside of Marcy that Danny trusted enough to bring there.

Fun time was over after about a half hour at the *"Big House"*. Danny was ready to leave. We kissed Mom goodbye and we left out. Walking downstairs, I didn't know what to think, so I didn't assume anything. When we got in front of the building, Danny reached his hand out to me. I reached my hand out as well, shaking his. He pulled me into him, hugging me and said...

"What's up partner?" (Smiling)

"I thought you said I had to talk to your mom before you decided on anything?"

"I didn't say that, I said I needed you to meet my mom. That way, I could sense a vibe, a reaction or something from you being around those I love. If I can trust you around my family, I can trust you with my freedom and my life. With that being said, here's how we moving forward from here on. We already partners, merging Red-Hook and Marcy Projects together. I'm cool with that and you've been helping me with the eleven spots I have throughout Brooklyn. The deal that I'm proposing to you is that, you continue to help me run my spots with you getting nothing off of them. I had them before you came into the picture, but any spot from this point on, we break down the middle. You need to expand outside of your comfort zone. I feel that we can tap into a lot of areas if we do it together and do it the right way. What's most important, I just got off the phone with my partners and set up a meeting for us to meet tonight. We have

a plan to stage a four-corner take over starting in Brooklyn, with an eight party group divided into two. That's why it was important for me to be sure about you. I was on a timeline to have my partner. I'm bringing you to the table, so now we can get started. You've proven to me on every level that I'd hoped you'd be at. What cleared my conscience of you was when you didn't sell ya man Jus out for money or anything else. I respect that. I know you're ready, and so you know, the deal is non-negotiable. The call is on you right now to take the deal or not?"

"Man, I ain't got a problem with the deal at all. My hand was all in with you when I started my movement in Red-Hook. We good, let's take over!"

The night of the meeting, I felt like I was on top of the world. Danny and I were doing the double date thing for the first time. I took this girl from Nostrand Avenue, named Almina and Danny took his date Deidre. He made reservations for us at Benihana's in the city. Before we left he gave me a gift. It was a fully loaded .45 automatic with a shoulder holster. This was his weapon of choice.

I put the holster on, holstered the gun and then we were on our way to the meeting. We took the battery tunnel, heading into the city. I had to get used to wearing a shoulder-holstered gun. I always wore my gun on my waist, but it was all good. We both wore bulletproof vests, but upon reaching our destination we took them off.

We walked up the stairs and inside the restaurant. We were then escorted to our table. We sat the ladies down and then Danny excused us for a minute. I followed him to the back area, which was more of a private setting. I realized he was taking me to the meeting. I came into view of his people and recognized them instantly. It was Blaze and Duke. Blaze tapped Duke to get his attention and they both got up as we walked towards them. Blaze said...

"Yo! That ain't who the fuck I think it is! Danny. You can't be serious? This is who you was talking about all this time?"

"Yea. I told you it was Klein."

Duke interjected...

"Yo, this our man! Where the fuck you been? It's been a long time!"

"Yea. I know. I got locked up in '84 and just got out this past summer. The last time I saw ya was in '83."

"You right. Blaze just came home this past summer too. Yo Danny, you gonna have to find you another partner, this our man yo, he gotta roll on our team."

"Oh hell no! Duke I ain't going for that. We been side by

side these pasts few months and I'm all out of options on who to bring to the table. Klein is my best option."

To be honest, it sure felt good being in the middle of a bidding war between two Brooklyn heavyweights. It wasn't hard to take notice of how much respect Danny held for Duke, which was well deserved. Danny looked at Duke as a mentor. What I liked most of all was that all parties in the group were their own bosses. Blaze was Duke's right hand man, as I was to Danny.

The meeting went great. Dinner with the ladies went great. The closing of the night was the icing on the cake and the cherry on top.

The following morning, Danny was at my mom's crib bright and early. We had a lot of work to do. We had to come up with a regimen that would suit both of us. We structured our plans, going over things until we felt we understood each other.

Once we agreed on everything, we set out in route to meet up with Duke and Blaze on Fulton St. and Kingston Ave. It wasn't long before we got there. We all embraced and chopped it up for a while. I recognized just about every strong-arm from Brooklyn in attendance. The meeting didn't take long because everyone was previously briefed on the subject. The meeting was basically to confirm that all parties were on one accord. We were ready to devise the plan to take over. Everyone agreed to respect the areas that were claimed by other members of the group.

The meeting was also to prevent any of us from stepping on each other's toes by having our people beef with each other. A face to face for all to know; we were part of the same team. If anyone crossed the line, matters would be dealt with according to the violation. With this level of ruthless talent assembled and ready to descend on the city, no one was safe outside. No one was safe inside either.

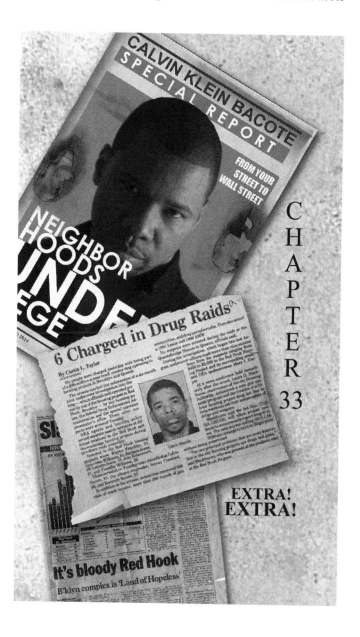

Extra! Extra! Read all about it! Judgment day has come and the word spread like wildfire. King Allah's reign has come to an end. His world came crashing down on him when New York State Law Enforcement apprehended him. He was charged for allegedly kidnapping the wife of Fat Cat Nicholas. He was on the run for a brief stint. He ran his course and finally hit a dead end. King eventually rolled the dice and got a speedy trial. Unfortunately, the evidence was stacked against him. Fat Cat's wife eventually took the stand. She testified against him and identified King as the one who had taken her captive.

Her testimony was obviously very damaging. She chose the system as her weapon of choice. She was making a point to King and his constituents. This was her way of getting back and making him pay for what he did. Her testimony ultimately sealed King's fate. It didn't take long for the jurors to deliberate and come back with a verdict. The judge slammed his gavel down on his hardwood as the verdict was read. Guilty of all counts! King Allah was sentenced to fifteen years to life in the New York State prison system.

"King has since served out that sentence and was released in the year of 2010. He lives as a walking testament and advocate against the lifestyle he once lived. He's doing well for himself in his renewed and restored way of living. Freedom is far more important to him in his elder years. A very wise man of knowledge, wisdom and understanding."

The life and times of the '80s were undoubtedly history in the making, a picture perfect era that set precedence for the future. For most blacks in America aspired to be a basketball player, a rapper or a major drug dealer. Many were brainwashed into becoming the latter. Being a drug dealer was the fastest way to rise up from the bottom. The stronger you got in the hood, the bigger your celebrity became. Everyone wanted to know and be around us. Flashing lights for the hood stars when we came through. We didn't blend in, we stood out. Most talked the life, but didn't really live it.

When we hit the block, everyone took notice. We didn't have to chase success. It chased us. If you were checking for the hood's current events, you were checking for us. We were the definition of being "Bossed Up". The borders were wide open and were flooded with drugs in every city throughout America. Drugs were imported on boats, buses, tractor-trailers, airplanes and even inside of human bodies. They were willing to sacrifice their lives to be drug mules. We were the superintendents with over a hundred keys on our key ring. We were backing the U-Haul truck up in the hood with product for the dealers and users.

Everyone conspired in one way or another, under the table, on the sides of the table, around the table, whatever way to get that money off of the table. Make no mistake about it. All levels of people played a role in the drug movement. When it got to the lower levels in the inner cities, the major players had already been paid. We worked for and often killed each other for merely the crumbs off the brick.

Could you imagine the Old vs. the New? From the Roman days to the Wild, Wild West to today? From the horse and carriage, to cars, trucks and motorcycles. From the gladiators, cowboys and warlords, to street thugs, gangsters, drug dealers and gang members. Being in the battlefield with land mines, to being in the streets, the block and the hood. From having to wear breastplate body armor, to a Kevlar bulletproof vest. From carrying a 6 lb. razor sharp stainless steel sword, to a stainless steel 40 caliber hand gun.

As the 4th quarter of 1986 closed out and moved into 1987, progress for Danny and myself accelerated. We ran through Brooklyn like wildfire, opening up, shutting down and buying into everything. If you were not down with us or someone on our team, you had very few options. Get down or lay down! You worked with us or for us. If your re-up was half a key, you got to keep your money and was fronted a whole key on consignment. You had no more than four days to move the product and pay your debt.

That deal was considered one of the better options. You couldn't beat that. You got to keep your $10,000 and we fronted you $10,000 more. We called that buying you out and merging you into a 50-50 partnership. The other option was to give you $20,000 worth of drugs bagged up and we would take 70% to your 30%. You would have to flip everything within two to three days. We were cool with them choosing either option. If you were offered the deal, you chose one or you strapped up and prepared for war.

The Bosses re'd up together and purchased hundreds of kilos a month. The connect gave us the benefit of the low price of $14,500 to $15,000 per kilo. Whatever amount each group purchased, they received half that amount on consignment. The asking price on the streets at the time was $10,000 per half key. If the whole key was bagged up and sold in Red Hook, the return would be $56,000. We saw about $41,000 once we deducted the salaries of the sellers, lookouts and other workers. It was a pretty good return for a $15,000 investment.

At that time, no one seemed to have been able to master the cooking game. A lot was being lost off of each key. That was, until a dude I grew up with named T-Rock gave me the formula! When I first started with Danny, I didn't know how to turn the coke into crack and T-Rock came highly recommended. At first, I was reluctant in dealing with him because I knew that he was getting high. I didn't wanna cross lines and have him try to play me. I really had no choice though, so I went at him with an offer.

If it was 125 grams that I needed cooked up then that's all I wanted back. I let him keep anything over that amount. He agreed to that deal. Everything was working out great with him on my team. Once he recognized my need in his skills, his greed kicked in. He wanted to renegotiate the deal and wanted more. Obviously, this was ludicrous. I told him the deal was as it stood. I went further into saying that I pretty much had his formula down to a science and could do it on my own. It was just time consuming and I didn't mind keeping the deal as it was.

We went through the cooking process a few more times, when all of a sudden he shut down on me. He refused to cook anymore. I thought we both were getting the best out of the deal. I most certainly wasn't budging from my previous offer. He was hard pressed for more money and his greed did him in. I thanked him for the formula he'd given me. Although we weren't much in favor of one another, we still respected each other's gangster.

When he did his thing, it was like magic at its best. I nicknamed him T-Rock Hard. He used no extra additives other than cocaine and baking soda. He never had to use anything else because it was top grade coke. I really hoped he would reconsider my offer, but he shut it down. Unfortunately that was the end of us ever doing business together.

Unbeknownst to T-Rock, his formula was half the reason I became so successful in the '80s. I went around doing my thing with Danny, opening up about twenty-two more locations, not including the eleven he already had.

It took me to heat up and cook the mixed substances. After about seven minutes of cooking, the coke was in oil form and was coming together. Most of the baking soda fell to the bottom of the pot. The final step, after taking the pot off of the stove, was to slowly add cold water so the substance would harden into the drug better known as Crack.

With most customers, I kept all the overs and gave them what they were supposed to get with no losses. They were more than happy with that deal. Business was great! Danny and I racked in over $250,000 in a two-day flip. We collected and delivered every two to four days. The hardest part of it all was bagging up all of those drugs. I had an all girl bag up crew in my hood that bagged up in eight-hour shifts, receiving $500 per person. It was all in a day's work, an everyday process.

The lowest pay went to the lookouts who got

around $150.00 for a twelve hour shift. The crack heads normally looked out and got half of that amount. Everyone was an important piece to the puzzle, even the crack heads. They would put the rental cars in their names. Those cars were popping in the hood. They had a New York Z plate and everyone in New York had one. It cost $200.00 to rent for one month. Metro Sky pagers were popular for correspondence as well. You needed a lot of quarters back then. When someone paged you, you had to use the pay phone to return the call. This was a way not to get traced.

My man KP propositioned me to go to Connecticut to get money. He was already out there with CD. They often ran out of drugs too quick. He made the offer to purchase from me and in return I would give him half of what he purchased on consignment. We would then split the consignment profits 50/50.

I upped his offer. I said, *"Keep your money and I'll give you everything you need up front. We'll split the difference down the middle after all expenses are paid"*. I told him my crew would bag up for him. This would lessen the consumption of his time at the table. No one wanted to be at the table wasting time and money bagging up. I used the bag up crew service for others and turned a profit for bagging up their work. The deal with KP was a better one from my perspective. There wasn't much for either of us to think about. He agreed to the deal. New London, Connecticut here I come!

I told Danny about the Connecticut deal, but for some reason he declined, which was unlike him. He voiced his concerns and told me to leave the deal alone, but I went through with it anyway. This was my first OT spot of my own. By having this deal, I was to quadruple my money. I used the extra drugs I cooked up from my side hustle. I felt this would make up for the eleven spots I was not getting paid for.

Danny and I expanded each day. I opened up a spot in the front of the projects and set up shop in Building 94. This was the same block that the NBA basketball superstar Carmelo Anthony grew up on. My boy Ed Fresh was the lieutenant of those two spots. Ed was tall and slim, with a dark skinned complexion. He was very quiet, but hardcore quiet. He very rarely cracked a smile.

What I liked most about Ed was that he was responsible and well respected amongst his peers. He stayed in the freshest gear. That was the reason why he was given the moniker Fresh. He was a good dude who was about getting money. Not that I needed to, but I wanted to make a statement to everyone including Jus. I wasn't there holding down the fort for him. He knew I wasn't a hoax. I was just as strong, if not stronger than he once was. I knew he was watching me. I wanted to make a bold move by setting up shop on the block he once claimed.

I didn't really care for his block, but I was playing mind games with him. Building 31 was his safe haven. I didn't necessarily want to be second in that building's history, so I opened up shop next door in building 37. I set out to make my own history on that block. I had dudes regularly posted up on the roof with guns. The weapons weren't in plain sight unnecessarily. If there were any problems in the hood, this block was likely the safest to be on.

My crew quickly grew. Everyone wanted to be down. I felt there was enough money in the hood for all of us. I wanted to show that I had the ability to service everyone. I was bold enough to say, that even in a drug drought, I would still keep the flow steady. I said that things weren't spread around correctly when the last nigga was in charge. I made a note to plant that in their heads.

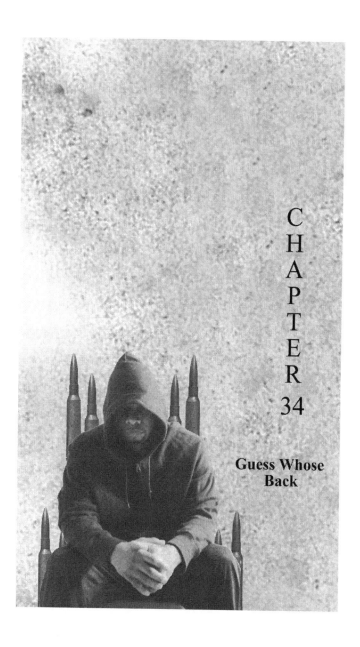

C
H
A
P
T
E
R
34

**Guess Whose
Back**

I knew the day would come that Jus would reappear. I just felt it. I knew he was itching to get back to the hood. He lost a lot along the way. His brother got locked up and he lost face value in the hood. Regardless of the fact, he wasn't able to walk away, not as long as he was still alive. The beef between him and King exposed him in many people's eyes, but like I said he was still alive. As long as he had life in his body, he was certain to find his way back home.

It wasn't long after King's arrest that Jus resurfaced and came back to the hood. When you're away for a while some things are destined to change. It had not been long, but a lot had changed. He knew he couldn't just strong-arm his way in, so he took the political approach. I wasn't hard to find, so we linked up quickly. It felt more awkward now than it did the last time we saw each other in Fort Greene. There was a lot of tension between us as we went back and forth on where he stood.

He said, *"I see you're doing your thing. You set up pretty much everywhere in the hood. I'm not getting into the small talk with you. The last time we spoke I told you I was coming back and here I am. All I want is the spot I built and we good. I'll put my work on the block and may the best product win."*

I told him, *"To be honest with you, I'm glad this day is finally here. Just so we're clear, I don't want 31. That's your spot, but I'm your next-door neighbor now. My spot is 37 and I'm not closing that down. Do you! You earned that. Me shutting down my spot on this block for you will never happen. I don't owe you anything but the respect I just gave you. That's a lot more than what you gave me when I came home."*

"Come on man, you know this ain't gonna work."

"You'll figure it out. Make it work. It is what it is. Neither one of us will do any traffic steering. Let the customers go where they choose. As for the lane, it's like it's always been, for the freelancers."

"Well I'm gonna open back up 31's. I'm going to strong arm the lane and shut down all the freelancers."

"That's none of my business. Do ya thing."

Jus walked away like he was stunned. To be honest, Jus and I both knew that if it were anyone else there would be nothing to talk about. We were very close at one time and neither one of us wanted to go at each other like that. We were just being bull headed for the moment. He wasted no time. He went on the lane with what was left of his crew in tow. He started directing all of the hustlers out off the lane. My crew and myself stood back and watched, curious as to how this was gonna play out.

At one point, Jus's presence and his voice put fear

into most, but this was a different day and time. King Allah decimated his reputation. Most knew that the only reason he was in the hood was because King was in jail. There was a lot of tension in the air, as he moved around trying to call the shots. No one seemed to move quick enough and he felt disrespected. Left with no choice but to make an example out of someone, he pulled out his 9mm and shot Lil' Pump in his leg.

As Pump laid on the ground, Jus and his crew started yelling out orders and demands. He screamed out *"I'm back."* In his mind, he thought he was laying down his laws and regaining his respect. Honestly, it was a bad look. Most thought, *"Why would you pick on the little guys when the big guy is over there, right on your block? Don't bully us, go over there and bully them."* Jus knew it wouldn't be long before the ambulance and police arrived, so he slid off. Later that night, he came back to the block and wanted to talk to me again. He tried to come at me with the guilt trip tactic. He said...

"I hear you fucking with that kid Danny real hard. I don't see why you gotta fuck with him when you and I can partner up and make some major moves. I don't know how much you're moving right now, but if we partner up you don't have to put up any money. I'll front four keys and we'll split it down the middle."

"Wow, I can't believe you yo. You my man. I'd love to partner up with you. That's how it was supposed to be when I came home, but you didn't' want that. Now I got somebody who helped me build what I got and I partnered up with him. Now you expect me to betray that for you? I can't do that. Dude has been loyal to me as I am to him. I can't walk away from that. I'm good yo."

"You know dude tried to come in the hood and attempted to kill me? What do you expect it to be when we see each other?"

"I expect both of you to do whatever you feel you have to do. Like I told him as I'm telling you, leave it alone! If it turn into a tag team thing and others get involved, you'll lose. Jus do me a favor; just get money man. I don't have a problem with you, you're my man and I don't wanna see nothing happen to you."

"This shit is taking a lot for me not to come another way, just because it's you. How about this? I see this working if you and I take over the whole projects. We won't let anyone sell any drugs unless they are selling exclusively for us."

"You mean you wanna cut out all the freelancers, middle men and any other spot that's not ours. No one can sell if they are not selling for you and me? What about the Panamanians? If I agree, I wanna shut them down too. They been here long enough, it's time we run them outta here."

"We can shut down everybody for now, but let's not fuck with the Pano's, we not ready to go at them yet."

"Nah man, with both of our crews together, we can run them out!"

"I'm telling you man, they way too deep right now. Let's shut down everything else first, then we go at them."

"What about Case and Real?"

"Don't worry about them, I got that. I'll deal with them myself. We can gather our crews up this time tomorrow night and make rounds through the hood and shut shit down."

"Let's do it! I'm all in."

Around this time, Danny had taken a business trip to Los Angeles. I had my hands full because I was not only handling my own business, but all of Danny's as well. The night Jus and I was supposed to meet up, I had my crew ready to go. I saw his half brother Jr. and I asked him...

"What's up? We're supposed to do this at 7:00, where's ya brother?"

"I think he's gonna be a little late."

"What you mean he gonna be late? He couldn't call me to tell me that? Yo, call this nigga right now man. I ain't waiting out here with all these guns on us not knowing what time he gonna

show up. I don't need him here. My crew can do this shit on our own. He said he wanted to be here and now we gotta wait for him?"

"Give me a second Klein, I'm calling him right now".

After a few minutes, Jr. had Jus on the phone and passed the phone to me...

"What's up wit you man? You're the one who set the time to do this. My crew is ready to go."

"My bad man, I got held up a little. The Cimarron got towed and I had to take care of that real quick. I'll be there as soon as I can, but Jr.'s out there..."

"Hold up! If you're not here, I don't have to be here either yo. I don't need Jr. and nobody else in ya crew to do this. Matter of fact, I'mma deal with this shit right now. I ain't waiting on you...Ay yo! Let's go do this ya! I don't need to talk to this nigga no more! (Passing the phone back to Jr.)

"Yo Jus, what you want us to do? Klein and his crew are going on the lane running down on niggas!"

"Go wit him! You gotta step up wit him! Don't let him do it by himself. Call me when ya done!"

I was mad as a motherfucker after speaking to that nigga. My adrenaline was on full blast. Me and my crew went on the lane, drew our weapons, spread out and started yelling out demands. This all came by surprise. As it was going down Jr. and his crew followed suit and yelled out the same demands. There was so much mayhem. People were trampling over each other trying to get out of the way. Resistance by a few was to be expected. We jumped right on top of that shit and started pistol-whipping a few dudes, making examples out of them.

Jr. and I hit the main lane where all the action was going down. I yelled out....

"There are new rules in the hood and no one can hustle unless they're hustling for me or Jus. Ain't no more freelance selling going on out here! I don't care who you wanna be down with, but if it ain't me or Jus, then it ain't gonna be in this hood!"

"Yo Klein, I lived out here all my life! I been hustling these blocks for twenty years, and now you telling me, I gotta work for one of you guys? I been out here too long, and that'll be the day I retire before I go for that!"

"Well guess what? Your retirement party's right now! As of tonight, you're officially retired! Now, get the fuck off the block before I blow ya brains out ya head! (Pointing a Tec-9 to his head). You should've had enough after twenty years anyway, get the fuck outta here!"

"Yo Klein, what's up with this? I grew up wit you man!

What's all this shit about me not being able to sell my shit unless I sell for you or Jus? You niggas can't be serious? Ya taking this shit way too far now man. I'm gonna do what I been doing man! Ain't nobody gonna stop me, fuck that!"

"*Dre, I wouldn't advise you to do that man. Not tonight! I don't want you to be the example! Trust me on this one. You my man, but this way bigger than you right now."*

"*So you saying I gotta pick between you or Jus as to who I wanna be down with in order to sell my shit?"*

"*That's exactly what I'm saying, but let it be known (I yelled out for all to hear), I don't want anybody who gets high working with me. All you crack heads can go do ya thing on Jus's side."*

The word spread around the hood quickly. Niggas thought Jus and I lost our minds. At first, I thought this was a good move. That was until Danny got back from his trip and I broke everything down and brought him up to speed. He was gone for three days, but a lot had happened during that time. This nigga lost his mind when I told him about the move with Jus...

"You did what!"

"Jus and I teamed up and took over the hood. Can't nobody do nothing unless they doing it for either one of us."

"What are you talking about? Do you hear what you saying? Why would you do that when you already got the hood! You just let him back in and gave him his strength back. He's playing you, knowing you still feel he's ya man. You in his way and he's playing you right now! The damage is already done, we just have to play this shit out and see how it go. I can't believe you did that."

I didn't necessarily see it Danny's way. I felt he was being too judgmental and critical towards Jus because of his past endeavors with him. As soon as things calmed down between Danny and I, he filled me in on his trip to L.A. He had just returned with a four-man team. He made a power move with the new West Coast connect. They were transpiring a major transaction of money and drugs. Once they got to the meeting place, the money and the drugs hit the table from both sides.

As the transaction was being made, all hell broke loose. The New York crew quickly went into motion, drawing their guns on the connect and his people. The connect never saw it coming. He was ambushed into a set-up. The estimated amount of drugs taken came close to the street value of nearly two million dollars.

I was disappointed that I didn't go on the trip. A bonus was given to those who went. I still benefited heavily once it all got back to New York. My chemist skills were in high demand. I was the best chef in town. All I needed was the work, a stove, a pot, a facemask, baking soda, water and a spoon and I was ready to perform magic.

Everything was business as usual and it was all good. So many bricks of keys were coming in that we could have built a brick house. I probably would have nicknamed it "The House That Keys Built". We didn't build a house, but we damn sure filled the inside of that motherfucker up with them. We were going super hard on the streets. Danny and I were going so hard that we never slept at the same time. He'd take a power nap for one hour. Once he woke up, I took my hour-long nap. We went through that system for at least nine months before having to get away and take a break for a few days.

We were on one hell of a mission to get money. We were chasing it for real. Neither one of us got high off of any type of drug. We didn't smoke cigarettes, nor did we do any type of drinking. We didn't party or hang out on the streets unnecessarily. This was one thing we both had in common. We stayed focused in devising a plan to make more than what we were already making.

I remember one day while at my mom's crib, Danny, Shamel, Supreme and myself had to bag up a brick real quick. We had to prevent Lil' Ra and Domanit's spot from drying out. Even with a bag up crew, we still seemed to have a problem. We could never have enough work bagged up.

As we bagged up, I went into my closet and pulled out about twenty boxes of sneakers. I told Sha-Ru's little brother to come get them. I was at the point where I only wore a pair of sneakers once and then I gave them away. As I was taking out the sneakers I checked them. I had to be sure I wasn't giving him my stash boxes, which were full of cash.

I had just recently moved my money out of my mother's crib, to a safer location. I was reluctant to keep a substantial amount there, thinking that a raid on the crib could happen at any moment. I didn't think anything would be there as I took out and opened the boxes. That was until I opened one of the boxes and it was full of cash. I asked Danny...

"Ay yo. Did you put a box in my closet recently?"

"I can't remember. Why?"

"There's money in this Nike box and I'm trying to remember if it's mine or yours?"

"How much is it?"

"It's stacked the way we stack it. All hundreds. $350,000."

"Since neither one of us can remember who it belongs to, split it. I'm sure we both can use some pocket money."

Where there's plenty money, there's plenty problems and that's what we had around us. Where there's fortune, there's fame and fame often goes to your head. You tend to think you're invincible. You find yourself being respected, loved and hated at the same time. We were the ones you pointed your finger at and whispered about all the time. For the most part, people in the community would turn their cheek to our wrongdoings, at least until someone innocent was tragically affected.

This would be the case when Blaze and his team got into a shootout with some dudes from Fort Greene. An eight-year-old boy, who was playing near his building got caught in the crossfire. The boy survived, but there was no way to control the effects this incident had on the crew as a whole. The whole team had a cloud of calamity over us after that.

Tragedy seemed to follow us. Lance who was a part of Blaze and Duke's team was first on the list. A rival went to his mother's house and knocked on the door. His brother Fred went to the door and looked through the peephole. He was unaware that he was looking down the barrel of a 9mm. He tragically lost his eye that day, but he was fortunate enough to still be alive.

Like I said, calamity was lingering over us. Shamel and Supreme were hanging out in Marcy Projects, playing Cee Lo with some dude. Shamel rolled himself out of a large bankroll. Although the money really wasn't an issue, Shamel warned the dude not to keep talking shit. Shamel rolled his last hand and lost. With respect to him losing over $10,000, he wanted to see if dude was going to respect him enough to give him a walk. Dude claimed he knew Shamel had money to throw away and he still kept talking shit to top it off, bad move.

Shamel pulled out his 357 magnum and shot him, lifting his ass in the air. Shamel picked up the money, counted $1,000 and pocketed it. He then threw the rest at the dude and walked away. Not long after that, I got a call from Supreme...

"Yo Klein, Panamanian Jack and like twenty Pano's ran down on niggas and shut everybody down. He said we couldn't sell in the hood no more!"

"Where you at?"

"I'm in the hood. He still out here on The Ave with Jus having a meeting."

"With Jus? I'm not that far, I'm on Atlantic Ave, cutting through Gowanus PJ's and I'll be there in five minutes."

I drove my Audi that night. As I pulled into the parking space, the meeting was still taking place between Jus and Jack. At this time, Jack and I had never met before. We really had no reason to. This was actually the first time we'd been this close since the day he ran down on my brother and pulled a shotgun out on him at the train station. I was already amped up as I got out the car, anxious to hear what was being said. Jack was speaking to the crowd that gathered around him. He spoke in his deep Panamanian accent…

"I hear there's some new changes made and some new people around making orders! Well, I'm here to tell you, nothing has changed other than what I'm telling you now. No one can sell they drugs out here unless you sell for me or Jus! You want weight, you buy weight from me or Jus! You want bag up, you get bag up from me or Jus! No exceptions! I don't care who you think you are! You want war, Jack will give you war!"

To be honest, I was stunned. I watched Jus's face while I listened to that bullshit. He had the biggest smirk, as if to say, *"I won!"* It felt like I was reading his mind, *"Yeah nigga. I played you! I used you to get my strength back in the hood. Checkmate! Game over!"*

That shit didn't sit well with me at all. All I could

hear in the back of my mind was Danny saying, *"I told you so!"* There was no need to stay there and listen to anymore of this foolishness. I told Supreme, Lil Ra and Domanit to get in the car so we could get up outta there. As I was walking away Jus had the audacity to call out to me. Everyone was watching...

"Yo Klein! Let me holla at you for a minute."

I had my back to him and when he got close enough, I spun around and reached my hand out to shake his. He looked at my hand, stuck on what to do. I told him...

"Look at you. You don't even wanna shake my hand in front of ya man, ya new partner." (Smile on my face).

"Naw, it ain't like that man."

Jus reached his hand out to me. Once our hands were firm in each other's grasp, I looked into his eyes with deep pain from being betrayed for the Panamanians. After a move like that, there was no trust between us at all and no way of reconciliation, I told him...

"You already know how this gonna play out right? I just heard I gotta cop my work from you or that motherfucker right there, right?"

"Klein, don't do it man. We can work together like you said. I just want back what I built."

"Jus, we ain't gonna get into who built what. You were fortunate enough to stay out here when everybody was catching bids man. If niggas was here, we would've put in the same work you put in to build for what you claiming is yours. It's obvious what it is, ain't nothing left to say. It is what it is. All I gotta say to you now is, be the flyest nigga at my funeral because I'mma be the flyest at yours. I love you man."

I pulled my hand back from his and told my crew to get in the car. What I said was in the moment, but everyone heard it loud and clear. Fly Ty repeated what I said, *"Oh shit! Did you hear what Klein just said to you? He just told you to be the flyest nigga at his funeral, or he gonna be the flyest nigga at yours!"*

I guess it took a moment for what I said to register in his mind. When Fly Ty repeated it he knew he had to come back with something and that he did. He said, *"Don't let the brick wall hit you boy! You can't fuck wit this! This shit too big for you to fuck wit!"*

I didn't see any reason in having a verbal battle. I did the only thing that was appropriate and instinctive. I blew a kiss at him and repeated, *"I love you man. Bye!"* before I got in the car. I was so deep in my thoughts as I sped off to my mother's crib, that I didn't even hear what Lil' Ra was saying...

"Yo, what we gonna do? We bout to go to war!"

"You got damn right! If I don't do nothing else, I'mma be the last motherfucker that Pano and Jus see before their last breath. That nigga got me fucked up! If he thought he went through a war before, he ain't see nothing like what I got for his ass. I didn't wanna have to go there with this nigga, but he got me fucked up for real!"

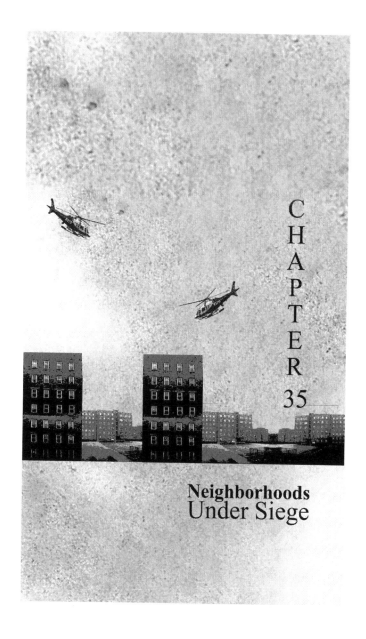

CHAPTER 35

Neighborhoods
Under Siege

Right before the beef went down with me and Jus, my brother moved back home. His girl had twin boys and now he was back in the hood trying to get his weight up and get money. A lot had changed since he was away. The biggest change was that, I was in position. I'm sure he felt it would've been easy for me to give him something and let him get back on his feet, but that was not the case. I felt a way about helping him, the same way he felt when I came home.

Karma's a motherfucker. His reason for not doing anything for me was that he was honoring his word to our mother. He told her he wouldn't do anything that would get me into trouble. I felt it should stay that way. Him getting on wouldn't come from me. It was kind of hard for my brother to get it together, being that he was in the same situation I once was in. He was told, *"Get it from your brother, he got it good".*

Anytime he came at me, I shut him down. One day I was handling my business with Danny, Supreme and Shamel, while he was in the other room trying to devise a plan. His level of frustration built up so high, that he would often pick fights with Danny. At this point, Danny felt like he was family and didn't want to get in between me and my brother's beef. He told me quite a few times to do something for my brother, but I refused. Against my wishes, Danny went and knocked on my brother's door. He went inside and they had a man-to-man talk. Danny came back into my room and told me...

"I don't know what's up with you guys, but that's your brother and trust me, one day, you're gonna need him on those streets. I know you mad at me, but you'll get over it. I did what you should've done. I gave him some work so he can get back on his feet again and take care of his family."

"You ain't had to give him shit. I can do what I do for my nephews myself. That selfish ass nigga shitted on me and disrespected me every chance he got when he was doing his thing. I don't feel sorry for him."

"For one, he's ya brother. For two, I hear he's one hell of a hustler. I respect that. I see the hunger and fire in his eyes to get back in the game. Plus, it don't make him feel any better that his own brother is all the way up and he's not. I hear what you saying, but whatever man it's done."

Now back to the Jus and Jack situation. I parked my car, moving swiftly, looking in all directions with an eagle's eye as my crew followed suit. We entered my mother's apartment and went into my room. I lifted my mattress, exposing a small army of weapons. Everyone in the crew grabbed a 9mm with extra clips. Supreme and I each grabbed Tec-9s. Before we left the crib, I made it clear that we were going after Jus and Jack. I instructed everyone to stay tight, fall back when told to do so, listen to each other and stay on point.

After all was said and done, we went downstairs and walked back to the block. We had our guns out as we walked. Everyone was still there. They saw us the same time we saw them. I locked in on Jus and Jack standing together. While in motion, I yelled out to Jack, *"You want a war motherfucker! You got it! Ain't nobody getting no money out here until one of us is dead!"*

My crew and I stood in the middle of the street side by side, letting off at least a hundred rounds. Everyone scrambled out of harm's way. We changed clips and closed in on them, as they returned fire. I did my best to get up on Jus and Jack, but I couldn't. Both of their crews were returning just as many shots. Everyone was ducking behind whatever they could to shield themselves. With not many options but for both sides to retreat, we knew we were at a stalemate. Most of all, we knew the police were about to flood the hood.

We got back to my mother's crib and spoke for a while. We were too amped up to be sitting in the crib, so we went back downstairs. We tried to creep up on Jus's block and hoped to catch him slipping. This was not the case. His block was deserted. No one was outside. At this point, it wasn't even about getting money. Going to war was a non-stop thing. Jus and Jack were looking for me and I was looking for them.

Somebody had to slip and when they did, game over!

I almost caught Jus slipping a few days later. He was on The Ave. with his crew. I was dealing with this Hispanic girl named Diana at the time and she lived on that block. They were slacking so badly. I slid past them and into her building. I chilled in her crib talking to her family for about half an hour and then I left. Once I got outside, I shielded myself behind a tree so that they couldn't see me. I started talking to my girl through her second floor window. She was scared that they'd spot me.

She couldn't believe that I was bold enough to come on her block by myself. Jus had at least ten of his boys with him. It wasn't long before a Pano came walking in my direction. I knew he didn't know who I was. As he was about to walk past me, he nodded his head saying, *"What's up"*. When he got a few feet ahead of me, I started taunting him saying...

"Yo Pano. What I say?"

"What?"

"What's up wit Cobin Klein? Kill Cobin Klein right?"

"Yea! We kill Cobin Klein!"

"Yo Pano, look! There go Cobin Klein!"

"Where?"

"Right here!"

I laughed as I drew my 45 from its holster and lifted up my Calvin Klein dress shirt, exposing a Mac-10. The Pano immediately ran over to Jus and started screaming my name, pointing in my direction. I came from behind the tree into full view for him to see. I raised my hands up in the air as if to say, *"What's up?"* Jus wasted no time. He knew he got caught slipping and now was scrambling to find something to shield himself with. His first reaction was to grab the closest person to him. He grabbed a girl holding her baby, but she quickly pulled away from him.

He rushed over to his worker JW and used him as a human shield, running off the block. I told my girl that I'd call her later and started walking to the back where I lived. I believe Jus didn't have a stand off right there because he felt I had him surrounded or maybe he didn't have any guns on him. Either way, I knew I was about to be under fire and outnumbered. No sooner than me walking to my block, Fly Ty called out to me. He was trying to catch up to me on a bike. Now mind you, I knew Fly Ty worked for Jus, but I also knew he wasn't into any gunplay.

This nigga was trying to stall me by making

conversation until Jus and his crew arrived. He said…

"Yo Klein, what's up man! You know you and Jus need to talk this shit out."

"We tried that already. I think it's obvious on both sides that there is nothing to talk about."

"Naw man. I think I can talk to Jus for you."

"Is this the same thing you doing for him? Talking to me? I got my spokesperson right here (showing my guns). I'm good. Ty, I gotta go now. Nice job trying to keep me here until they came through. I really think for your own good, you should mind your business. You need to go. I see them coming and you don't wanna get shot in the crossfire."

All of Brooklyn was talking about the beef I was having against Jus and the Panamanians. I had everyone reaching out wanting to be drafted if need be. Either they called or they had a face-to-face with me. There's many to give thanks to, especially Brooklyn legend, I-True. He came to see me and offered his life if necessary. He said he'd stand by my side to protect mine. This was loyalty at its best.

I-True and I had gone through the ranks together growing up in Brooklyn. We held a mutual respect as if we were blood brothers. I told Danny and I-True that I didn't want to bring a lot of unknown faces into the hood. They took it upon themselves one night to get together and run through Red-Hook with a team of a hundred strong.

Danny and I spoke about bringing in other sources, but I disapproved in doing so. I wanted to keep my team small. As long as I had the right people, six would feel like a hundred. All of that changed when I got a phone call from Jus one day...

"Yo, where you at?"

"Fuck you mean, where I'm at?"

"Look man, we gonna do what we do, but I'm not gonna cross the line that's about to be crossed. Jack's on his way to the back and talking about killing ya moms! I ain't got nothing to do wit that man. I'm calling you to put you on point that he's coming."

"You got everything to do with whatever happens! My moms die, ya moms die, I promise you that! You better do whatever you can to stop that nigga!"

I hung the phone up and drove as fast as I could to get back to my projects. I called Supreme and told him to make sure he had everyone under my mother's building and to be on point for Jack. I called Danny and I-True to meet me out there as well. Before I got to the hood, I called my sister. I explained that it was an emergency and for her to meet me somewhere safe so I can talk to her. Within minutes I got to the parking lot. I ran past Supreme and the crew and told them, *"I'll call you when I'm bringing my moms downstairs".*

That was one day I'll never forget. I unlocked the door and saw my mom in the kitchen. She was in her robe, cooking dinner. I ran up on her and she said…

"Hey sweetness."

"Ma, I don't have time to explain! You gotta grab a few things and I gotta get you outta here!"

"What you mean? What's wrong? What happened?"

"Come on ma, go in ya room and get a few things, I told you I don't have time to explain right now! You gotta get outta here!"

My mom laid her suitcase out on the bed, looking puzzled. She was trying her best to move as fast as she could, but she wasn't moving fast enough for me. I grabbed a hand full of things and threw it in the suitcase. I then went into her drawers, throwing a little bit of everything in there, closing the suitcase. That day, my moms left out of the apartment we were raised in, still in her robe and never returned back to Red-Hook ever again. I called Supreme to let him know I was on my way downstairs.

He cleared me to come down. When I got to the parking lot, my brother, Danny, I-True and about thirty other dudes were there. Everyone had their guns out ready for whatever. My mother couldn't believe her eyes as she got in my car and we drove off. I had about eight cars follow me out the hood and onto the Belt Parkway. As my mom and I drove off to meet my sister, I told her that it wasn't safe for her to live in Red-Hook anymore. I told her she couldn't make any calls to her friends or tell them where she was going right now.

We pulled off the highway before entering into queens to meet my sister. When she saw all the cars around us, along with the expression on my mother's face, she said, *"I don't wanna know nothing! Come on ma!"* I popped the trunk of my car and got my mom's bags. I gave her some money and gave them both a hug and a kiss. I told them that I loved them and would have all of my mother's things packed up and delivered to her as soon as I could. When they drove off, Danny and the rest of the team gathered around me. I told him...

"Jus called me."

"What he say?"

"He called to warn me that Jack was plotting to kill my moms."

"What!!!!!"

"Yea man, he asked me where I was at and gave me the heads up, saying he couldn't stop it and they were on their way back there at some point tonight."

"Well, if they don't know we moved her, maybe they still plan on coming back there. Let's go out there now and set up so if they do show up, we can end this shit tonight."

"Ay yo Supreme, drive my car, I'm riding back with Danny."

"Ok."

Danny already knew what I was thinking. Once my mom was safe, I had nothing to lose at that point. I always felt that men could handle themselves. I spoke with my father, brother and my cousin Bobby who was visiting from down South. Everyone knew to stay close to the building and not to go deep into the projects without having some of the crew with them. Danny sent his brother-in-law Metcalf to stay by my side at all times. I-True was doing his thing in Fort Greene around this time but made himself available on my behalf.

He met up with me everyday at some point to make sure I was good. It hadn't been two weeks since I moved my mom out. I was walking through the projects with about four dudes from the crew. I was on The Ave. and I saw Rakim. He was driving and pulled over when he saw me. He told me how scared Jus was. He was caught up in the moment and actually forgot he had Jus's sister Gina in the car with him. She tried to disappear into her seat. She looked like she was facing death. I saw her discomfort. I broke the silence and told her…

"What's up Gina? You ain't gotta look and act like you're scared when you see me."

"Calvin. You know you and Ditto (Jus) need to stop this."

"This grown man business. As long as I don't see you, ya moms or any of ya sisters on the phone around me, we good. As long as I don't see you, ya moms or ya sisters trying to point any guns at me, we good. I don't have a problem with ya. Ya brother know what it is. He's on the wrong side."

I didn't stay in one place too long. I kept walking through the projects. I walked past a crowd and they parted like the Red Sea. It seemed as if my presence had a lot of people on edge. My aura channeled death, to taketh or receiveth. I was at the point of no return. I didn't give a fuck about nothing and no one. I recognized all the people in the crowd, as I got closer, so I knew I wasn't walking into any danger.

I expected to walk by with no problem and that's

when I saw Jack's baby mother. To my surprise, she liked to get into grown men business. I had no intentions of using her as a pawn to draw him out. That was, until she came out of her face and got out of line. The bad thing about this was, I grew up very close to this girl and her family. Her mother used to babysit me and was like my mom's sister. If for nothing else, I felt she knew what her man planned to do to my mother. Although most men don't talk about certain things with their lady, pillow talk was a motherfucker.

I felt she had knowledge of the attempt on my mom's life and didn't respect our families' bond enough to warn me. Instead, she chose to be cocky. When I saw her, I had no intentions on saying or doing anything to her. I was going to keep it moving and then she tried to instigate a reaction from the crowd...

"I don't know why ya moving out his way like that! Like he some God or something. Calvin, you better stop acting like you looking for Jack before he find you and kill you!"

"What! I know this bitch didn't just say what I think she said? Who the fuck you think you talking to?"

I pulled my gun out and pointed it at her face.

"You heard me! Who the fuck you think you talking to?"

"I'm sorry! Please don't."

"Shut the fuck up! Bitch, get on your knees!"

"What?"

"You heard me. Get on ya motherfuckin' knees and open ya mouth!"

Once she was on her knees, I walked in closer to her with my gun leveled below my waist. I put the barrel of the gun in her mouth and proceeded to move it in and out. I made it look as if she was sucking my dick. Then I kicked her and told her, *"You tell that bitch ass nigga of yours I'mma kill him where he stand when I catch him. He ain't safe out here at all! I don't give a fuck what time of the day it is or who is around. I'mma kill that nigga and whoever he wit. You think he's tough, tell him to show his face. Tell him, I dare him to walk through the hood."*

I knew if for nothing else, she was scared and humiliated. She knew she fucked up when she came at me like that. To be honest, what she said really pushed me to go harder in pursuit of Jus, Jack and anyone else down with them. It wasn't even about Jus anymore; this shit was bigger than him. Although I had all this drama in my hood, there was still some other business to attend to. Danny called me and wanted me to meet up with him in Marcy Projects. When I got there, he briefed me on some issues he wanted to address in Fort Greene.

I wasn't much into asking questions. He had his reasons and that's all I cared about. All he had to do was tell me when and where and me and my guns were there. I thought he called more people to roll out with us, but that wasn't the case. We just took extra guns and clips. When we got to the Fort, we sneaked in through the back into the park. As soon as we stepped in the park, all hell broke loose. It was the middle of the day and we were having a major shootout. I'm sure they thought we had a lot of dudes with us due to all the firepower we were sending back at them. We were just fast at emptying out and reloading.

Whatever message Danny wanted to send, was heard loud and clear that day. He went to the table and negotiated his way into Fort Greene's action. At one point, it was almost impossible to think that any product other than the signature stamped Pony Pack was allowed on Fort Greene's turf. Household names like, The Lugo Family and Supreme Magnetic were synonymous to Fort Greene's reputation throughout the '80s. Fort Greene represented and was built tough like Brooklyn was supposed to be.

Like I said before where there was money, there

was problems and problems had to be dealt with the instant you took notice. One thing that was law in Marcy was that Danny ran shit. Danny was the Godfather of Marcy Projects, point blank, no questions asked. In any event, a violation was made and Danny called me to come through and deal with it. The pleasure was all mine. It was surprising to say the least that these dudes put work in the hood and didn't know whose toes they were stepping on.

Danny told me to come through hard and whenever he said that, I knew I had to put on my signature outfit. From my underwear to my socks, I wore all black. I parked a few blocks from the hood and walked the rest of the way. Before I turned down the lane on the Nostrand Avenue side, I drew my guns. I held two black steel 45's high in the air as I walked faster in the direction of the crowd. I recognized everyone except for two dudes, so I locked in on them. I waited to get closer up on them, so that I didn't make any mistakes.

I wasn't known for shooting from a distance and I wasn't going to start now. As I got closer, I saw Danny talking to the dudes. I was cautious moving forward. They saw me coming from over Danny's shoulder and their facial expressions changed. Danny turned around and saw me with my guns in the air.

Danny immediately took his hands and signaled

for me to shut it down. I instantly dropped my guns to my side, as I got closer and walked into their cipher. Nerves were tense as they saw me holster one gun and put the other at my side. Me coming through like that took them by surprise. Danny and the crew already cleared up whatever matters they had prior to my arrival. Danny knew he made a mistake by not calling me and telling me the change of plans.

The fortunate thing about it was that I wasn't a reckless type of shooter. I let it play out the way it did. If their expressions didn't alert Danny of my presence then it probably would've been a different story. The only reason I didn't shoot right away was because I didn't feel I was close enough. Danny tried to make the dudes feel at ease by getting back to the business at hand. He filled me in on who they were and what we were going to do moving forward. He started off saying...

"I know I should've called you to shut it down. My bad. I just bumped into them a few minutes ago and they were just telling me what their situation was."

"And what was that?"

"They just had a little bit of work they were trying to get off real quick. I didn't know they were from the hood until just now. I'm not making any excuses for them, but they not on the block trying to take over nothing. They stepped on feet and

didn't know whose feet they were stepping on. We were clearing that up before you pulled up. In fact, they have a spot in Jersey they say they can set up shop with us."

One of the dudes interjected...

"Ay yo Klein, how are you man? I just wanted to tell you like I was telling Danny, we had no intentions on stepping on anybody's feet or disrespecting anyone. We know what it is. We had something light we were trying to get off on our block and we were gonna keep it moving."

"I hear you, but as you see this shit could've ended up a lot worse than us standing here negotiating on making a move. I feel you when you say you got something light to move, but we out here moving something heavy and we here everyday all day. I'm not even from out here and I rep for your hood the same way I rep for my own. If Danny says we're good, we good, just so you know. If you're in the crew, I'll come through for you the same way, nothing personal. On that note, welcome to the family."

"That's what's up Klein."

"What's ya name?"

"I'm Jazz, and this my man Jay."

"What's up?" (Shaking their hands)

"We not out here as much, but we from the hood too. We're trying to get in where we fit in and rock from there. If we can get down wit the crew, that'll be a good look for us, we're all in. We'd rather roll out OT and not hustle where we live and rest our heads anyway."

"Ok. That's what's up. I used to feel that way myself not long ago. Not anymore. I'll go anywhere on the planet if I can. Well, I guess you'll finish working out the details with Danny, and we'll go from there. There's a lot of money to get, so let's get it."

Neighborhoods Under Siege   Calvin Bacote

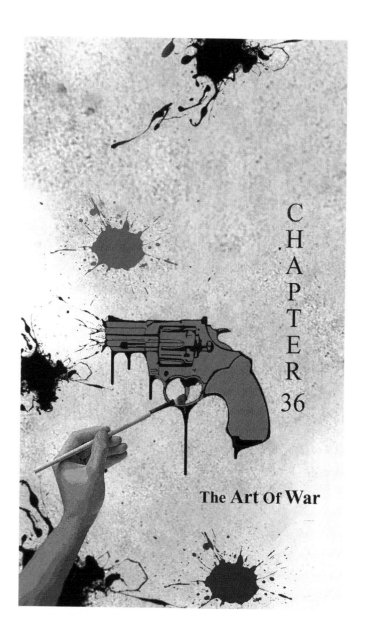

C
H
A
P
T
E
R
36

The Art Of War

After the meeting in Marcy, I linked up with KP and CD. They came down from Connecticut to assist me in the beef I was having in the hood. Things were still outta control. KP was use to being by my side in times like this. He felt he needed to come back to the city and do whatever it took to shut them niggas down. It was hot in the hood from the daily shootouts. The police were in hot pursuit; trying to stop all the violence. They didn't care if we killed ourselves. They were more concerned about the innocent bystanders becoming victims of circumstance.

Way too many shootouts occurred, no matter the time of the day. Jus and I knew each other all too well. He sent for his family members from Alabama and South Carolina to assist him in battle. He took a major loss already and knew that if he lost this battle, it would be the nail in the coffin. As soon as his family arrived, they were on the prowl, plotting to catch us slipping and that almost happened.

One night, Savior and I walked Shamel across the street, to make sure he got to his crib safely. Jus was in the cut stalking us. He made his move as my brother and I were walking back across the street to our building.

We saw a blue Grand AM with tinted windows and

South Carolina plates pass by when we first crossed the street. We then saw it again on our way back. The car attempted to make a U-turn. Before completing the turn the car stopped. The doors flew open and out came Jus, screaming...

"What's up boy? You want some of Jus!"

"What's up? You want some of Klein! Let's do it!

I pulled out my Tec and my 9 and Sav pulled out two 9's. We ran towards Jus, exchanging rounds. All of a sudden, my brother yelled out to me. He saw something I didn't...

"Calvin! Nooo! Come back! It's a trap!"

Savior was right. Jus was baiting me and I went for it. When I ran at him, my Tec jammed on me and I almost emptied out my 9. I was forced to turn back around as Savior kept them at bay firing back. We felt like they were closing in all around us. We needed to get back to our building. Our building had a front and back entry. We ran through the front, not knowing they were coming from the back waiting for us.

A hail of bullets followed. Fortunate enough, their timing was off and they missed us. We ran up the stairs as fast as we could, with them in hot pursuit.

For the first time, Jus was in my building. He broke through our force field. We made it inside our apartment knowing it was a close call. I never told anyone besides my brother, but I never felt closer to death. One of Jus's bullets came so close to my head that I heard it zip past my ear.

I had an out of body experience. It gave me the worse feeling I'd ever felt in my entire life. It felt like I saw my whole life flash before me. I couldn't get over the fact that it was such a close call, me losing my life. The more I thought about it, the more I became enraged. The sound of that bullet in my ear had my mind going crazy.

I knew what I had to do and I was about to turn it up. Somebody had to die and it wasn't going to be me or anyone down with me. The next night things were much different. The crew was ready to go.

Supreme, Shamel, Lil' Ra, Domanit, Sav, Metcaf and myself strapped up and went on The Ave. My brother decided he wanted to go another way. I told him that if he wanted to go another way that was on him. I wanted everyone on The Ave. We tried to take them by surprise, but one of the Panos saw us and ran off to warn the others. We ran around the building and came out from the side they were on. In a split second all hell broke loose.

Shots rang out! We stepped from behind the cars and went out into the middle of the street. They fell back, running into the building. For a few minutes, there were no shots being fired. Then all of a sudden, we heard a massive amount of gunshots go off in the back where my brother was. Supreme screamed out, *"Savior!"*

Supreme sprinted off, running in the area where he heard the shots. We were in their line of fire. The Pano's started shooting back at us again and we returned fire. All of a sudden, I saw Lil' Ra leaning over like he might have gotten shot. I ran over to help him and luckily he wasn't hurt. We all rushed to get to Supreme and my brother.

My girlfriend Diana was looking out her window the whole time with her cousin Millie and Millie's boyfriend Man. They saw Jus's crew posted up on the side of the building. That was the same side we were about to walk down. If not for them we would've walked into a trap. They yelled out, *"Nooo!!! Don't go that way! They're on the side of the building! Go the other way!"*

By the time we got to the back of the projects, my brother and Supreme were waiting for us. Sav told me Jus had him caught like a deer in headlights and could've shot him, but didn't. He said Jus yelled out his name to let him know he had him. Sav kept rambling off about wanting to set up a meeting. He said he wants me and Jus to have a sit down and talk things out. I was quick to tell him…

"You should've never gone off on your own. It's all good. Now you out here going to war with us, but this my crew not yours. We doing this my way. I'm out here on the front line and however it goes, that's what it is. You can wave ya white flag and sit down if you want, but don't think you speaking for me when you do."

"It ain't about raising no flags! Niggas trying to get money, when all you wanna do is go to war. Jus ain't trying to kill us! He had me and let me go."

"I bet you if he had me like that, he wouldn't have gave me a pass. When he sees me, he's shooting directly to hit me! He's not pointing in the air and not pausing to shoot. So I'm not gonna think that he ain't shooting to kill."

I didn't like how close Jus was getting and I was considering bringing in more people to match him and the Panos. Little did Jus know, one of his crew members JW broke rank and crossed the line. JW went behind his back and tried to form a truce with me. He came towards my block, lifting his shirt up to show that he was disarmed, yelling out…

"Yo Klein! I wanna talk! Don't shoot! I wanna talk!"

"What you want man?"

"Klein, I'm not trying to die behind Jus's bullshit man. I know he can't fuck with you and it's only a matter of time before it's the same thing that happened with King. All I'm saying is, I don't wanna die behind this beef you got with him."

"If you're there it's likely you'll die. If you're not there, you have nothing to worry about. I can't believe you have the balls to come on my block like this and sell your man out. I wonder if Jus sent you to say all of this? I should kill you as a return message?"

"Come on Klein! I came on my own. I'm telling you, I don't want no problems man."

"Ok, we'll see. Now you can get off my block, before I change my mind."

Lil' Ra jumped in...

"No Klein, don't let him go, let's kill this nigga!"

"He don't count to Jus. If Jus did send him that goes to show the value he has in him. This the same nigga Jus used as a human shield, so no he doesn't count. Trust me on that. Worst case, if Jus didn't send him and he finds out about this little meeting, he'll kill him himself."

To be honest, I was disappointed to see this act of

cowardice come from JW. He broke from his rank as one of Jus's most trusted soldiers. I guess he didn't pay much attention to why they lost the last war. At one point, I respected this dude for the love and loyalty he once had for Jus. All of that went down the sewer when he crossed the line and betrayed Jus behind his back. It showed bad character. When I saw the weak link in their chain, I knew they would be easily broken.

They really had no legs to stand on. I had to hit Jus where I knew it would hurt. I needed to strike his heart. My target was Jus's Uncle Sonny.

I went outside only when it was necessary. When it got dark, I would cut out all the lights in the apartment. If Jus or anyone else looked up at my windows, they couldn't tell whether I was home or not. Most of the time, I'd be there watching movies. I got caught up and was amazed, watching nothing but gangster and black exploitation flicks. I made the crew watch them too. I would compare us to the people in them. We were either going to do what we just saw or be who we just saw.

I had my mind caught up in those movies so bad; I was literally acting them out in real life. We watched those movies so much that one of the crew members started to complain. I backed my gun out on everyone in the room and yelled out...

"Who the fuck got a problem watching these movies? You? You? You? I didn't think so. This us and if you don't know who you are; then you don't know how to be! That bullshit Ra did the other night getting drunk, could've gotten all of us killed! I don't give a fuck what you do, but if you wanna be down with me, there's no drinking or smoking from this point on. We have to be aware at all times and can't let nothing be a reason to have clouded thoughts out there. It's serious out there! My life is in your hands just as much as yours is in mine! So, if you don't wanna watch these movies with me, you can go find another crew to be down with".

Neighborhoods Under Siege   Calvin Bacote

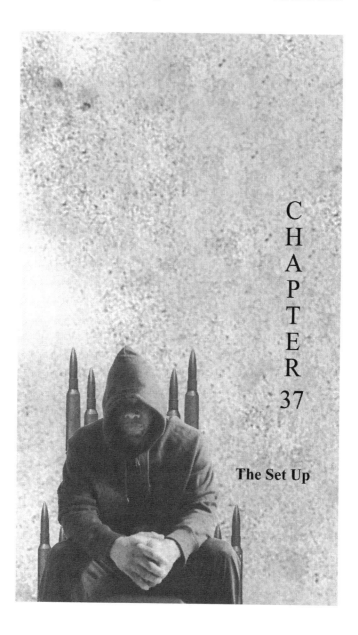

C
H
A
P
T
E
R
37

The Set Up

Due to the war going on in the hood, money slowed. I arranged for Domanit and Barkim to go to Connecticut with CD and KP. Domanit was not happy about this at all. He wanted to stay for the war games. I explained to him that he was needed just as much out there as he was in the hood. On their first trip, I sent them up with half a key. They flipped it within hours. After that showing of progress, I sent them at least five keys within a week's time. I was cashing in big on this move. My turnaround was double that of New York's.

After about three weeks of doing well in Connecticut, I decided to go out there with CD. I wanted to get away from the city for a minute so I could clear my mind. Once we got to New London, CD pulled over after recognizing some dude. Being that my seat was on the same side as the curb, CD rolled down my window and asked the dude a question...

"Yo, what's up man? You seen KP out here?"

"Naw man. What's up with you? You good? What you g..."

I interrupted him...

"Yo my man, go around on his side and talk to him."

He ignored me and said...

"What you got man? I'm trying to make some money man. I was out here waiting on ya for a while. I'm trying to get this work so I..."

"Ay yo! You fucking spitting on me! I told you to go on the other side of the fucking car!"

Don't you know that after I warned this dude the second time, he ignored me and kept talking. He was so caught up in his conversation; he didn't take notice. I unlocked the door and pushed it open as hard as I could. He stumbled back on his feet, cursing. CD couldn't stop laughing. That pissed me off even more. I was mad as a motherfucker and didn't find anything funny.

I got out of the car and started walking towards him. Once I got close up on him I punched him square in the face. He hit the ground. I wasn't pressed to jump all over him. He got up and stumbled down the block, holding his jaw. KP was walking up the block and saw the dude walking away from us. He asked him...

"What's wrong with you?"

"I was just asking CD a question and that motherfucker right there punched me in my face!"

"Who punched you in the face? That dude right there?"

"Yeah! That motherfucker right there!"

"Oh, Ok."

This dude thought KP would check me for hitting him. Never in a million years did he think that KP would do the opposite. KP dead punched him in the face. Dude went down and hit the ground running. It was like he hit the ground and bounced up. We laughed our heads off after seeing that. KP came and gave me a hug, then briefed me on what was going on. KP and one of the lil' homies named Vern got in the car with us and we drove off.

CD called to check on some girls that were waiting on us to come through. He told his girl's friend that he wanted her to meet me. Before we went to get up with them, we went to Domanit and Barkim's hotel room. They weren't there, which was unusual for Domanit. He was one, if not the most trust worthy of those who were around me at the time. KP checked on them earlier, but they never got back up with him. Something had to be wrong.

I told CD to take me to my hotel to check in and we would come back to check on them again before we headed out to see the girls. I checked in, made a few calls and then we headed back to check on

446

Domanit and Barkim. This time when KP went to their room the curtains were moved and the room was more visible. The room appeared to have been ransacked. Their clothes seemed to have been thrown all over the place. I suspected they were in the room for a few weeks and made a mess of things.

I quickly excused the thought of anything uncharacteristic on their part and gave them the benefit of the doubt. I thought they would be much more responsible knowing they had two kilos on them. Something was wrong. I felt it. There wasn't much we could do, so we went to go see the girls. I took a power nap during the ride. Upon reaching our destination, which was in a sub-division, I woke up to a 9mm in my face. The police pulled us over and claimed there was a description of our car involved in an assault earlier that evening. Normally, we would've stayed calm, but Vern and the car were dirty.

Vern had a bag full of crack and a stash behind the gas tank door. It felt like a setup. The K9 dogs were already on the scene so it didn't take long before they found everything. We were all arrested. CD told the arresting officers that we had no knowledge of what was on the lil' homie or in the car.

Fortunate for KP and myself, the laws in Connecticut were on our side. Being that we were the passengers, we got a very low bail. The lil' homie's situation was obvious. He got caught with the drugs on him. CD received a high bail because he was the driver of the car. KP and I got out that night and bailed CD out later that next day. Vern was remanded with no bail, so he went to the county.

While in the bullpens you won't guess who we saw, Domanit and Barkim! When we saw each other, we acted like strangers. It was hard to do that when the officer said me and Domanit gave the same address. The officers were trying to put both cases together. We stated that, just because we lived in the same building didn't mean we knew each other. I told them I never saw him a day in my life. That was the best lie I could come up with and we both stuck to our guns.

It wasn't hard to figure out what happened. The dude I punched earlier, told the police and set us up. Some bullshit! That evening turned out to be the worst. Oh well. Dude was gonna pay for this, one way or another.

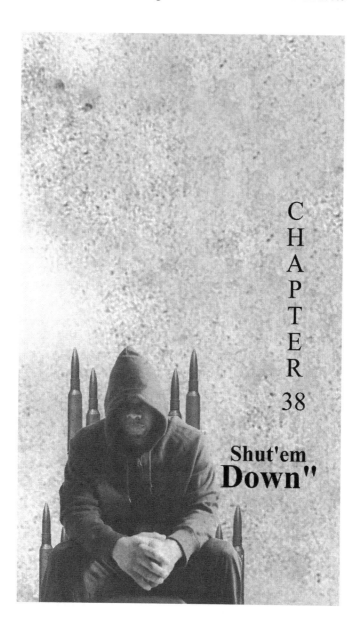

C
H
A
P
T
E
R
38

Shut'em
Down"

So much was going on in New York. If it wasn't one thing it was another. Either way it was business as usual. The latest toys were moving around town. Pathfinders were the new hustler's whip. Danny bought a black one, my brother had a red one and I had a grey one. Jus even had a two-toned grey and burgundy one. Things didn't settle down in the hood at all. Everyone was waiting to see who would get caught slipping. It didn't take long. The first one to slip up was Jack.

One afternoon, I crept up on Jus's block. I was on the prowl, lurking for whomever. I almost got my prize package. Panamanian Jack. Jack's baby mother lived on the same block as Jus. I saw Jack coming out of the building alone. It was very rare to see him by himself, but never the less I was on his ass. As soon as he saw me he ran down the block and onto a side block. The only vehicle on the block was his burgundy Cherokee truck. He did everything he could to get away. There was a little distance between us so I really didn't want to start shooting. I needed to get close up on him. I was hoping to get this dude real bad.

Eliminating this dude would be a huge notch under my belt. I was aiming for his head, ready to kill his whole movement. I wanted to get this dude ever since he pulled that shotgun on Sav. Unfortunately, he got away and that was last time I saw him alive. Most would say; I ran him out of town. Whether I did or didn't, I know I played a major part in him taking his show on the road and out of Red-Hook.

He moved to D.C. in 1987 and not long after, he died. I have reason to believe that the cause of death was a cocaine overdose. Oh well, one down and one to go. Jus was still on my radar. Like I said, I was gonna hit him close to the heart first. Our beef was personal.

On this day it rained most of the day and into the evening. I got a call from some dudes from the hood that wanted Jus dead just as much as I did. They called and asked me to meet up with them. I did and didn't like anything they were talking about. They paid some dude named Jose to kill Jus and wanted to fill me in on the details.

I told them they could've given me the $50,000 payment, being that I was gonna get him at some point anyway. The dude they hired served a lot of time for killing a cop. They already made an agreement with him and paid him half of the money. They were afraid to void the contract being that Jose was still there.

I didn't like Jose because of an incident six years prior. The police were chasing Sha-Ru, Lil' Ra and myself after the F train robbery. We barely got back into the hood and had to hide under some cars until a fleet of cops drove by. We knew we couldn't stay there and made our way into the hood. We got on, Jose's block and stashed our guns and some of the stolen goods. This motherfucker saw us stash our shit and caught us for it. We strapped up, went to his mother's crib and had some words with him. His mother was so scared. She made him give us our shit back. I never liked him after that night and we never bumped into each other again until now.

This dude had these niggas fooled with that cop killing rep. They just knew he was the truth and was gonna solve all of their problems. I couldn't say anything to persuade them otherwise. Jose and his man left the crib to go out on their mission. I told the guys, *"Ya just got beat for twenty-five stacks, don't let them come back and beat ya for the rest."* I was so suspicious of Jose and his man that I called KP to meet up with me so we could shadow them. What happened next was unbelievable.

If these dudes really planned to kill Jus, they had the perfect opportunity. When they walked on the block Jus was standing in front of building 31. KP and I watched these dudes walk on the block, shake Jus's hand and then walk off the block. Seconds later, they let off a few shots and ran. KP and I fell back for a few minutes before we went back to the crib to let the dudes know that they've been played. As soon as we walked in the crib, they jumped for joy saying Jus was finally dead.

I told them not to pay the other twenty-five stacks. It was too late they just did. Jose and his man left minutes before we arrived. The dudes couldn't believe they just took a loss of $50,000, just like that. I told them. *"Now we gonna show you how it's done for real."* KP and I left the crib. We went on the block across from 31's and laid low. We were waiting for Jus or his uncle Sonny to come out. It was pouring down rain. I knocked the light out above us to have a clear view of 31's.

We stayed there for about twenty minutes before we decided to go make our rounds. About a half-hour later, we went back into the building and waited. Before we knew it, our prize package came out. Uncle Sonny! He had a full-length black leather jacket on and was walking towards us. The hallway was dark and we had on all black. We had a clear view of him, but he couldn't see us. We waited for him to get closer. I was ready to run out from the darkness and hit him up, but KP whispered in my ear and said...

"Let him pass us. Don't hit him in front of the building. We'll hit'em when he gets on the side of the building."

I zoomed in on this dude with tunnel vision. I had a Tec-9 in hand. Once he reached the side of the building we pounced on him. By the time he heard us splashing through the puddles of rainwater it was too late. I yelled out, *"Ay Sonny! Got you!"*

It seemed like nothing could go wrong, but it did. I didn't realize that I discharged the bullets that were in the chamber just minutes prior. This careless mistake gave him time to reach for his gun. I only had seconds to reach for my other weapon. Within those second KP put his 9mm over my shoulder and hit Sonny straight and center with about half of his clip. I was already in motion with my 45. I let the shells spit hitting the bull's eye.

He looked like a rag doll. His body was stumbling back and forth from the force of the bullets. Once he hit the ground, I stood over him and dumped a few more slugs into his chest. It was just a little extra assurance that he was a done deal. I turned to KP and told him, *"Come on let's get outta here!"*

We were about a block away when we heard a shot go off. We turned around and to our surprise this motherfucker Sonny was on his feet with his gun in his hand! I was about to go back to finish him off, when he fell down to the ground. I figured that was his last ditch effort before he gasped for his last breath. My regret at that moment was that I didn't aim straight for the head. On these dark streets you gotta think all or nothing. You're either going to get killed or do a life bid for killing.

I felt the damages were detrimental. I knew Sonny wouldn't be able to sustain after the abundance of rounds that ripped through his torso. With out a doubt this hit changed the whole dynamic of Jus's movement. I wanted him to see that I wasn't going to stop until I succeeded in taking him down. In my mind, he drew first blood. All I was doing was closing out what he started. This was an enormous hit on his heart. His mother's brother had been taken down.

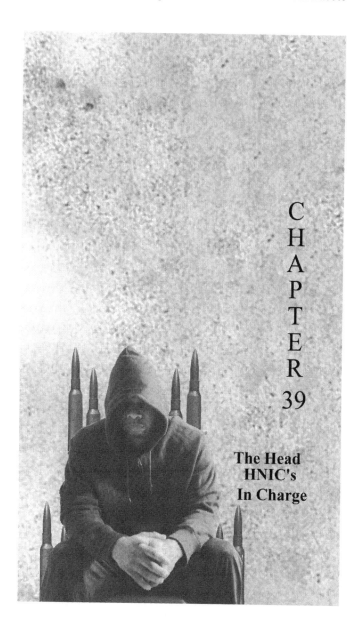

CHAPTER 39

The Head
HNIC's
In Charge

Back in Marcy Pj's, Danny had a few decisions to make. He had to decide who was going to fill the position of Lieutenant. A lot of people expected it to be Metcalf or Tareo, but it was neither. The biggest shock came when he announced that it would be V.I. The hood was baffled by this move. A lot of dudes were very upset and rightfully so. A lot of people stood by Danny's side and were in the trenches with him every day. They put in all kinds of work to prove themselves to him and the movement. A lot of backlash followed suit behind this move.

Danny's close affiliates felt betrayed. He chose someone who put no work in the streets, was never tested and had no type of street credibility. This move was mind boggling, but Danny knew very well what he was doing. He knew V.I.'s loyalty was with him and no one else. Danny felt that although V.I. held no weight in the hood, he would come into his own once he saw how much strength he had through Danny and myself. An added bonus was that Danny was dealing with V.I.'s sister.

The hood was not comfortable having V.I. pull the reigns. He endured a lot of pressure from the crew. This was almost enough to break him down and have him resign. Danny was quick to dispel any of his pleas to quit. He told him to man up. V.I. learned to let the words roll off his back and grow tough skin. He didn't want to let Danny down. Nothing got past

Danny, thanks to V.I.

It was impressive to say the least, to see V.I. be able to endure the torment and remain focused on the business at hand. He didn't care what anyone thought or felt. Him satisfying Danny was all that mattered. As long as he knew Danny had his back, he had no reason to fear much anyway. He wasn't a gunman so he wasn't responsible for putting any work in. He kept things in order and that's all we expected him to do.

It didn't take long before V.I.'s younger brother Pezo, aka Success became intrigued by the way we were doing our thing. He saw us making it rain in the hood. We were straight gangsta with it too. I knew how contagious it was, especially being so close to the movement. Success had a vigilant eye to the dangers around him. At the young age of sixteen, he had a huge edge over his older brother.

Success reminded me so much of myself when I was his age. It became easy for me to bond with him. I needed him to be patient and not follow in our footsteps. Easy to say but hard to accept when that's all that's around you. The burden of our presence victimized him and swallowed his imagination. It was hard to fight against his enthusiasm and will of wanting to get in the game. It was only a matter of time before he'd break through.

Before a prosperous life had a chance to blossom into greatness it withered away. Success lost his freedom for more than a decade, due to the loss of another young kid's life. It's unfortunate that these two lives where taken before they could even get started. His life came to a temporary halt when he was charged for the alleged murder. The other kid's life came to an eternal halt when he was murdered. Success was now forced to become a man and face the gruesome reality of living the street life.

I stepped up for my lil' man and got him the best lawyer money could buy. Mr. Robert Siegel, esq. I did everything I could to give him comfort while he awaited his fate.

Next in line to prove their loyalty and become a trusted Lieutenant was Ty Ty. I can't say enough about how great a move this was. Although Ty Ty was young, he went through the trenches and the ranks. He proved his ability to be able to hustle side by side on "The Lane" next to best of them.

The Lane was where the best hustlers from Marcy established their reputations. It was like a terror dome. From drugs to murder it all went down in the Lane. You entered into a 10-yard long, 12 feet wide lane that swallowed you whole. There was no in between, either you manned up or you were a man down. You were quickly chewed up and spit out if you didn't contain the right ingredients to make a hustler. You were in or you were out. There was no straddling the fence in Marcy at all.

To control Marcy Projects you had to be strong enough to control The Lane first. Many have tried and many have failed. You'd stay out if you knew what was best for you. As for myself, I garnered my name in Red-Hook and it followed in Marcy and abroad. I owned half the stock in Marcy since '86 and I didn't play any games. Other than Duke, I was the only partner Danny had in his New York hustling career and there was no one after me.

Danny's trust was in no one other than Duke and myself, when it came to doing major business. One should never get a workers role mixed up with that of a Boss. The titles are a far stretch apart. Danny trusted no one outside of us. Make no mistake about it, some have attempted to bask in our success, but you must remember one thing, their story will never compare.

"You know who you are. You live your life in fictional fame that ended in five minutes. A fabrication of your perception of a story that you were an extra in. Very artistic to say the least, but we don't believe you, you need more people."

Back to business as usual. Drugs, money and guns

were the ingredients to success in the hood. The streets were flooded with so much money and drugs it was hard not to get wet. All Danny and I had on our minds was getting more. Once we got more, we wanted more than that. So much money was coming in it was hard to keep count. We used money machines and triple beam scales to keep track of our earnings.

It took a whole day to count our money. We separated all of the denominations and then separated that into stacks of $10,000, to use as weight references. We would grab stacks of money and weigh them against our weight references. When it balanced out we knew we had $10,000. It took the same time to calculate our money on the scales as it did with the money machines. It was a long process, but the system worked well with only a few glitches in the end. We counted our money this way everyday.

Neither Danny nor myself were a fan of dollar bills. We rarely kept any of them. Those that did slip through went into a Hefty bag and were set aside. Within a two-week time frame the $1.00 bags held at least $50,000 or more. We'd have around seven to ten Hefty bags full. We only kept one hundred and fifty dollar bills at our stash spots.

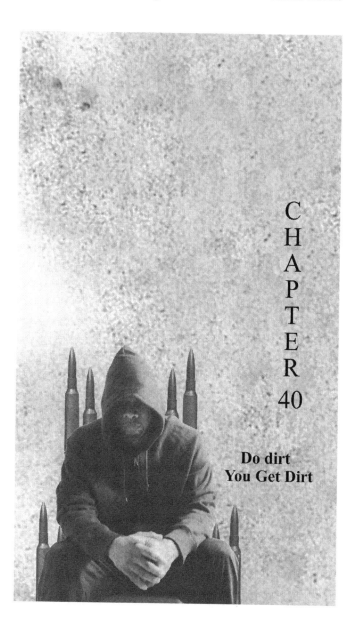

CHAPTER 40

**Do dirt
You Get Dirt**

Surprising news. Sonny was still alive. They say black cats have nine lives. I guess Sonny didn't use up all of his. We skinned the cat, but he wasn't ready to meet his maker. He out witted the reaper for the moment. Word on the street was, Sonny had on a bulletproof vest. If for nothing else, Sonny was completely out of commission and wouldn't be hitting the battlefield any time soon. Mission certainly not complete, but a job well done.

Time waits for no one and it was moving fast. The case for Connecticut was up and I was pissed off. Not so much about the case, but more so towards the dude I punched in the face. He took his vengeance to the police. Little did he know; this would be one of the worst choices he'd ever make in his short-lived life. It's often said, when you do dirt, you get dirt.

The case had gone quite quickly. It was really cut and dry. Domanit and Barkim took a few years for the drugs in the hotel and Vern took some time for the drugs in the car. All other charges were dropped on CD, KP and myself. Since that was behind us, we were back to business as usual. A lesson learned was the last thing we felt regarding that case.

Once I got back to New York I turned it up some more. I not only sent more drugs to Connecticut, but I sent one huge problem, Supreme. Preme was an enforcer and had no problems imposing his will on any one who violated. A rude awakening hit the town when he landed. New London and Hartford were affected by Brooklyn's venom. It didn't take long before my team started to converse with the big dog hustlers and mingle with the baddest females in the town. Business was very good.

I was trying to get Danny to get in on the action, but for some reason he was reluctant. I wasn't mad at him. I was making way more money in Connecticut than in New York. I just wanted to spread the wealth with my partner.

I wanted to go to Connecticut and get away from New York for a few hours. My boy Lord Supreme from Nostrand Ave. came to my hood to check for me. He had just copped a candy apple red 3Series BMW. He wanted to put it on the road, so we went to Connecticut that night. We went straight to New London to a club called The Palladium. The club was popping. The biggest hustlers and the baddest chicks were in the building.

Everyone was flossing and stunting in their own way. I pulled up on this sexy caramel cutie and started dancing with her. Our chemistry was instantaneous. We spoke into each other's ear, doing our best to hear over the loud music. Just as we were beginning to vibe, we were rudely interrupted. I couldn't believe my fucking luck. Her man stepped in between us. It gets even better, it was the dude I punched in the face.

Dude and I exchanged a few words and then security stepped in between us to diffuse the altercation. This was my cue to exit. Lord Supreme and I rolled out and headed back to the city. I didn't want to make too much of a scene in the club. In the back of my mind, I vowed to get at this nigga sooner than later. Sooner came faster than I planned.

Some other issues came up in New London that had to be addressed. I figured I'd strap up, just in case. I rolled out with my boys Case and Dee from my hood. They came up there with me in hopes to get back the $40,000 Supreme beat them for. Case, Dee and myself hit the block and pulled up to where Supreme was. I only addressed it because Case was my cousin's boyfriend and he knew Preme was my homie. He didn't want to take other options and wanted me to mediate the issue. Truth be told, I was hoping to see the dude that I punched in the face.

It didn't take long before the enemy came on the block. I spotted him and was stalking his every move from that point on. His first move was the wrong one. He went to the phone booth on the corner and started dialing with his back turned. He didn't see it coming. I ran down on him and hung the phone up. Gun in my hand, I laid the barrel on his chest. He started singing like a bird and denied getting us locked up.

I thought he was calling the police to alert them that I was in town. He dismissed that claim and told me he was about to call his girlfriend. He asked me if I wanted to speak to her. Can you believe the nerve of this dude? He was so scared that he was willing to push his shorty on me. I wanted to hit this dude and leave him were he stood, but I knew that wouldn't be wise. There were too many people standing around.

I threatened him and told him I never wanted to see him again. Willing to say anything to get away, he agreed and proceeded to walk down the block. One of the spectators spoke out and said…

"Man, I don't know why you let dude go and walk down that block?"

"Why you say that?"

"That's the block him and his boys be on and they got plenty guns in that building."

"I got to get to him before he get to that building then right?"
"Well, I guess so."

I was mad as a motherfucker at myself. I gave this dude way more passes than he deserved. Enough was enough. He had it coming. He was about to get it. I pulled out my 45 auto and put it at my side. I sprinted down the block in his direction. He didn't bother to look back and didn't see me creeping up on him. He got in front of the building and instead of going in he went to a car that was parked out front.

I figured he was getting a gun from whoever was in the car, so I moved with heavy precaution. He got in the car and closed the door. I wasted no time. I took my gun and reached inside the rolled down window. I placed the barrel on his lap and pulled the trigger, shooting him right in his private part. The echo of the gunshot and the loud screams rang through the air.

The driver didn't know what was going on and he jumped out the car, screaming. I put my gun in his face and told him to get back in the car if he didn't want to die. He quickly got back in. The dude I shot was screaming at the top of his lungs. I walked away from the scene as the bystanders ran past me in dude's direction.

I put my gun back at my waist before I hit the corner. As I walked past the eavesdropper, I thanked him. I told Supreme to call me if dude died. To be honest, I wasn't really trying to kill him. In my mind he was the type of dude that deserved to suffer and that he did.

I immediately went back to New York, never to return to Connecticut again, still till this very day. The dude I shot survived, but one thing for sure his sex life would never be the same. In my mind, he got what his hand called for.

Neighborhoods Under Siege   Calvin Bacote

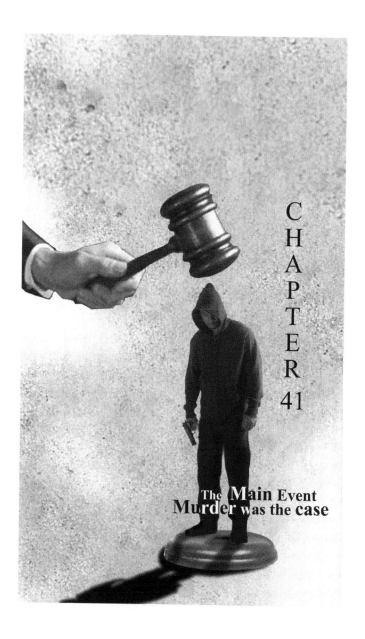

CHAPTER 41

The **Main** Event
Murder was the **case**

Back in New York, The money game was at an all time high. Drugs were flowing everywhere. Crack addicts and dope fiends tore the city down trying to hustle their way to their next fix. All the dealers did whatever they could to provide the product. Whoever was strong enough to take a block, took it. Whoever was strong enough to take a hood, took it. The war games were wide spread and the gunfire was a constant reminder.

It seemed like 88' was one of Brooklyn's worse years. The murder rate was off the Richter scale and Red-Hook Projects was leading the pack. It held the crown for the most murders. The ambulance, morgue vehicles, news vans and almost every cop car in the 76th precinct were constantly in the hood. When I got back from Connecticut I found myself smack dab in the middle of some major beef. It seemed like every week there was a boatload of about a hundred Panamanians flooding the hood. Everywhere you turned, they were there. As soon as they got off the boat they were programmed, *"Guns, Drugs, Kill Cobin Klein!"*

Red-Hook was considered to be one of the largest hoods in the city, but it seemed over crowded and was becoming very small. Everyone knew the hood was now infested. Most were scared and felt that there were way too many Panos to overtake, so they accepted it for what it was. '88 would change all of that. All it took was for something major to happen and that it did. It's often said that the loss of a life can initiate change.

This was the highlight of my life. I was caught up in one of Red-Hooks most infamous times. A lot of heat surrounded the hood since LIFE magazine printed a story about its crime rate. Channel 4 News was covering *"A SPECIAL REPORT/ NEIGHBORHOODS UNDER SIEGE"*. Uproar ensued from both the city council and the community board members. They demanded an immediate take down of everyone involved in the organization of underworld crime.

For Murder Of The Year, the award goes to.... The one and only, the Brooklyn Don himself, Calvin "Klein" Bacote! This was certainly not an award show, but it sure felt like it with all of the attention that followed.

I assembled a group of very dangerous enforcers who were prone to violence. They had every intention to cause and inflict bodily harm on the Panamanians. We had M-16 machine guns, AK's, 9's and a few of what we called, Israeli machine guns. The target, no ifs, ands or butts were the Panamanians. We had nothing but murderous intentions in our minds and settled for nothing less than that. We strapped up and set out on our mission. I was leading the charge. We based our war tactics on the element of surprise. A surprise it was. They never had a chance.

Death was lurking around the corner about to swallow the enemy whole. We walked down the block like cowboys from the old westerns. The first shot rang from its handgun, hitting one of the Panamanians point blank range in the face. His head instantly went back from the force as it punctured his skull.

The bystanders on the block ran for their lives. Frantically, every one scattered as best they could for safety. Bullets were flying through the air seeking a place to land. Most were certainly praying not to be one of the targets. People ran behind cars and some slid under them.

One of the known leaders of the Panamanians made an attempt to get away. He ran down the block known as The Crazy Corner. He got picked off and chopped down by a hail of bullets from an AK 47 assault weapon. I ran up to his body that was lying on the ground. I dumped another round into him, making sure there was no way of survival.

It didn't take long for the Panos to round up and retaliate with a barrage of bullets. They chose to take it out on everyone they saw and shot more than a dozen innocent bystanders. This was the worst nightmare in Red-Hook's history of violence. Death loomed in the air. Screams of horror and pain resounded to the heavens.

Where there's death, there's often a murder trial to follow. This case was no different. An arrest came in less than forty-eight hours. Manny and J-Rock were arrested. The rest of us were on the run. I stayed as low as I could. My thirty-day run came to an end when I was arrested in Freeport, Long Island. I was charged with five counts of Weapons and two counts of Murder in the second degree. I was housed on Rikers Island while awaiting trial.

Not long before the start of my trial, I was hit with the worst news ever. This trumped any news that I've ever received to this very day. Tragedy struck my family hard within two weeks. The murder charge I faced was small compared to this news.

One morning while in HDM/2-Block I read a story in the newspaper about a young woman and her baby being killed by her estranged boyfriend. She told her boyfriend that she planned to take her baby to visit his father who was in an upstate New York Prison. This news seemed to be a little too much for him to handle and he snapped. He acted out in a vengeful rage. He went over to the two-year-old and started stabbing him repeatedly.

The little boy's mom ran to his defense and was stabbed repeatedly as well. As they clung on to what little life they had left, the boyfriend left the home. With no intentions to help them survive, he returned shortly with a container full of gasoline. He   poured the gasoline over them and set them both on fire.

Although the guy was arrested, I didn't see that as fit punishment. I intentionally got into trouble just so that I could get transferred to C-74 were he was housed. He was in 3-Upper, The Bing.

I was transferred to C-74 unit 3-Lower. I was two floors under the dude that killed my cousin and her baby! It didn't take long before I entered the unit and went in attack mode. I didn't unpack my property because I had no intentions on staying.

I needed to make a call. I went to the phone and called my brother. He told me about the preparations the family was making to lay my cousin and her baby to rest. The more I heard, the more I began to boil up inside.

Some dude who thought he had some status in the unit pulled up on me. He told me I was using his phone time. After 4 p.m. only the dudes with the most respect were able to use the phones. They called it slot time. I was very much aware of the system. I already took an hour from one dude and now here comes this one. Oh well, I guess you already know what happened next. I took his time too. He stood off to the side talking to his man, acting like he was a tough guy.

My brother overheard and told me to chill out. I told my brother that I was going to tear that nigga's head off when I got off the phone. Once we ended our conversation, I went looking for the dude. He was in his cell. I walked in and confronted him. We had words, for a few seconds and then I spit a razor from my mouth. I grabbed him and cut him from ear to ear. He ran out of his cell and down the hall screaming for help.

I left out of his cell with my hood over my head. I walked up to the bubble where he stood with his boys. I asked them if they had a problem with me. They fell back from him as if he had done something wrong. The riot squad showed up a few minutes later and I was standing there waiting for them.

I figured that this incident would be more than enough to get me upstairs to 3-Upper, but that wasn't the case. A few things came up. One, I had a family member who worked in the same building. Two, I had a high bail and a high profile case. The system became well aware of my mission to get to 3-Upper. My family member that worked in the building was transferred from their post and I was immediately transferred out of the building.

It seemed like every building was refusing me. I went to C-76. They didn't want me. I went to C-95. They didn't want me. I went back to HDM. They said they didn't want me. The only place left was North Facility and they took me in. In the mist of all of this moving, I was hit with even more bad news. Danny was dead!

I was told Danny was in DC, on his way to Virginia to renew his license. He was with CD and another dude from DC. It was known that Danny and myself were speed demons behind the wheel. My mom once told us that our death would be on our own accord.

My mom's prediction would hold true. Danny was speeding on the highway, racing another Pathfinder. He was doing well over a hundred miles per hour. He was about to pass his exit when CD made him aware of that. Danny had only a split second to make his exit, but that second was not enough.

Danny hit the divider on the exit ramp. At the rate of speed he was going, the impact sent the truck spinning multiple times in the air before it landed on the ground. Unfortunately neither Danny nor CD wore their seat belts. Danny was ejected from his seat and went through the sunroof. He cut his neck, piercing his jugular on the way out. CD was ejected out of the passenger window, breaking his neck.

The passenger in the back seat broke his leg, but sustained nowhere near the injuries of Danny and CD. Danny had to be airlifted to the nearest hospital and was pronounced dead on arrival. CD was rushed to the hospital as well and had to undergo a major operation to not only save has life, but also to prevent him from becoming paralyzed.

Danny's body was transferred from VA. To N.Y. Everyone was in shock. Brooklyn was in mourning. Danny was very close to his family as well as mine. The impact of his death was way too much for his mom to bear. My mother stepped in and took care of all of the burial arrangements as if he was her own child.

One of Brooklyn's greatest had been taken. People had to find someone to blame and the rumors started surfacing. Some were saying Danny's break line was cut. Others said it was CD's fault and many death threats went his way. It was bad for him because no one had seen him nor did anyone know the extent of his injuries. A lot of speculations surrounded him, but he'd soon put all of that to rest.

CD didn't care what the cost was. He had the hospital in Virginia transfer him to a hospital in Brooklyn. CD was not going to miss Danny's wake.

He held true to his word. On the day of Danny's wake, with all of Brooklyn and plenty of people from out of town in attendance, CD showed up. People couldn't believe their eyes.

CD walked into the funeral with the help of two people. His body was very weak. It had only been days since the accident. He snuck out of the hospital to pay his respects. CD had an operation on his neck days prior. He wore a head and neck brace and had two bolts screwed into his forehead. Not only did it pain me that my partner was dead, but it pained me even more that I couldn't be there to see him off. In some ways, It felt better not to see him like that, because my thoughts still hold to this day of his life and not his death.

I was held on Rikers Island, under heavy security. I started in C-95 CMC in the same unit as P-man and Freeze from Queens. I was then transferred after stabbing another inmate, to HDM /MAX B where they held the infamous Fat Cat from Queens. Kool Rock from Marcy Projects and Pappy Mason's nephew Meatball were there as well. There was only about six of us in total on the floor. Puerto Rican Hound Dog was housed upstairs from us. Under us was the Max-A unit, where one person was held, Larry Davis.

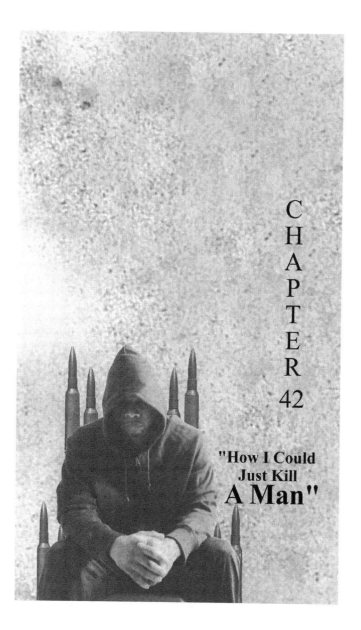

C
H
A
P
T
E
R
42

"How I Could
Just Kill
A Man"

The day of the murder trial was here. So much was going through my mind. It seemed like the odds were stacked against us. An acquittal seemed out of the picture. Everyone from Bush, Nook, Pike, Sid and Mark Spark were placed in the same bullpen as Manny, J-Rock and myself. We all had one thing in common, murder charges.

Manny, J-Rock and I were called to start trial. We knew things could go one way or the other. We felt that our lives were on the chopping block. Juries of our "peers" were to decide our fate, but we didn't see one person that came remotely close to being one of our peers. In regards to that fact, the cards were dealt and we had to play out the hand.

Going to trial felt like a main event and we were the underdogs. There were nine witnesses and only three were in our defense. The one advantage I had on my side was having the best lawyer and legal team that my money could buy, Robert Siegel/ esq.

It took ten-months to come to this day. Everyone was in attendance besides one person who chose not to come, my brother. We weren't on good terms, due to a difference of opinions regarding my actions. He didn't like the approach I took, so he kept his distance from me.

I felt no matter the issue, he should have put it

aside and showed face. This was the crossroad between my freedom and spending the rest of my life in prison. Desperate times called for desperate measures. I told my mom, *"Tell my brother I said thank you for not finding time to attend my wake. Maybe he'll find time to come to my funeral when I get sentenced."*

I almost wish I didn't say that, but I knew if anyone could get to him it was my mom. I saw the pain in her eyes as soon as the words left my mouth. She knew she raised us better than that. Times like this, family needed to set aside any quarrels and come together. The situation I was in was much bigger than either one of us. It's never good for siblings to become rivals. Those in the middle feel the hurt, often times more than the ones who are bickering.

The previous version of the Panamanian murders you read above was the best story the prosecutor could conjure up from her imagination and self claimed investigation. She depicted that version of events in her opening arguments for my trial. She attempted to paint a gruesome picture for a sole purpose. She wanted to plant a seed in the minds of the jurors. She wanted them to know that we were a very dangerous group of young men. She plead for justice and expressed that we should receive the maximum penalty, life in prison without the possibility of parole.

The prosecutor wasted no time. As soon as the first witness got on the stand to testify, she asked them to identify the killers in the courtroom. They concurred by pointing out the three of us sitting at the table with our lawyers. Someone in the audience screamed out a death threat to the witness. The court erupted. The judge banged down on his gavel and demanded order in his courtroom.

Once things came to a calm, the prosecutor continued with their witness. All of a sudden, the doors to the already crowded courtroom swung open and my brother walked in with two of his boys. He sat next to our mother, but I directed him to sit across from the witness stand. Since he was there, I wanted him to have the best seat in the room. If for nothing else, my brother's presence made a lot of the witnesses very nervous. They still tried to get me convicted, but it was very uncomfortable for them to do so.

It seemed like things weren't looking too good for the prosecutor. Prior to trial, I hired a private investigator. I gave him most of the names of the witnesses that were testifying against me. I attained this important information when I received my DD5 discovery documents from the courts.

This information was key. It was one of the many turns in my favor. It was one hell of a battle though.

Every round was close. Most of the witnesses had inconsistencies in their statements. They told one version at the precinct, another with my private investigator and now a third in court. This depleted the credibility of their testimonies.

The prosecutor had some tricks up her sleeve and came up with a surprise witness. He was a recovering crack head. I couldn't believe this shit! A fucking crack head had my fate in his hands. I only saw this dude twice in my entire life! Once in the streets when he was scamming rent-a-cars and the second time was when he was working in the law library in HDM. He was in on a violation.

When I ran into this dude in the law library we made small talk about my case. I didn't go into any details. I told him that I had a witness who could verify my whereabouts. This would prove that I didn't murder who they said I did. I thought nothing else of that conversation, until my lawyer Mr. Siegel asked me did I know an inmate in HDM named Charlie Vee. It didn't hit me at first and then I realized who he was talking about.

My ears didn't seem to serve me well. He told me this dude Charlie Vee contacted the prosecutor and told her I confessed to him. Charlie Vee said that I told him that I committed the murder. WOW!

My lawyer told me, "*If this guy takes the stand and testifies, it won't look good for you.*" He kept asking me questions about the guy. I didn't know much, other than him being a crack head that came to the hood to get rent-a-cars in his name for the homies. I also knew that he was from the Bronx. That's all I knew of him.

I didn't sleep well that night. The next morning, when I walked into the courtroom my mind was focused on this dude and the lies he was about to tell. Up until that morning, the prosecutor acknowledged, but never commented on my attire. I wore a different suit every day of the trial. She said, "*Nice suit, Is that Armani?*" I said, "*Thank you and yes it is*". I knew she was being sarcastic. She felt that she had trumped us with her new witness.

My lawyer must've been reading my mind. He attempted to ease my conscience a little. He said, "*Don't worry kid, I been up in the Bronx doing a lot of research on this Charlie Vee guy. He's a very interesting character, but don't worry, that's what I'm here for* ".

Although there were quite a few people who took the stand against us, I had a bad feeling about this Charlie Vee guy and my intuitions were clear and precise. The prosecutor felt this witness would some how put the nail in my coffin. The questions she asked made him seem very factual. Even worse, he had the jury seemingly convinced.

I felt crushed, but my lawyer kept trying to convince me otherwise. He told me that things weren't as bad as they appeared. Aside from that, we were about to present our rebuttal against the witness. I felt much more comfortable when my lawyer spoke with Manny and J-Rock's lawyers. Their lawyers decided that they would only ask basic questions then let my lawyer take over.

My lawyer started questioning Charlie Vee and I couldn't believe what I was hearing. The questions he asked were making this guy look even better. Even I was impressed by Charlie's imagination. They were having mutual dialogue as if they were long lost buddies. My lawyer had the nerve to come back to the table to ask me...

"How am I doing Kid?"

"What are you doing? You're making this guy look good!"

"I know. That's my point. Don't worry. I got this. Oh yeah, by the way, I like that suit. When you get home, you have to buy me a few of those."

As he walked away, my lawyer smiled with confidence. He was playing this guy. He was making him feel comfortable enough to put his head in the lion's mouth. Soon enough, the lion would catch this guy right between his teeth.

Siegel knew this guy worked in the HDM Law Library as an inmate clerk. Siegel made small talk about the law and he respond as if he was some type of lawyer himself. Siegel got him so comfortable that he never saw it coming. It was like a Monet, a work of art.

To everyone's surprise, when Siegel asked him about a prior murder case he was involved in back in 1979, this guy blatantly stated...

"Yeah I killed him! And I'll kill 'em again if he came back to life!"

"What happened?"

"The motherfucker tried to rob me! I ran to my car, got a tire iron from my trunk and I beat him with it!"

"Oh really. I can understand how you would feel under those sorts of conditions. You felt you were defending yourself I'm sure"

"You got damn right I was!"

"Sorry to have made you so upset in asking that question, but let me ask you another question, if you don't mind me. Did you

have a license to carry a weapon in 1979?"

"Yes I did. I was in the service around that time fighting for my country!"

"I see. I understand, but where I got lost at was when I read your criminal record. It stated that you were arrested for a weapon soon after you were released, awaiting the trial for murder. Out of curiosity. Where did you get that weapon from?"

"I took it from the deceased. He pulled a gun out on me and I took it from him."

"I want to be clear on this, this is the same gun you were arrested with and around the same time you had a permit to carry a weapon? See what I don't understand is, why would you get arrested for carrying a weapon when you were licensed to carry? Don't worry, no need to answer that. I will assume that you can explain just about everything about yourself, but to be honest we are not here for you today. We're here regarding these three young men today. Do you recognize any of the three young men, for the record?"

"Yes I do. That's Manny, that's Jeff and that's Calvin Klein. I know all three of them. Calvin is sitting there trying to look all innocent. (Looking at the jurors) Don't be fooled by the baby face, Calvin has killed plenty more times than this."

"Your Honor, I object! Your honor, if there is anything else in

regards to my client's past, it has no relevance to what he stands trial for today. I request that that statement be stricken from the record."

The judge chimed in...

"All counsels come to my desk now!"

Siegel had me walk up there with him. He said I had the right to do so. (Seconds later the judge spoke).

"I will advise the jurors to disregard that last statement, but there are grounds for a mistrial if anyone so chooses, say so now."

Siegel interjected...

"No your honor, I speak for all counsel and by no means do we want a mistrial."

"Okay, so be it. Okay, ladies and gentlemen of the jury, I am making it clear to you that you are directed not to take in any of this witness's last statement. As counsel Siegel stated, his client is only here for the charges before you. Mr. Siegel, you may continue."

"Thank you your honor. Now back to you Mr. Vee. I have only a few more standard questions then you can go. I know you've been sitting on that stand for awhile."

"Yes it has been a while."

"I understand. Okay, I probably could answer this question for you being that you seem to be a man of a sound mind, but have you ever had any type of nervous break downs recently or any time in your past?"

"Oh no, not me, never that."

"Oh, Ok. Now, have you ever been addicted to drugs at any point in your life?"

"I've used drugs at some points in my life, but never addicted."

"Oh really."

Siegel paused for a moment. He then took a paper from his files, looked at me and said...

"He just fed the lion."

Siegel then proceeded to walk to the court officer and handed him a letter, which was passed to the judge to review and document into evidence. Siegel asked that the court officer pass the letter to Mr. Vee as well for confirmation.

"Mr. Vee, can you confirm for us on record that the letter you are currently holding was written by you? You wrote this letter to your sentencing judge for the murder charge you faced in

1979. You stated that you were having a nervous break down and you were asking the judge to release you on bond due to your health. You lied to the judge then and your lying to the judge now!"

"No I'm not! They did kill that man!"

"No, we've heard enough. These young men have a life to live. You for your selfish reasons are up here trying to get a deal with the prosecutor to go home at the expense of their freedom.

"That's not true just let me explain!"

"We don't need you to. You had your turn. You lied to the judge then and you're lying to the judge now! You told us you were never addicted to drugs. You lied to the judge then and you're lying to the judge now!"

The judge spoke…

"Mr. Siegel, say no more, I heard enough. Step off of my stand Mr. Vee."

"But your honor, I can explain"

"You've said more than enough, now step off of my stand".

Looking into the eyes of the jury the judge said…

"Ladies and gentlemen, I want you to disregard any and

everything this man has said. His testimony will be stricken from the record in its entirety. Like Mr. Siegel has stated, this is a very serious crime these young men are facing. The decision you make will determine their fate."

After the jury was redirected to follow the new instructions, all the defense lawyers and the prosecutor went in front of the judge. Siegel told me to come stand up there with him as the judge spoke of some major concerns. The judge wanted to know if anyone had any concerns regarding a mistrial due to Mr. Vee's testimony.

All of the lawyers were in favor of moving forward and refused a mistrial. Even Manny, Jeff and myself were feeling pretty good about the chance of an acquittal, but deep in the back of our minds we had second thoughts. As soon as the prosecution rested their case, our lawyers went into overdrive. It literally took just two defense witnesses to counter all of the prosecutor's case.

All sides made their points, then Manny, Jeff and myself had to go back down stairs to the holding cells to await the deliberations. Forty-five minutes later our names were called. The jury had some questions about me that they were still unclear of. They were curious as to my actual whereabouts when the murder occurred.

We all went back into the courtroom to clear up their concerns and then we were escorted back to the holding cells. A little more than an hour passed and then our names were called again. The verdict was in. Our nerves were all over the place. I remember all the guys that were in the holding pen awaiting their cases. Derrick Bush, Sid, Mark Spark, Nook and Pike were all telling us that it was a good sign to be called early.

In any event, our moment of truth had come. We stood before the judge and jury. It felt like we were standing before a firing squad, waiting for the trigger to be pulled. I was holding my breath thinking it was going to be my last.

The prosecutor seemed more interested in my verdict and asked the courts to read mine first. The judge refused that request and had the verdicts read in the order of the arrests. Manny's was read off first and he was found not guilty of all charges. I was beyond happy to hear that. The crowd in the courtroom erupted. They were more than satisfied with that verdict.

The crowd followed with the same response when Jeff's not guilty verdict was read. The juror read my name off, and then he took a deep breath before continuing. Not guilty! The courtroom exploded for the third time, but they went to another level this time. It was so loud in there, no one heard the judge hammering the gavel or calling order in the court. It took a few minutes before control was regained back in the courtroom.

There was so much commotion that no one realized that the juror didn't finish reading my verdict. He said that I was not guilty for the two counts of murder. He then followed up by saying I was also not guilty of the five counts of possession of weapons. Siegel turned around to face me as I gave him a hug. He said, *"Kid, this was a close call. You got your life back, now keep it."*

Manny and Jeff walked out of the courtroom. I had another case and had to go back to the Island. My brother came and immediately posted my bail. Finally a free man! One would think that I learned my lesson after such a close call. They thought wrong.

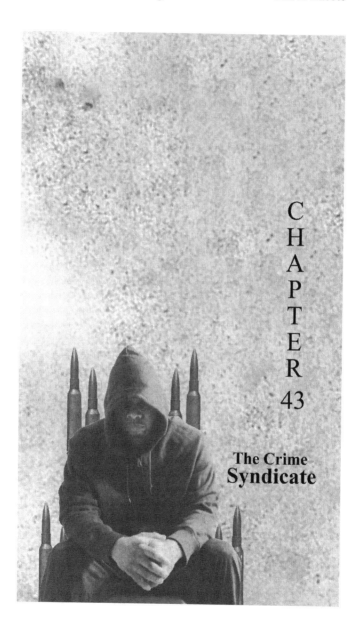

CHAPTER 43

The Crime
Syndicate

It was the first day of my release and I was on a mission to get my weight back up. Danny died and I felt tremendous pressure, like the whole borough was watching me. They wanted to see if I would be able to function the same without my partner. That fueled me to turn my game all the way up to another level.

It wasn't so much about the money or the power for me. Things weren't the same with him not around, but I moved forward not wanting to disappoint him. At that point I was an empty shell. I really didn't want to be in the game anymore. I only stayed because I too wanted to see if I could do it without him. I had a point to prove to myself.

There were two major problems starting out. One I was broke and two I had no connect. That all changed in a day. The first thing I did was move to St. James Pl. and Fulton St. This was the same block Biggie Smalls and Jr. Mafia grew up on.

1989 was the start of a new dynasty. I linked up with my man who linked me up with his connect. I was moving so fast within my first days home that I didn't know what to expect. Danny's fortune had surprisingly disappeared. The only thing left was our list of IOU's.

I inherited the list and it was worth major figures. I rounded up my crew and we ran through Brooklyn like tax collectors. I got back a good portion of what was owed with no resistance. I put those that owed on a payment plan. They had to give me most of their profit each time they re'd up, until their debts were paid in full.

My profit was almost one hundred percent for at least two weeks. That gave me way more than enough room to get my weight back up. The neighborhoods were under siege once again. I held a meeting in my hood at the Red-Hook pool. Not only did every one from the hood show up, but Ty Ty, Conan, the Marcy homies, the BK homies and the Queens homies came through to show support.

It was a rally of some sort. I laid down the laws of the hood and dared any one to violate them. Some were happy that I was home, while others weren't and I knew it. It gave me that much more of a reason to push my power around.

After a while things were as if Danny was still alive. I wanted to let people at least feel his presence through me. I went hard on some dudes. I felt those on the list disrespected us. They weren't going to pay their debts until I came around to collect. Many thought that since Danny was dead and I wasn't coming home from the murder case that they would just keep what wasn't theirs. If you know you owe, don't pretend to mourn on one side while celebrating on the other.

I didn't change much from when Danny and I first started. I kept Red-Hook and Marcy together. That was where most of my strength on the streets came from. I linked up with Dehaven and Jay-Z not long after my release in 1989. That's when I decided to pull them into my team. We already established somewhat of a rapport a few years past. It was an automatic go, no questions asked. Dehaven saw that I still had my weight up after Danny's passing.

He saw me talking to his connect one day. He was shocked when he found out that I was his connect's connect. Dehaven made his move right then and there and shut his line down. At that moment, he started dealing with me directly. He cut the middleman out and that's when him and Jay started seeing some real major money. They were going OT on a mission. They knew they were in a major circle at this point. The game changed for them. When you have a connect that can keep your flow consistent. There's no ceiling. The sky is the limit.

They were my out of towners. They went hard burning up the road. I had teams coming and going in all directions, New York, New Jersey, Connecticut, North Carolina, DC and Maryland. Dehaven took his team from Marcy on the road with him. He had a strong force of selected individuals that would hold court on the streets and protect the team under any condition, especially Moets. Moets's presence and bully styled tactics caused some friction among them, but they all stood tall against the odds and kept it New York. They knew it was key to stick together when they were out of town.

Around this time, Big Daddy Kane was holding Brooklyn down strong in the rap game. I was cool with him and Biz Markie. We hung out often. I went to their shows with my dude Hawk, who was part of Kane's camp. The girls were always heavy in attendance.

This was around the time Jazz-O was trying to spread his wings in the music industry with the homie Jay-Z. Jay had a gift that was way before his time. Time had to catch up to him. He was just too great for his own good. He gave me a demo of him, Big Daddy Kane and Jazz-O. They recorded it in a basement studio. It was a short session but it was a platinum demo to say the least. The way Jay delivered in that session was phenomenal. He had so much poise it was like he was a vet. He had no fear in laying a verse down with Kane and Jazz.

I was chilling up in Harlem one day and bumped into KRS1 outside a club. Biz Markie was performing that night. I pulled up out front in my 535 BMW banging the demo through my system. KRS and Biz started talking about it as soon as they heard it. KRS asked me, *"Who was the last kid that was rapping on that track?"* Biz knew who Jay was but KRS didn't and he was highly impressed with his style and delivery.

I'll be honest, if that demo came out on this very day, it would have been a number one single. It would've shut down the number one rap single out to date. That's how hot it was. That was the best verse I ever heard from Jay's mouth. It was timeless.

I played that demo the entire summer of '89. I remember my cousin Tiz from Woodside, Queens took the cd from my car. I went on a manhunt trying to find it. Out of curiosity, I called and asked him if he had my cd. He said he did, and begged me to let him hold it until the next day, so he could make a copy. I went to Queens that night to get my cd. I gave him a copy the next day. I damn near made and gave away a million copies that summer. I was promoting and stamping Jay as being official.

Biggie Smalls use to be on the corner of Fulton St. and Washington Ave. hustling and hanging out with his boys. I would see Big all the time since I moved in the area. Un Rivera had a record store a few blocks down and I would always run into BIG and the Junior Mafia there as well.

One day to my surprise, while on my way to the

bodega on Fulton and Washington, I saw a small cypher around the kid Big. Not in a million years would I have thought to see or hear this kid rap the way he did. I judged him off of appearance, most people did. He was a secret weapon. He was unexpected.

I can assure you, me playing that Jay-Z demo on Saint James St. all the time had some type of influence on Big. Jay was on my team so I was a bit biased. Un and I had a few conversations back then regarding who was the better of the two. I'd big up Jay and he'd big up Big. Un invited me to bring Jay to his record store for a battle with Big. If time permitted I would have, but at that time we were going so hard hustling on the streets, in and out of town. It was impossible.

Around this time the drug and music games merged, each feeding off the other. I remember having a meeting with Biz Markie, Jazz-O and Jay. Biz and Jazz wanted to launch a record label and have Jay as their first artist. They wanted me to fund them a budget. We had various talks during that summer. We planned to resume talks later. Due to my legal issues, I was somewhat reluctant to put that type of money into a new project not knowing the fate of my freedom.

1989, I was at the height of my drug career. Life couldn't have been better. I bought my first house in

Brooklyn with my girlfriend Karen. We were spending countless amounts of money on cars, clothes jewelry and anything else we desired. I felt I had so much money I stopped counting it.

Every store I shopped in, I would buy their stock out. I bought everything in my size from head to toe. No matter what it was, I never wore the same thing twice. From the best stores to the best boosters, whoever had it, I bought it.

I partnered up with a store in Brooklyn on Atlantic Ave. and State St. called Pro Line Sporting Goods. Manny, Lionel and myself went there to shop one day. We told them to bring us everything they had in our sizes, from head to toe. Shocked at our request, they asked us how we were paying. We looked at each other and started laughing. We took out our money and dropped it on the counter. I dropped close to $20,000 and they dropped $10,000 each. I told the lady at the counter *"If that's not enough let us know"* and walked away.

We had their full attention. They locked the front door and then called the owner of the store. Minutes later the owner came and introduced himself. After about an hour of talking business, I assured him that I would have all his stock bought out every month, even if I had to buy all of it myself.

I had one condition. He had to let me buy into his company. We followed up with another meeting that weekend and we brokered a deal. I was in control of the entire stores inventory. I dealt directly with the representatives of Nike, Timberland, Sergio Tacchini and all the other major outlets.

Upholding my part of the deal was easy. Aside from ordering for myself, I took in orders from all of the crews in Brooklyn and Queens. This was far more than enough to meet my quota each month.

Just when you think all is good. Just when you think you've seen and read all the signs around you. You miss that one sign telling you to slow down, there's a bump ahead. You cant slow down quick enough because you're moving too fast. Point in case for me. I was moving at lightening speed. I felt the need to fall back some, at least for a few days.

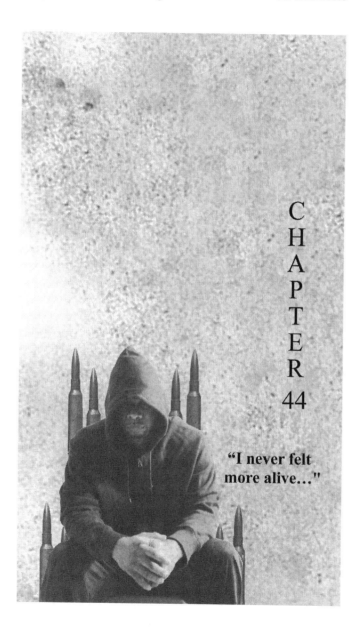

C
H
A
P
T
E
R
44

"I never felt more alive…"

An opportunity presented itself when Moets said he was going to Maryland. I told him I would go with him. I pulled out my green 535 BMW and we hit the road. As soon as we got to Maryland I made a stop in Landover to take care of some business. We stayed a few hours, and then we were back on the road. When we were about ten minutes away from our destination we got pulled over by the highway patrol.

It was after 8 p.m. and it was dark on the side of the road. I showed a valid license and insurance and the highway patrolman still made us get out of the car. He called for back up and went into a full search of the vehicle.

The only reason he did all of this was because we were young, black and in a nice car with New York plates. It got even worse. They took everything out of the trunk and opened up a Nike sneaker box containing $9,000 in cash.

I had $5,000 more in my pocket and Moets had about $5,000 in his. He called for the K9 unit to come on the scene after that. At that point, Moets wanted to run. I told him not to. I asked the officer to go through my wallet for my bank information. It would vouch for the money we had. He didn't want to hear that. He waited for the dogs. He swore he was going to find some drugs in my car and prove he had drug money in his possession.

I went on a rampage after that. I threatened him with a lawsuit. I said I had the best lawyers money could buy and that he was making the worse mistake of his career. I told him that I would have his job once I filed my harassment and racial profiling suits.

By the time the dogs arrived, he started having second thoughts. I told him, *"When they finish sniffing my money, let them sniff yours. We all got dirty money if you ask me"*. The dogs went in a frenzy when they came near our money, as expected. The officer's back up patted him on the back like he was certain of an arrest, but the officer still had second thoughts. The officer took his own money from his pocket and put it on the floor. The dogs sniffed it and had the same reaction.

I told the officer, *"I take it that you're a drug dealer too"*. He saw my point and confiscated the $9,000 in the box and $1,000 of my pocket money. He then gave me a receipt. He gave us the remaining $9,000 and told us we were free to leave.

We left, but I was mad as a motherfucker. Freedom was more important to me, so we kept it moving. You can't make up a loss, so I just wrote it off. I knew why he collected $10,000. If I went back to claim that money, I would have to prove where it came from not only to them, but to the IRS as well.

As soon as we got into town, we went straight to the car wash, then to a hotel to check in. We went to the spot were the team was set up and chilled for a few to take care of business. I ended leaving out with about $100k. Moets and I went back to the hotel, then out on the block.

I saw Jay and we shook hands. He was surprised to see me because I never came out there before. He asked me if I was coming out to the party later that night. Everyone knew I wasn't the partying type, but I was out of town and wanted to chill with the team. I told him I would be there.

Later that night, Moets and I pulled up to the party in my BMW. It had 17inch Pirelli tires with chrome Schnitzer rims. Kid Capri's mix tape was pumping out of the 6.000-watt precision power amps. Dehaven and some of the homies pulled up on motorcycles. I didn't see what Jay was pushing because he was already inside.

The party was packed. New York was about ten strong in the building. Moets and I went inside. We saw Dehaven, Jay, Righteous and the homie Emory from Maryland chilin' in the cut. Moets and I started walking through the crowd embracing some of the NY homies as we passed.

The crowd was packed heavy in the building. Jay strong armed the booth and took the mic. He turned the spot into a Brooklyn party. He started shouting all of our names out in his rhyme. He yelled out, *"Brooklyn's in the building!"* It didn't take long before we became the center of attention. The females were flocking all over us. As I was talking to one female, some dude walked past bumping into me.

I grabbed him by the arm and asked *"We know each other from somewhere?"* He looked at me and said, *"Why, do we?"* Enough said; I was on my Brooklyn bullshit. I passed the word for all the Brooklyn homies to meet outside. One of the homies whispered in Jay's ear and he put the mic down. It was obvious to all of the partygoers that something was wrong. We were all outta there. Everything at that point happened so fast.

Every one of us was ready for battle that night. We knew the odds were against us, but we were all posted up, ready for war. It didn't take long for the battle to begin. Dehaven set it off. He stood on the side of the door. When one of the dudes came out, he hit him straight in the face with his helmet. All hell broke loose after that.

It was only ten of us going back-to-back, trying to fight off about three hundred people. Fist, sticks, helmets, knives and razors were swinging everywhere.

Bones were broken and blood was all over the place. All of us got away except for Righteous. To be on the safe side, we went to the next town. It wasn't long before we got there that I was ready to go back to N.Y. I didn't want to stay out there any longer than I had to.

Moets kept arguing with me about staying. I told him I was leaving. I told him to bring the money back with him and I'll see him in the morning. Jay told me, *"I don't think it's a good idea for you to leave now like Moets is telling you, but if you're going back to N.Y. I'll ride with you so you don't have to go by yourself."* That's all I needed to hear. Jay got in the car and we were outta there. I was glad Jay came with me. He knew how to get back home from where we were. I wasn't familiar with the area.

We weren't far into the ride before we started talking about the main event of the evening. As we played everything out, we started laughing. We agreed on how close a call that was, since the odds were so overwhelmingly stacked against us.

We drove down the highway, nearing the location of the incident. The fight was no more than two hours prior. I couldn't believe we had to actually drive past the scene of the crime in order to get home. Jay said, *"This is the only highway that will take us back to New York from where we are"*. Within seconds, Jay told me,

"Look over to your right." We drove right past the club. It was deserted. No one was in sight.

It seemed as if our thoughts were intertwined. We asked simultaneously, *"Where is Righteous?"* This was the topic of conversation when we all left because no one saw where he went. I told Moets to call me if he heard anything from him. A few hours passed and there was still no word of his whereabouts. This warranted some major concern.

We continued driving up the road. We were making small talk about the hustle life, Jay's music interest and other things. Neither one of us took notice, until it was too late. The police came out of nowhere and crept up behind us.

The thought of a police chase ran across my mind for a second. I didn't voluntarily stop, I kept it moving with them trailing behind us, but I stayed within the speed limits. I was trying not to give them an obvious reason to stop us, but they made their move anyway.

The cop car pulled into the next lane and sped past us. They got in front of us and started gradually slowing down until we came to a complete stop. By this time, another patrol car pulled up behind us. Within seconds, we had The State of Maryland Highway Patrol surrounding all sides of the car.

They screamed out for me to cut the car off. They then proceeded to pull us out of the car. They claimed my car was identified in an incident at a club earlier that evening. Obviously we denied any involvement, but they weren't hearing it.

They left my car on the side of the highway and then transported us to the hospital. It seemed like everyone from the party was up in there. We sat in the back of the patrol car handcuffed, while the officers brought out at least six people to identify us.

How coincidental was it that the first person they brought to the car was Righteous! He was acting like he was a victim. He walked up to the car, with a broken arm. He winked his eye at us, and then told the officer that he never saw us before.

The guy that bumped me in the club, walked up to the car next. He had stitches on both sides of his face. He looked at me and said *"See you on the streets"*. The next guy to approach the car was his brother. He walked up to the car, and said *"Yeah! That's them! He's the one who cut me and he's the one that was swinging the stick!"* Game over, Jay and I were officially arrested.

We were transported back to the precinct to be processed. We were read our rights and were told we were being charged with attempt murder, attempt murder to maim, battery, assault and possession of a deadly weapon. They came at us with those trumped up charges because we were from New York. New Yorkers had a reputation for being troublemakers and weren't highly favored by judiciaries in other states.

If you got caught, you were made an example out of. They wanted to show others what would happen if you committed a crime in their town. Most small town people had a certain disdain for big city folk. With not much hope left for Jay or myself, I made a last ditch effort to save our freedom.

We sat in the holding cell, while the officer prepared to fingerprint us. I was determined to mess with the plaintiff's mind. I attempted to have some dialogue with him. I did all I could to convince him that this was just some big misunderstanding. I told him that it could be resolved another way. He sat in the chair, waiting for the officer to return and then blurted out...

"Ya better not think about going to trial. I'm going all the way with this. Ya were wrong for what ya did. Ya gonna pay and go to jail for a long time."

I said...

"Come on man, you don't have to do it like this. Sending us to

jail won't help you or your family get through this. It'll cost us at least $50,000 in lawyer fees. I'd rather give that to you if you don't follow through with pressing charges on us. That should cover any emotional damages right?"

"Naw man. One of ya gotta go to jail! Whose car is that you was driving?"
"It's yours if you want it. Just drop the charges"

Jay and I looked at this fool like he was crazy. I was finally able to persuade him to drop the charges on at least one of us. To my surprise, Jay stood tall. He said he would take the weight for the case. He knew I had just got acquitted for the murder case months prior. He told me, *"Klein, I got this one. Go get the lawyer Siegel and come bail me out tonight".* There was no way I could have predicted my future at that moment, but I felt Jay had a promising future in the rap game. If he took the fall he wouldn't be able to pursue the talent God had given him.

We spoke a few minutes longer before the decision was made. As agreed, the dude dropped the charges and Jay was released. Jay went back to New York and immediately contacted my family. He made sure that arrangements were made for my $50,000 bail to be posted that night. Four hours after being fingerprinted I was released. A few hours later, I was back in New York. The attention turned up to another level.

Things went back to normal. I was living the high life vacationing, attending Broadway shows and splurging on any and everything I wanted. Those eighteen months came and went. '89 and '90 were moments of the past. When things are going great, time tends to pass by so much faster. My new reality was facing the trial for the Maryland case.

I was facing a lot of time on this case, and I had some real concerns going in. I was from New York and had a bad criminal record. There were so many witnesses against me. The only ones I had to testify in my defense were Righteous and Jay.

Jay was scheduled to go to Europe on tour with Jazz-O the day of my trial, which was detrimental to my case. Jay spoke with my lawyer before leaving. They made arrangements for Jay to be available the day of my trial. Jay faxed over his testimony to the judge's chambers. After all was said and done, I blew trial. I was less disappointed than the prosecutor. I didn't get the forty years the prosecutor was aiming for. I received four years instead.

IN THE CIRCUIT COURT FOR TALBOT COUNTY, MARYLAND

- - - - - - - - - - -x

STATE OF MARYLAND   :

    vs.   :   Criminal No. 4465

CALVIN D. BACOTE   :

- - - - - - - - - - -x

                                Circuit Courtroom
                                Courthouse
                                Easton, Maryland

                                Monday, August 27, 1990

    The above-entitled matter came on to be heard as a jury trial at 9:01 o'clock a.m.

BEFORE:

    THE HONORABLE WILLIAM S. HORNE, Judge

APPEARANCES:

    On behalf of the State:

        MARIE ELISE HILL, ATTORNEY-AT-LAW
        Deputy State's Attorney for Talbot County, Maryland
        Courthouse
        Easton, Maryland 21601

    On behalf of the Defendant:

        JO ANN D. ASPARAGUS, ATTORNEY-AT-LAW
        P. O. Box 2028
        Easton, Maryland 21601-2028

```
 1              MS. ASPARAGUS:  Okay.

 2              BY MS. ASPARAGUS:

 3       Q    Were you able to determine why Mr. Bacote and the

 4    other gentleman -- I believe his name was Sean Carter -- were

 5    here?

 6       A    Um, they were at the party, that's the only thing

 7    that I was able to find, that they were at the party at the

 8    arena.

 9       Q    Okay.  Were you able to determine where they were

10    staying?

11       A    One of them, uh, I believe he  said they were

12    staying at The Greens, here in Easton.

13       Q    Okay.  And where would that be?

14       A    Be on North Washington Street, in Easton -- or

15    correction, South Washington Street.

16       Q    Could you -- were you able to determine if they were

17    related to anyone?

18       A    No, ma'am.

19       Q    Okay.  So after you talked to Sean Carter, took him

20    to the hospital --

21       A    Um-hum.

22       Q    -- then he was released, and out.

23       A    Yes, ma'am.

24       Q    Okay.  And during the course of your investigation,

25    were you able to determine if there were ever any more than

                              59
```

1 identification for me. The doctor said he could. I brought

2 the victim out to the car. The victim looked at the

3 defendant. He said, "That's the one who cut me, and he

4 had the stick." He pointed to Mr. Bacote as the one who had

5 cut him, and the gentleman, the other suspect that was with

6 him, as the one who had a stick.

7   MS. HILL: I have no further questions at this

8 point.

9   THE COURT: Mrs. Asparagus.

10   CROSS-EXAMINATION

11   BY MS. ASPARAGUS:

12   Q Detective Green, in Detective, or Deputy Ross's

13 statement he quotes Mrs. Guy as saying a car-full of boys

14 from New York arrived. Is that your recollection of the

15 conversation with her?

16   A Mrs. Guy said that it was a BMW with New York tags,

17 some boys from New York in a BMW.

18   Q Okay. More specifically, did she say New York or

19 New Jersey?

20   A She said New York or New Jersey, one --

21   Q Okay. And she also said that it was a silver BMW,

22 is that right?

23   A That's correct.

24   Q And what in fact was the color of this BMW that you

25 stopped Calvin Bacote in?

     74

1   trying to look -- to stop him; I just passed him until I had

2   some assistance.

3   Q   Um-hum. Okay. When you are in a marked or unmarked

4   car following anyone, isn't the normal, or would you say in

5   your experience that people have a tendency to slow down if

6   they think someone's following them?

7   A   Well, if it -- they do do that, if they know someone's

8   behind them.

9   Q   Now, was Mr. Bacote wearing a black and white shirt?

10   A   That's correct.

11   Q   And at that time did you observe any blood stains on

12   his person or any of his clothing?

13   A   No, I did not.

14   Q   Okay. In his hands or anyplace?

15   A   No, I did not observe any blood.

16   Q   When you asked Mr. Bacote to accompany you, accompany

17   you to the hospital, did he in fact agree to go, along with

18   the passenger?

19   A   That's correct, he did.

20   Q   And did you determine what the passenger's name was?

21   A   His name was Sean Carter.

22   Q   Okay.

23   A   Sean Corey Carter, I believe.

24   Q   And did you learn from your investigation why

25   Mr. Carter was in the area?

                              76

1   A   Mr. Carter just advised me that he came down with

2   some friends.

3   Q   Um-hum.

4   A   He said this had been the first time he'd been in

5   the area, he came down with some friends.

6   Q   And what about Mr. Bacote?

7   A   That was his same response, too, they just came down

8   with some friends.

9   Q   All right. And they both advised you that they were

10 unfamiliar with the area.

11   A   Yes.

12   Q   Now, you've indicated that Robert Guy -- it was

13 Robert -- said that Sean had a stick?

14   A   He didn't call him by his name.

15   Q   Right, the other gentleman.

16   A   The other -- the other subject had a stick.

17   Q   Okay. Was he charged with any crime?

18   A   No, he wasn't.

19   Q   Okay. And at the hospital was there any other attempt

20 to identify Mr. Bacote?

21   A   That's correct, it was.

22   Q   And who tried to identify him?

23   A   I had -- it was another subject that had been injured.

24 His name was Richard Gibson. I asked him could he identify

25 either of the persons who he had claimed that had hurt him.

                              77

1   He said no, he could not.

2   Q   Okay.

3   A   I -- I -- he did allow me to bring him out to look

4   at the subject, but he could not identify him.

5   Q   Okay. When you said, "He did," you mean the

6   defendant, Calvin Bacote, went with you to look at the other

7   subjects?

8   A   No.

9   Q   Okay.

10   A   I brought Mister -- Mr. Bacote and Mr. Carter both

11   stayed in the patrol car. I went into the hospital and

12   brought the subjects out.

13   Q   Okay.

14   A   When I brought Mr. Gibson out, he was very reluctant

15   to identify, he said he couldn't identify, he didn't even want

16   to walk up to the car.

17   Q   Okay. So he could not identify.

18   A   He could not identify.

19   Q   All right. And did you also ask Richard Guy?

20   A   Yes. He could not identify him either.

21   Q   Uh --

22   A   Uh --

23   Q   Go ahead.

24   A   Yes, Richard.

25   Q   Okay. And Richard would be the defendant of Robert --

78

1   I mean the brother of Robert.

2   A   Brother.

3   Q   Yes.

4   A   Yes.

5   Q   Okay. So that the only person who said that he

6   recognized the defendant would have been Robert Guy.

7   A   That's correct.

8   Q   Okay.

9   A   The only person that would give me a statement.

10   Q   The only person --

11   MS. ASPARAGUS: Otherwise, I'm moving to strike the

12   balance of that statement as being nonresponsive to the

13   question.

14   THE COURT: Well, re-ask the question. The witness

15   may re-answer it.

16   MS. ASPARAGUS: Okay.

17   BY MS. ASPARAGUS:

18   Q   The only person who identified the defendant was

19   Robert.

20   A   The only person identified him was Robert Guy, yes.

21   Q   Thank you. Now, did you hear Robert Guy say anything

22   to Mr. Bacote when he came to the car?

23   A   No. All I heard was -- I was standing right beside

24   him.

25   Q   Um-hum.

79

A   The only thing I heard him say was that, "You're
the one who cut me, and you're the one with the stick."

Q   Okay. Did Mr. Guy say anything about the automobile
that Mr. Bacote was in, at the car? (Pause.) Did he mention
the car?

A   When I talked to him in the hospital, yes; not when
I brought him out to make the identification.

Q   Okay. About how many people were at the Hog Neck
Arena when you arrived?

A   (Pause.) I would say -- it's just guessing -- I
would say approximately 150 were in the area. There was a
party or something going on.

Q   Were there fights going on when you got there?

A   No, I --

Q   The crowd was dispersing?

A   The crowd was out front, and the -- because the
ambulance was there and people were coming out. I didn't, uh,
witness any fights. I went straight to Mrs. Guy, me and
Sergeant Ross, and talked to her.

Q   Did you notice if there were any scratches or anything on Mr. Bacote?

A   Not that I noticed, no.

Q   Did you assist with the search of Mr. Bacote's car?

A   That's correct, I did.

Q   Was there luggage in there?

80

As a last ditch effort to keep my freedom, I told my lawyer to ask for an appeal bail. She debated with me and told me to be grateful for the end result. Grateful I was, but she was retained by me and I wanted a request for bail. To my surprise the appeal bail was granted. Little did I know; I was released so easily because I was under a federal investigation that was being held in Red-Hook Projects.

It didn't take very long. From the moment I left my house, I was being followed. Most of the time I wouldn't leave the house. I tried to lay low and stay out of the way. I relieved myself from pretty much everything.

I passed the reigns unto my two top lieutenants and told them I was done and out of the game. They made it seem like I just told them I had terminal cancer by their reactions. I only asked for one thing that day. I wanted them to gradually disassociate me from any activities and claim them as their own doings. I didn't want my name on the streets as a drug dealer any more. I was heavily considering taking Biz Markie and Jazz-O up on their offer to fund them the record label money.

Christmas of 1990 was the best ever. I played Santa to everyone. I spent over $250,000 on my family and friends. I was showing my appreciation, as I made myself believe I was bowing out of the game for good. I had all I wanted and needed and had no desire to further my hustle in the drug trade.

Danny's death among many other things ran its course in my mind and heart. I had enough and reached the end of the road. I thanked all of the people who stood by my side while I was out on those streets risking my life and theirs as well. What I hoped to be happier times would be short lived. The roller coaster ride had come to an end.

I didn't realize that I wasn't the one who actually controlled the on and off buttons of my own fate. I had nowhere to run and nowhere to hide. On February 12,1991 the Feds came in hard from every direction and it all ended. They got me!

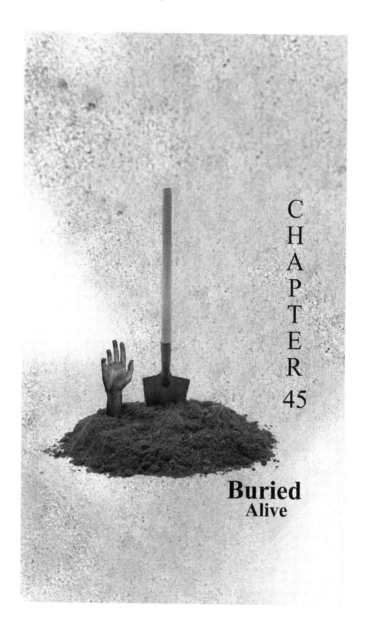

C
H
A
P
T
E
R
45

Buried
Alive

"All rise; As the Honorable Judge Elaine Spielberg enters the courtroom!" Those in attendance, stood up as the judge entered the room and took her seat. The court officer instructed everyone to be seated. Soon after, the judge informed the court officer that she was ready to proceed. The court officer directed the US Marshals to bring out the first case on the docket.

As my brother and I entered the courtroom, the court officer yelled out for all to hear, *"Court is now in session! On November 8, 1991 The UNITED STATES vs. CALVIN BACOTE and KENNETH BACOTE on charges in violation of title 21 U.S.C. Sections 846 and 841 (b)(1)(b)(iii), a class C felony. Today is set for the sentencing of said defendants."*

COURT PROCEEDINGS:

<u>THE COURT</u>: *"All right, we have certain steps that must be gone through before sentence can be imposed under the guidelines. Let me ask you counsel, have you fully reviewed the probation report and had a chance to talk it over with your clients?"*

<u>MR.SIEGEL</u>: *"Yes, I have with my client Calvin Bacote, Your Honor."*

<u>MR.HOROWITZ</u>:*" I have as well with my client Kenneth Bacote, Your Honor."*

THE COURT: *"Are there any facts contained in the report to which you wish to take exception, other than those that have already been addressed by the court?"*

MR.SIEGEL: *"No, Your Honor."*

MR. HOROWITZ: *"No, Your Honor."*

THE COURT: *"I don't believe there are any outstanding legal issues now that we've resolved the question of withdrawal of the guilty plea, is that correct?"*

MR. SIEGEL: *"That's correct Your Honor."*

MR. HOROWITZ: *"Correct, Your Honor."*

THE COURT: *"Is there any dispute as to the probation department's guideline calculation, other than those you've already noted?"*

MR SIEGEL: *"No, Your Honor."*

MR. HOROWITZ: *"No, Your Honor."*

THE COURT: *"All right. For the reasons I've stated in this case, I find that the defendant Calvin Bacote's total offense level is 34 with a criminal history category of 6. The guidelines provide for 262 to 327 month term of incarceration, a 4 to 5 year term of supervised release, a $17,500 to $2,000,000 fine and a $50 order of special assessment. Other than those* *objections noted, any further objections Mr. Siegel?"*

MR. SIEGEL: *"No, Your Honor"*

MR. SHEFFIELD: *"Your Honor, for the record, The Government is taking the position in requesting that both defendants receive the top of what their guidelines require."*

THE COURT: *"All right, noted. Mr. Siegel, if you're prepared to go forward, I'll be happy to hear you as to anything you'd like to say on Calvin Bacote's behalf."*

MR. SIEGEL: *"Yes, my client's a twenty-five year old that has obviously made some very bad choices in his life. He is very much aware of what is at stake here today Your Honor. He can either face the minimum, serving every year that he has lived thus far or the maximum, serving his natural life in prison. We ask that the courts take that into account."*

THE COURT: *"All right, Mr. Bacote, while I cannot speak to the issue in large terms, I do think that the net result of everything in this case results in a very harsh sentence for you, someone who has plead guilty to this crime. Although I feel I may be giving you too much time, 262 months is the least that I will be able to impose to you under the guidelines. As I said, I already think that's too severe."*

MRS. BACOTE: *"Excuse me, Your Honor, I'm Calvin and Kenneth's mother. Did you receive my letters?"*

THE COURT: *"I know who you are Mrs. Bacote and yes I did receive your letters. As a mother, I do understand what you must be going through. I am simply telling you that 262 months is the lowest amount that the law allows me to impose on Calvin. I see no reason to impose anything more on him. It's already a very, very harsh penalty. But I did get your letters. You do have to understand that your children have committed some very serious crimes, Calvin more so."*

MRS. BACOTE: *"But that's my baby!"*

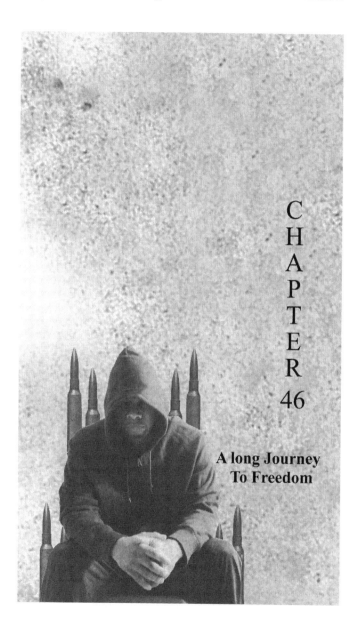

C
H
A
P
T
E
R
46

**A long Journey
To Freedom**

The journey doing federal time in prison was unimaginable to say the least. In an instant I went from being rich in freedom, to being poor in incarceration. My life and the lives of the people I loved were frozen in time. I was sentenced to twenty-five years.

I was in the MCC jail in Manhattan and was transferred on a plane to Laredo, Texas. I felt like I an animal or even worse, a shackled slave. I was transported from one place to the other in chains, sometimes up to twenty hours at a time. After being in Texas, I was transferred to the Terre Haute Indiana Prison. It didn't take long before I settled in. I teamed up with the legendary Boy George, from the Bronx and a group of New York homies.

Although I was in jail, that didn't stop me from picking up on old habits. I started selling drugs on the inside. I was making more money on the inside than the average hustler in the hood. Around this time I had a jailhouse lawyer looking over my case. I gave him over $10,000 to work with my lawyers on the outside. The additional help was worth the money.

The jailhouse lawyer provided research to my outside lawyers in 1992 that would reopen my case in Maryland. He presented such a strong argument that the case was overturned and dismissed. I quickly presented a 2255 motion into the Federal Court. I attached the documents from Maryland showing the courts the dismissal. The Maryland case took off four years from my sentence, leaving me with twenty-one years to serve out. In addition, the Federal Court took off six years from an enhancement for the Maryland case. That left me with fifteen years to do.

I served over thirteen years doing time in various prisons and facilities such as, Terre Haute, Lewisburg, Schuylkill, Farrington NJ, Estill SC, Ray Brook, Fort Dix and Butner NC. Not only did I serve that time, but my family and friends served that time with me. They were serving it when they came to visit me and they served it while awaiting my return.

That day finally came, May 2004, a moment in time I'd never forget. It was a day of rebirth. I was breathing free air once again! I finally got my life back, the start of a new beginning. At least, that's what I believed.

After a thirteen and a half year hiatus, traveling the United States, shackled in chains through different facilities, the worst of my days had come to pass. My release date finally came. The morning of May 14, 2004, I was released from the federal custody of Butner Camp in North Carolina. As happy as I was, I was only released mentally because I was physically transported to a halfway house.

As I opened the front door of the facility, I stepped into the warm embrace of my mom and stepdad. They came to pick me up and take me to the halfway house in South Carolina to serve out my last five months. We were elated and overjoyed that the worst phase of my journey was behind me.

Although my freedom was temporary, I felt ecstatic for the time being. I inhaled a deep breath of that fresh air of freedom and shouted a quote from the late great Martin Luther King Jr., *"Free at last. Free at last. Thank God Almighty, I'm free at last!"* As we drove from North Carolina to South Carolina, it was thrilling to say the least. We laughed, cried and most of all we thanked God for giving me yet another chance. As my mom often said, *"Thank God for Jesus".*

Throughout the years, while in the belly of the beast I've tried to rebuild my mind, body and soul. I wanted to be and do better. I wanted to think well in the decisions and choices I'd make in my renewed life. As we drove down the highway, my eyes took in all the sights, but my mind was wandering. I was busy thinking about what I should and shouldn't expect as a free man. Knowing who I used to be, my peers set the bar very high and expected me to surpass that. This was one of the challenges that I feared the most. Truth be told, I was very nervous and scared. I had the fear of the unexpected weighing heavily on my mind.

I felt like my faith was strong in the Lord, but my thoughts of transgressions often lingered. Everyday I tried to stand steadfast in my faith and take it one day at a time. I was unsure of when and where I would bump into the devil, but I knew that day of reckoning would eventually come.

The devil and I use to be friends. I wondered if he knew I didn't want to be his friend anymore. I made no future plans to conspire with him or his followers in their reckless antics. I'm sure the devil didn't care how I felt one way or the other. He felt we were blood brothers and he was happy to see me. In his mind, we had plans and by no means would he allow me to foil them. He didn't care that I came home and found Jesus as my Lord and Savior. As far as he was concerned I was on some self-proclaimed bullshit.

The devil knew a lot about me. At one point in my life, we were inseparable. I knew he wasn't going to be as forgiving as the Lord. I no longer had blood in my eyes. Everyday I had to keep the devil from believing we were of the same flesh and blood. Only time would tell when our paths would cross again.

My thoughts came back to reality in the car with my mom and stepfather. We had a few hours to waste before I had to go to the halfway house. My mom's house was nearby, so we went home. They wanted me to have the feeling of being home before they dropped me off.

We pulled up into the circular driveway. I stepped out of the car and walked up to the steps of the house. I felt a great sigh of relief knowing that I was home. I walked through the front door and into the foyer. The beauty the house bestowed blew me away. I immediately felt at home. Being around steel bars twenty-four hours a day was a distant memory.

My mom and stepdad took me on a tour of the house and then we went into the dining area. My mom had a home cooked meal prepared for me. I longed for the day to be able to eat my mother's home cooking again. There was so much food on the table it felt like it was Thanksgiving.

We sat down at the table, said grace and proceeded to eat. There was one problem though. I saw pork in some of the food. I said, *"Ma, is that pork in the food?"* She looked at me with the biggest smile of pride on her face. She was finally sitting down having dinner with her baby. My mom said, *"Yes Sweetness,"* her smile fading somewhat. She said, *"Is there a problem?"* My response was very quick. I didn't want my mom to think that I didn't appreciate her efforts, time and hard work in preparing this meal. I began to eat some of everything on the table, enjoying every bit of it. I said, *"No Ma, everything is perfect".*

During dinner, my aunts and other family members stopped by to see me. It felt really good to be in the presence of those I loved. I grew up around this kind of love, but when I was in jail the love often felt distant and lost. There was very little love shown while I was in there. I felt a lot in the beginning, it faded out in the middle and then it came back in the end. I made a vow at the start of my time to try not to have hate or resentment in my heart towards my unsupportive family and friends. If I loved them when I went in, I wanted to love them when I got out. I refused to let the system kill my spirit.

The brief family reunion came to an unfortunate end. I had to get ready to go to the halfway house. My mom had already prepared a room in the house for me. She told me to go in my room and get the two bags of clothes she neatly packed for me. I took the bags, went in the garage and put them in the trunk of the car. I then said my goodbyes to the family. Me, my mom and my stepdad got in the car and were on our way to the halfway house. It was less than a fifteen-minute drive, so we got there quite fast.

We arrived at almost 4p.m. There were a few pre-released inmates sitting out front taking a cigarette break. As I was about to enter the building, I acknowledged them and said, *"What's up?"* I opened the door, walked inside and went up to the receptionist desk to turn myself into the custody of the Florence, South Carolina halfway house program for the next five months. I filled out some paperwork and then I was able to go back to the car to get my bags. Awaiting me was a great big kiss and hug from my mom and a bear hug from my stepdad. We said our final goodbyes for the evening, then I watched them drive off as I walked back inside the building. The day was very draining, but overall it was beautiful.

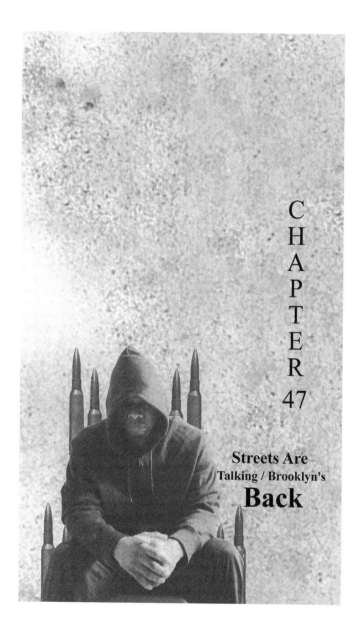

C
H
A
P
T
E
R
47

**Streets Are
Talking / Brooklyn's
Back**

I started to take in my surroundings. The facility was unisex. The rooms were set up in dorms, with lockers that could house up to thirty people. The women slept in separate sleeping quarters, but we all shared the kitchen, eating area, work area and recreational areas. It was short staffed with no more than six staff members during the day and three staff members after 4p.m.

As I started to unpack my property and store my belongings, one of the staff members called out, *"Bacote, you have a phone call!"* I hadn't been in the building a half-hour and I got a phone call already. As I picked up the phone, I wondered who it was. I said, *"Hello?"* The voice on the other end said, *"Welcome home brother!"* I recognized the voice immediately. *"Kev!"* He laughed and said, *"Yeah, welcome home!"* It was Kevin Chiles, the CEO of the infamous street magazine, Don Diva. He is hands down, one of Harlem's renowned greats, a household name in his own right. We became very good friends throughout the years.

Kevin's a very wise man, whose opinion always meant a great deal to me. He was a very knowledgeable man and when he spoke, you listened. Not one to disappoint, he had some very wise words to deliver that day. This advice I carried close to heart. He said, *"I know how scared you may feel and trust me, it's natural. It's a transitional phase that everybody goes through.*

Trust in the experience you've just endured and know that you've grown into being a better you."

He said, *"You went in young and came home much older. You can't have wisdom without acquiring a certain level of knowledge."* He continued by saying, *"Don't count the days lost, make the days to come count. You can't remove your past, so just move forward with the confidence that you are a smart enough hustler to win again, the right way."* He told me to incorporate my hustler's instinct into my legit business ventures and everything would be fine.

What stood out most of all was when he said, *"Don't look for people to do anything for you. The streets are talking and there are plenty of myths, rumors and rhetoric in regards to who is going to want you on their team. The bid for you to be on anyone's team at this point is very high. Your reputation precedes you. This is your moment. The red carpet is rolled out for you and I'm confident that you will walk the walk. Whatever anyone does for you will be a blessing, but don't set yourself up for disappointment in looking for it. It's sad to say, but you have more people expecting you to do for them than you have people wanting to do for you."*

In the closing of our conversation, Kevin made it clear to me that he would be there in any way he could. He said that the streets had the same old scenes, dope fiends, crack fiends and wannabe hustlers.

I placed the phone back on the receiver and went back to my dorm room in deep thought. I was unpacking my things when a few guys came around me to make conversation. We introduced ourselves. Reggie was from Philly and Travis was from South Carolina. I told them I was from New York. It was expected of them to come over to me because I was the new dude there. We fed off of one another's vibes immediately and a bond of respect formed on the spot.

Being that I just got there, I asked them how the system went and how long it would be before I'd be able to go home on a weekend pass. Reggie said, *"Man, if you got money, ain't nothing you can't do while you here. The case manager is on the take and once he get to know who you are and he feels he can trust you, you good."* I guess that was good news to hear. At least I had some leverage and a window of opportunity. I guess these five months wouldn't be that bad after all.

While they continued to bring me up to speed on how things went on in the building, the staff called me again, *"Bacote, you have a phone call."* As I walked to the phone, I heard the staff member sarcastically tell another staff member, *"He got somebody on the phone asking to speak to him, saying their name is Jay-Z".* When I heard her say Jay's name, I picked up the phone suspecting a prank call from someone in my family.

I picked up the phone and said, *"Hello?"* The voice on the other end said, *"What's up? This is Jay, welcome home!"* Surprised I said, *"Who is this?"* I wanted to be sure he was who he said he was. He said, *"Jay, welcome home!"* I said, *"Hahaha, Hov!! What's up? This is a pleasant surprise, thanks for calling man. I knew I'd hear from you at some point, but I didn't think it would be this soon."* He said, *"Yeah man, I just wanted to welcome you home and get it out of the way".* I said, *"I feel you on that".*

Jay made it clear on how he felt about me doing my halfway house time in South Carolina, as opposed to Brooklyn. He said, *"I wouldn't have called you right away if you were in the halfway house in Brooklyn, across the street from the hood. It's crazy how your homecoming is being received on the streets. I've never seen anyone besides 50 Cent and myself who both dropped albums, have such a buzz on the streets like this. I almost wish you were a rapper, hahaha."*

Jay's tone got a little more serious as he continued, *"Klein, I've come a very long way in my career since we've last seen each other and I want to be honest with you. I'm sure you're aware of the situation with Supreme (Supreme team) and Irv (Irv Gotti/Murder Inc.) getting locked up with a federal investigation. I watched that whole situation unfold. Irv is not doing well just from trying to be there for Supreme since he came home from jail. For some reason, I feel this is a similar scenario with you and I. To be honest, it scares me."*

With respect to what Jay just said. I told him, *"I've*

547

heard many rumors in jail and on the streets, in regards to our relations. Whether true or not, I want you to know You Don't Owe Me Nothing!".

When I said that, I heard Jay take in a sigh of relief. I asked...

"Why you sound like that?"

"Klein, you don't understand all that's going on with rumors regarding you and I. To hear you say, I don't owe you nothing makes me feel more at ease."

"Back in the days, in my time, I had the lead in making it happen for the team. I know all the pressure you feel in feeling you have to be responsible for all the lives around you. I been there and you're there now. I'm not gonna stand in your line and wait for you to do anything for me. I'm a hustler!! I'll find my way somehow. I didn't come home like Supreme did, with split thoughts on doing good or bad. I don't want you to categorize his or my fate as being one in the same. Furthermore, although I do see your point in comparison to Supreme and Irv verses you and I, but Supreme came home and did it his way. I'm not a reincarnation of him! I'm not trapped in a maze or stuck in a warp. I took the proper precautions in taking better calculating steps to assure that I don't relapse back into old habits. I'm home now and it's my turn and I'm doing it the right way. I don't owe the streets nothing and the streets don't owe me. All I can ask from anybody including you is for a chance to prove myself and show *that my mind is a lot smarter than the stigma that's on me of being a drug dealer. Give me the benefit of the doubt because I'm more versatile than that. Someone gave you your chance and if you will, give me mine."*

We spoke further, in great length. We laughed, joked and spoke about back in the days. We were about to hang up the phone, when Jay said, *"I wanna help you Klein and I will! I'm gonna make you larger than life! I got you, jut let me figure how I'm gonna work things out and get the things together that I know you need. I'll call you tomorrow to follow up on how you're doing and we'll go from there. Holla!"* His last words, I'll never forget.

After he hung up the phone I sat reflecting, *"Make me larger that life, what did he mean by that?"* When he said that I really didn't understand what he meant by it, but I would've been a fool to debate it and I didn't. There was no reason to doubt the words from Jay himself.

I went back to the dorm thanking God for the blessings that were being bestowed upon me. I wasn't sure what to expect or what was in store for me, but I liked my chances even more now. Jay was taking interest in endorsing me. I've been away from the real world for a very long time and to have some one of his magnitude step up and mentor me back to life, was a wonderful thing. I never was the lazy type and never leaned on anyone. I was certain in my work ethics and the value I held. I knew I would be a key component to anyone's team!

I was hard pressed to get in the work field, roll my sleeves up and put my brains and creativity on the table. I wanted to show the hustlers and corporate America what I was made of! I felt I had a big point to prove and in more ways than one, I did. The first move I made would really determine what circle of people I would attract in the near future. I knew people saw me as an asset opposed to a liability, so that wasn't the problem. I needed to do other things and be productive at them. I needed to be able to shake the stigmas from my past, in order to have a positive prosperous future. Now, all I needed was an opportunity.

When I got back in the dorm, it didn't take long for the rumors to start swirling. Everyone had questions about where I was from and who I was. I thought that coming to South Carolina, I'd be able to relax and not be the focus of everyone's attention, boy was I wrong.

Travis, a tall, slim, dark skinned kid whom I met upon arrival, came in my area to finish talking. He seemed like he was trying to remember where he knew me from. He said, *"I knew you looked familiar! I didn't put it together until the staff called you for the phone saying the Jigga man was on the phone calling to talk to you. I know who you are. You tha dude Calvin Klein that's in the Vibe Magazine that Jigga was talking about and he even mentioned you in his songs! I read the Don Diva magazine article on you too!"*

When Jay dropped, "The Black Album" aka his "retirement" album, a lot of attention circulated around me. He mentioned my name in the song, "Allure." The fact that he did that was a rebirth for me. My stock sky-rocketed in a phenomenal way to the masses. Although I was still in jail and been away from the public's eye for more than a decade, my identity resurfaced back to the top again.

I couldn't believe how many rumors were going around. One of the biggest ones was that Jay was pissed at Dame and Biggs for signing Cam'ron to Roc-A-Fella Records against his approval. They said him and Dame were parting ways and he was waiting for me to come home, to partner up with me. Haha.

That rumor, like many others were so far from the truth. Although the rumors were false, they still raised my value in the game to an all-time high, very high to say the least. I saw that I was able to capitalize off of nosey people's suspicions.

After reading into Travis and peeping his swag, I discovered that he was a rapper from the Dirty South. He went by the name of, Trigga Play. He told me, he had a family member that was in the music industry and he was doing it real big. He said his name was Akon. He went on about Akon having a song and video out with Styles P from the group, The Lox. The song was called, "*Locked Up*". I heard the song before. It was getting heavy rotation on the radio. At the time I didn't know who Akon was nor did I see his video, but all that was about to change.

Afternoon faded into night and morning came fairly quickly. I woke up, brushed my teeth and took a shower. I put on some Mitchum deodorant, then splashed on some Polo cologne. It really felt good to put on my own clothes rather than a jail outfit. I put on some Evisu jeans, a Purple Label dress shirt, a matching alligator belt and a fresh pair of all white Nike Uptown's. Needless to say, I was feeling myself!

I went to the receptionist desk so I could sign out for the day. Once I did that, I was able to leave the building for work. I checked the forecast the night before and it was expected to be sunny throughout the day. It was around 7:40a.m. when I left the air-conditioned facility. The moment I walked outside, I felt the humidity instantly. As I started walking down the street, I felt awkward. I tripped and lost my step a few times. The pavement felt slightly different than the yard full of dirt and gravel. I got to the end of the block and waited for the light to change. I found this task to be very difficult, as well.

Mind you, I have not crossed a street in almost fourteen years. The damn light and the moving cars were sort of confusing. I thought I had the right of way and walked out into the street. A car almost clipped me. I tried a few more times, only to have cars beep their horns at me. I walked down to the middle of the block. I timed the cars going both ways and then ran across the street. Wow! This was one hell of a reality check.

I realized that, even the simple things in life were going to take some getting use to. This made me reflect. Whenever I inquired about what changed while I was away, everyone was quick to say, *"Nothing, you ain't missing nothing but your freedom."* In the back of my mind I'd say, *"Everyday something changes and I'm missing everything if I'm not there."*

Fortunately for me, my mom already lined up a job for me. She asked a distant cousin of mine to provide employment for me upon my release. As promised, he did. I was to start work at The Fatherhood Families Engagement Program, a non-profit, community based program. They did home repairs to deprived homes, helped juvenile delinquents and conducted motivational speaking engagements among many other things.

As soon as I got to the job, I had to call the half

way house and report that I reached my destination. At the end of the day, I had to call the half way house to report that I was returning back to the facility. I was allotted thirty minutes to get to and fro. I had to be responsible for my whereabouts at all times. If I wasn't where I was suppose to be or if I took longer than expected to get from one place to the other, I would be penalized. They could even charge me with an attempt to escape charge.

My cousin Robert and I had our first meeting. We brainstormed for a few hours. Once the meeting ended, we knew what we were able to provide each other. We left out of his office and hit the ground running!

He had a fabulous staff. Their hearts were into helping others in need. At times, it shocked me how they came in every day with no motives for personal gain. They were about helping the people that were in dire need. For me, this was going to take some getting used to.

I needed something to be my daily motivation. I changed my mind frame and went in with different thoughts. I told myself that although this was not where I was born or raised, it didn't matter. I could rebuild a village to make up for the one I destroyed, Red-Hook.

As the day wound down, I felt sort of relieved. It felt good to finally do something positive and make a difference for a change. I didn't have any selfish agendas anymore. I was more than willing to give back in any way possible. I had five months left in the half way house and I vowed to at least finish the program out that way. I wasn't in any rush. I knew life came in stages. The streets taught me to take things in moderation, but also to have a lot of patience. *"When the surface of a lake is still, one can see the bottom clearly."* This jewel of wisdom has proven itself to be accurate as I traveled along my journey.

True to his word, Jay called me that following day. He called both the half way house and my mother's house, leaving messages. I was unable to catch his call because I was at work. I had to wait until I got back to the half way house to call him back. I had his direct number. I dialed his number and he picked up within a few rings.

Ring...ring...ring... *"Hello?"*

"Jay, what's up, this Klein."

"What's good with you? I tried calling you a few times today, but I guess you was busy."

"Yeah man, my moms got me a job working for my cousin at a community based program. It kept me busy pretty much

throughout the day. No complaints from me, I'm cool with it."

"I hear you, that's a good way to look at it. I just want you to know I'm still working on how I'm gonna go about doing what I'm gonna do for you. My question to you is, what don't you have that you need right now, while you're in the half way house?"

"As far as clothes and all the basics, I'm good. All I need is some money to hold me over until I'm able to come to New York."

"Ok, I hear you. To be honest, as I told you before, I'm scared to make certain moves for you, but I just wanna play my steps close so nothing will come back to me."

"I feel you, but I have to say this again, you don't owe me nothing! I can't say this enough for you to feel comfortable in dealing with me? This shit about Supreme and Irv feels like a fucking black cloud over my head, yo! There is nothing in the back of my mind that wants to do wrong. Common sense should tell you that if you do something for me and position me right, I wouldn't have anything negative on my mind. If I did have any thoughts in the back of my mind, you erased them by extending your hand legitimately. So why would I compromise that?"

"I told you I got you and I do. You said you good for now and being that you in the half way house for at least five more months, there's no rush to do anything major yet. This will be

more than enough time for me to figure how I wanna do this for you. Again, like I said, I got you man."

The week was moving right along. I went through pretty much the same routine everyday. Got up in the morning, took a shower, changed clothes, signed out the half way house and went to work. I even enjoyed the office work.

One morning, staff was short and my co-worker A-Money asked me if I wanted to go out in the field with him to do some home inspections. A-Money was in his early 40's and very slim built. At first glance, you'd assume he was a super nerd; that was until you got to know him. You couldn't tell this dude he wasn't hip or cool.

He had a list of homes that were in extreme need of repairs and he needed some assistance. I agreed to help him. He said, *"They really need our help."* There wasn't much money provided in the budget to do much of anything. The state only gave a total of $5,000 for each emergency fund. To be honest, I jumped at the opportunity to get out of the office so that I could start mingling with some new people.

When we left the office, we stopped at the Home Depot to get the things listed for the repairs. Soon after, we pulled up to the residence and were met by an older woman. She was the grandmother type. She was very nice in her demeanor, with the type of southern hospitality that would make you feel like you were family. She was a little short in height, but reminded me of the Tyler Perry character Madea at first glance.

As she escorted us towards her home, I couldn't believe my eyes. It looked like an episode of Hoarders. I couldn't fathom someone actually living in this trailer home. We walked up to the steps and sitting out front was a pretty young girl around nineteen years old. She was well developed for her age. She was reading a college book. A-Money and myself both said hello as we passed to go inside the home.

When we walked inside, I damn near fainted. The home was most certainly not habitable, not even a squatter would live there. My heart dropped. I thought I saw it all, but this was way too disheartening, even for me. I pulled A-Money to the side and said...

"There's no way these people can be living here. There's gotta be a way that we can do more for them."

"I understand that this may be a bit too much for you right now, but there's a lot of people who live in far worse conditions than this. Besides, we don't have the funding to do more than what we're doing. Believe it or not, they're happy they're getting

this much."

"I hear you, but it seems to me that it would be easier to get them a new trailer than trying to repair this one. This home is not even sturdy enough to walk around in. There's no solid foundation under us. They have bricks in all four corners to balance it out."

"They can't afford a new trailer. I tried to brace you for this. I told you not to get personal out here. Do your part in doing the best you can. Lets do our job and move on to the next one."

I tried my best to snap out of the shock, but every move I made in that home was depressing. To make matters worse, I had to use the restroom. I asked politely, to use her restroom. She raised her hand and pointed her finger saying, *"Down the hall, first door to your right,"* I said, *"Thank you."* I walked down the hall and opened the first door to my right. I walked in, closed the door and was devastated. It felt like I walked into one of those small filthy gas station restrooms off of the highway.

There was no way I could physically do anything under these conditions. There was shit inside the toilet and smeared on the seat as well. The smell was overbearing to say the least. I felt so ashamed for this family. I held my breath for as long as I could and pretended to use the toilet. I opened the door and raced outside, passing the girl sitting out front. I needed some fresh air in the worst way. A-Money came out behind me and said...

"Are you alright?"

"Yo, get in the truck. Let's go and come back in a half hour. I still gotta go to the bathroom."

"I thought you went already?"

"No! I couldn't. It was shit all over the toilet and I couldn't bare the smell in there."

"Hahaha! Come on man. Lets go."

We drove off, screaming out...

"We'll be right back!"

Within a half a hour we were back at the lady's home to finish working on the trailer. I did my best to regain my composure, gathering myself quickly. I didn't want to embarrass the young girl in any way. She didn't seem fazed by our swift departure, not one bit. She stayed focused on her studies the entire time.

At first sight, she had such a radiant beauty about herself, but that quickly changed. If you saw her in a club or anywhere away from this trailer, you would not guess in a million years that she was living this nastily. She lifted her head up from her book, looked at me with innocent brown eyes and said...

"I wanna thank you guys for helping us and doing what you can because we really need it."

"You don't have to thank us, I wish we were able to do more, but with the budget we have from the States program, we don't have much to work with. I promise you we will do our best and all that we are capable of doing. I take it that you don't live here?"

"I use to before I went off to college, I'm in my freshman year now and came to visit her for the holidays. My grandma raised me and I know that if I do well for myself in life, I will be able to help her do well too. We only have each other. I know we don't have much, but this is all we have for now."

"I can assure you, we will make the best of what you have and we will make your grandma as comfortable as we can. I don't want you to have no reason to be distracted from doing your thing in school. You are both blessed and anointed in your journey, so don't put too much on the things you have no control of. Do your part and leave the rest up to the Man above. Ok?"

"Ok, thank you so much."

I have to say; we did a whole lot with what little we had to work with. A-Money and I worked side-by-side and salvaged as much as we could. We took bags and bags of garbage out of that home and cleared up a lot of space. It wasn't in the budget to buy cabinets, so we purchased lumber. We then built and painted cabinets. Anything else in need of paint we painted. We fixed the septic system as best we could. We cleaned up the landscape around the perimeter of the home and bought some accessories.

We went back to the Home Depot to spend the rest of the budget on a few miscellaneous things. A-Money and I came out of out pocket and bought more things for the grandmother to use over the coming winter. As we finalized the finishing touches on the home, both the girl and her grandmother hugged each other. Then they hugged A-Money and myself, shouting praises to the Lord.

A-Money and I got in the truck and gave our final waves goodbye. We drove away feeling great pride in ourselves for the work we were able to do. That place was now decent enough for someone to call home. At the end of the day, it was our reward. *"All praise and glory goes to the most High and Mighty! God is good. All the time!"*

The week was closing quite fast. I looked forward to getting a weekend pass. In order to qualify for one you had to be there for at least a month, have a job and do all that was expected of you. You would leave Friday night and come back Sunday evening.

The case manager Mr. Williams, who had been there for a while, worked himself up quite a system. A system he felt he had control over. He did all he could to take advantage of both the system and the inmates. He got his hustle on big time. Mr. Williams was about 5'10 weighing around 185 lbs. He was dark skinned with a bald head and always dressed very well. He was a straight shooter and didn't make unnecessary conversation unless he felt you held some significance.

Reggie mentioned to me a few times prior that I didn't have to wait the required time to get a weekend pass. He warned me that I had to be willing to pay for it though. This was my second week of seeing everyone leave for the weekend. I refused to be left behind this weekend. I told Reggie that I wanted him to set up a meeting with Mr. Williams. We wasted no time and went straight to Mr. Williams's office. Mr. Williams wore his game face. He directed me to have a seat; then he asked Reggie to excuse himself from his office.

"I'm sure you are very much aware of the rules and regulations around here, as I am sure you are aware of the benefits as well. I've been through your files and I see that you are from New York and you are paroled here in the South due to your mother living here now. Am I correct so far?"

"Yes sir."

"Ok. Let's skip past the bullshit! I want to be as clear and straightforward with you as I can possibly be. I run a tight ship around here. I've been around the system a long time. If you don't know, now you know. You will not be able to bullshit a bull-shitter. You will lose and I will send you back to jail where you came from. You make mistakes. I don't. You will do the remainder of your time back inside if you don't play by my rules. Our business here is our business. There is no middleman. I am the front, the middle and the end! There is no in between in here. I am all you got here and all you need. I want you to know that you have no one to answer to or explain anything to other than to myself. Don't concern yourself with any staff speculations. If anyone has any concerns in my decisions, I will deal with them accordingly. Now, if there's nothing further to say we can close out with the better part of business. As I'm sure, you're aware my fee is $500.00?"

"Yes Sir."

"Ok. How soon can you have it?"

"I have it on me now, but only if I'm able to get the pass to go home this weekend?"

"You haven't been here a whole two weeks yet and I'll need more time to submit your paper work. I'll just use the excuse that you have the weekend pass for a personal family emergency, but in your case I have to be very careful. For all of

what I've seen in your files and due to you having a high profile case out of New York, I'd prefer to put you in for next weekend. There will be some major concerns if someone else opens your case file and reviews your background. I'll have to do this a certain way and keep this one close to my hip. I know you were expecting to go home this weekend, but the approval will be more certain if we wait until the following week. I don't wanna raise any red flags when your file goes through. Is that fine with you?"

Obviously I was upset with his decision, but understanding at the same time. I knew in order for it to go right, he had to dot the i's and cross the t's. I told him…

"Nah man, no problem. I understand you have to cover yourself around the board, so I'm fine with it."

"So, I guess our business is done here. It's a pleasure doing business with you. I will make it as comfortable as you can afford. I hope you enjoy your stay here."

Mr. Williams stood up and I did the same. He shrugged his shoulders and straightened up his posture, while buttoning his suit jacket. He almost didn't have to say anything because his body movements made a clear statement. This meeting was over. I put my hand in my pocket making a statement of my own. He walked around his desk and extended his hand.

565

I took my hand out of my pocket to extend mine as well. I had five crisp $100.00 bills in the palm of my hand and I made the pass off. The exchange was made and the deal was done. We both got what we wanted. I felt relieved that things went well in the meeting.

When I walked into the dorm room I gave Reggie a high five and told him I was good. I told him I would more than likely get the pass the week after next. Travis joined in and gave me a dap to show he was happy for me as well. It was late in the afternoon and still pretty hot outside. Trav, Reggie and some of the other guys went out front to take a cigarette break and catch some sun. On the other hand, I wanted to stay inside, layback, relax and chill under the air conditioning.

Just when I was about to take a power nap, Travis came barging in the dorm room yelling...

"Yo. Klein! Get up Yo!"

"Why? What's up?"

"My cousin's outside he wants to meet you."

"Your cousin?"

"Yeah man I told you Akon my cousin. He came to visit me. I

told him you was in here."

"Ok, that's what's up. I'm ready, let's go."

Trav and I walked out the door. We saw just about everyone from the halfway house, staff included standing around this short dark skinned dude who was signing autographs. I stood off to the side with Trav watching his cousin do his thing. Trav had his Trigga Play swag on one thousand. You couldn't tell him anything at that moment. He was smiling from ear to ear with tremendous pride in his family and rightfully so. It was well deserved.

Akon was signing autographs. Without looking up, he said to me...

"Yo Klein, What's up my nigg!"

"Taking in some of this free air Goodfella. No need in asking how you doing, I can see it's all good."

"I thought cous' was bull shittin when he said you was here with him."

"Yeah man. I'm here for five months. I felt it would be too much pressure and expectations to do this in New York. Plus my mom lives down here and asked for me to come here. So, I had to honor that. You know how that go."

"I already know. Did you hear from anybody yet?"

"Haha, (smiling) who haven't I heard from, but yeah man I had quite a few people get at me, Kevin Chiles, Jimmy Henchmen, Jackie Roe, Dee from the Ruff Ryders and Eric B. That's just to name a few. I just got off the phone with DJ Clark Kent a little while ago."

"That's what's up! (Smiling) That's my dude. The next time you talk to him, tell him I said to holla at me.

It seemed like it was gonna be a few more minutes before Akon was done taking pictures and signing autographs, so I backed up against the side of the building. I pulled out my cell phone, which obviously wasn't permitted in the halfway house and called Clark...

"Klein! What's good my brother! How you doing?"

"The greatest DJ dead or alive! Clark what's up Goodfella! I'm halfway home, I can't complain, what's good with you?"

"All is good my dude. The streets is talking real heavy right now about you being home. You got New York in a frenzy! That's all everybody's talking about, Klein's home. It's crazy right now. We have to hurry up and get you out in the field and position you into some major moves."

"I'm all in for that. I can't say it enough, how thankful I am

for you taking the time out of your busy schedule to mentor me into the industry. The experience you gave me while doing my last four years inside gave me the confidence I needed to have coming home."

"Listen my dude. You're my brother and I told you before coming into the game a powerful dude. I'll work you into the right circle. Your time is not going to be wasted by not having the right blueprint to start your movement. There's no hard part with you. You're a brand and you are your own product. There's a demand for you already and the buzz is crazy."

"Yeah bro I feel you. You know this is all new to me, but I trust following in your footsteps and seeing where they lead me. Oh yeah, by the way, you know the dude Akon?"

"Yeah, why what's up?"

"He said to tell you what's up?"

"Tell me what's up? I didn't know you knew Kon? Where you see him at?"

"I just met him today. His cousin is in here with me and he stopped by to see him. He's in front of me now."

"Say word?"

"Word!"

"Yo, tell that nigga I said what's good!"

"Hold on. Yooo Kon! Clark said to tell you what's good"

Akon responded...

"Oh word! You doing it like that my nigg! Tell him I said I'll be in New York in a few days and we gotta get up."

" I heard him. Tell him I said what's up with…"

"Yo bro. He's a few feet away from me. Let me put him on the phone so ya'll can chop it up without the third party thing. Hold on."

Akon was about to take a picture with a fan. He asked me to hold on for a second. I fell back. When he was done he came over and gave me a hug, then he took the phone…

"Clark, What's up my nigg! What's good with you" (Pause) Yeah, I know we pushing hard with this video and making some noise along the way. We got heat in our camp. It's our turn now dude (Pause). Thanks man, I appreciate that coming from you. You been in this game and seen some talent. For you to put me up there already when I feel like I'm just breaking the surface of the ice feels good to hear. I'm humbled. Thanks again my nigg (Pause). Oh yeah, Klein already know. When I get off the phone with you, we gonna chop it up. We gonna get him up and running to do his thing. He already know (Pause).

That's what's up. You got my number hit me up in a few days when I'm in New York so we can link up (Pause). Ok. That's what's up. Talk to you then, hold on.

Akon passed the phone back to me...

"Hello"

"Yooo my brother! I hope you know you got a gold mine in front of you! That's the hottest nigga in the game right now and will likely keep bringing hits for the next ten years! I don't know how much interest he might have in you, but don't take him lightly. He's up and becoming very powerful! His movement is crazy. All eyes are on any move that man makes right now. You would wanna be by is side if you can."

"That's what's up! Yo let me get off the phone so I can chop it up with him. I'll call you back."

"Ok. I got you later."

I hung the phone up. Kon and I shook each other's hand and embraced with a hug. This was a sign of respect for one another. To be honest, his aura gave me the vibe of a long lost relative. He imposed his concern regarding my welfare. He wasted no time...

"My nigg. What's really good? It's a good look that everybody is reaching out to you. It's well deserved. But I guess the real question would be, did Jay-Z reach out to you yet?"

571

"Yeah. He reached out to me. Actually I just spoke to him yesterday. He told me to fall back and he got me, so I guess I'm on his time and have to trust him on his word."

"Man, I don't know what that's all about, but if he don't sign you or do something I'm gonna pull you in with my team. It should be no hesitation on what to do. You guys got history together and its hard not seeing him doing anything for you when he been biggin' you up in one way or another throughout his career."

"I feel you, but Jay don't owe me nothing."

"What? You gotta be joking? Him associating himself to your reputation throughout the years kept the hungry wolves off of him. To further that, a rapper is a storyteller. They either depict scenes from their own lives or the lives of other around them. There's not one person in Jay's past history that has the type of street cred and status that you and ya partner Danny had. He used all of that to create his style and the lifestyle he presented to his fans to make himself believable. Don't ever say Jay don't owe you nothing."

"Damn my dude, you know a lot."

"I know my history my nigg. I know the streets!"

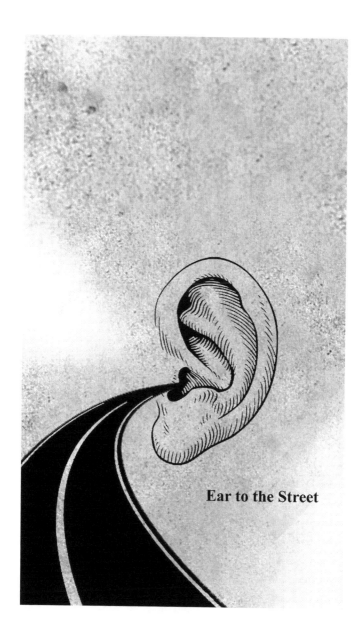

Ear to the Street

Once life is given, one never knows the journey set for them to travel. I was born into this world to become something that only God knows. The privilege of life is just that, a privilege. The life I lived, many would not have been able to endure. This roller coaster ride was filled with many fabulous uphill moments that were overshadowed by steep downhill slopes.

I allowed you, the reader to travel inside my mind and look through my eyes. I hope that you read through *"Neighborhoods Under Siege"* and learned from all the mistakes I've made. Hopefully you will not have to write a book emulating this one. I didn't write this book to preach to you, I wrote it for my own personal therapy. I hoped that after I wrote it and read it, I would learn from it without being prejudice. I wanted to read it from the reader's perspective.

Glorification is far from my intent. I went deep into the depths of my soul and etched out to you, undeniably the realest story ever written. I express no pride in how I lived parts of my life. Some would say, they wouldn't change anything in their life because they wouldn't be who they are today. I feel otherwise. I would change a lot about myself. I would change all the wrongs I've done and make them right. I could have lived a far better life than the one I lived. Don't get me wrong I embrace the life I lived, but only because of the course God has set for me moving forward.

I am currently on the largest stage I've ever been on because of my past life. It's not by coincidence that I am as relevant today as I once was in the height of the 80's. Not many have survived through that life and times. Another reason why I wrote this book was because I felt so many people were made to believe they were like myself and dedicated their life to wasted choices.

At some point in my life I lost my connection with God and stopped dreaming. That became my biggest mistake. My bright star turned dark and in that darkness I became very cold. I lived in that tunnel for many years until I finally found a way out. Although I had all the family support one could imagine, I had to find my way out on my own. I had to reconnect with God on my own terms.

After many, many years of losses and mistakes, I'm here still in the flesh to deliver my message from a blind state of mind. It took a lot throughout the years for me to learn to adjust my vision. Addicted to the street life, I couldn't stop living a certain way just because everyone wanted me to. I could only stop once I felt I had enough of living the way I was.

In life, you either take heed to advice or you have

to learn through experience. In my case, I had to learn on my own and that was the hardest way imaginable. It took a substantial amount of risks and having to do over twenty years in and out of State and Federal prisons to be at the point I'm at in my life today.

Today is a beautiful day. After all is said and done, I have my life and my freedom. Everyday is a work in progress for me to continue building. Not only did I add author to my resume, but I also added business owner, motivational speaker and executive producer. At this phase in my life, I have no more excuses. I am so above and beyond focused. My mind is finally where it needs to be, on myself and my family. There is not enough temptation in this world to make me stray away from that.

I've seen it all, the traps and the pitfalls and by no means will I allow any of that to intervene in my circle ever again. I don't owe anything to anyone but God. I often ask myself, was I born to be this way? I don't think so. I come from very good parents and I made myself this way. All I can do at this point is lay down the original blueprint of my story and pass it on, in hopes that no one follows these footsteps to nowhere. Trust me, you can be far more successful by thinking other ways and you can still break through any hold poverty may have on you.

There's nothing wrong with having a hustlers state

of mind, but don't be a fool and hustle your life away to sex, money, murder, or power. What awaits you in the mist of all of that is, ashes to ashes and dust to dust or the strongest steel bars in the world. There's greater knowledge gained in paying attention to a person's defeats rather than their successes. If you focus on the failures then you will be far more prepared on what awaits you through your own successes.

Make your own rules, live by them, stand by them and believe in them, even if you're the only one to do so. You are the number one priority at the end of the day. Don't try to change the world, change yourself. If there is any sort of greatness in you then greatness will follow. Everyone, including leaders are looking for someone great to blaze the path.

Everything I did in my life was predetermined. Although I am no longer a child and have grown into a man, I am still a child of God. I was once climbing a mountain that was very high. It had fortune and fame at the top, but I had to carry a lot of people on my back during that journey. I am proud to say that I cut that mountain in half and I no longer have to carry people who are capable of traveling their own journeys. Although there's still fortune and fame at the top, I am better equipped and much more mature. I can now handle the responsibilities that come along with being on top.

I know how important it is now for me to have and appreciate my partner. I don't see myself as a product, but as a brand. I won't do anything to jeopardize that. I got to think for the dummy, even if that dummy may be myself at times. Although I am unable to turn back the effects of time, I will move forward and focus on my future. I can't and I won't try to justify how I lived my life.

Life is ten percent chance and ninety percent choice. All that I went through was to prepare me for now. Just so you know, I'm dreaming again and I see the future of my dreams. The deepest darkness inside of me has produced the greatest light. I have the knowledge and wisdom to understand that the light I have is not mine. It was given to me.

Calvin Bacote is a successful business owner, motivational speaker, talent manager and author of "Neighborhoods Under Siege". He is a former notorious gangster and drug lord hailing from Brooklyn's Red Hook Projects. Calvin has since turned his life around and is dedicated to giving back. He is involved with organizations such as, The Young Presidents Organization (YPO) and The Guns Down Life Up tour where he acts as a motivational speaker.

Calvin managed international pop icon Akon and r&b singer Ray Lavender under the Konvict label, which he helped build. His documentary Gangsta Chronicles: The Story of a Brooklyn Don / Calvin Klein Bacote is the number one street dvd sold to date, grossing more than two million dollars. Calvin is mentioned in songs by artist such as Akon, Jay-Z and French Montana. He also signed a contract with Universal Studios to film his biopic. Among all of his accomplishments Calvin has added the greatest of all to his resume, being a devoted husband and father.

Calvin Bacote

63943094R00323

Made in the USA
Middletown, DE
08 February 2018